Globalization and the Welfare State

Edited by

Bo Södersten
Jönköping International Business School
Sweden

palgrave
macmillan

First published 2004 by
PALGRAVE MACMILLAN
Houndmills, Basingstoke, Hampshire RG21 6XS and
175 Fifth Avenue, New York, N.Y. 10010
Companies and representatives throughout the world

PALGRAVE MACMILLAN is the global academic imprint of the Palgrave
Macmillan division of St. Martin's Press, LLC and of Palgrave Macmillan Ltd.
Macmillan® is a registered trademark in the United States, United Kingdom
and other countries. Palgrave is a registered trademark in the European
Union and other countries.

ISBN 1–4039–1894–5 hardback
ISBN 1–4039–3257–3 paperback

This book is printed on paper suitable for recycling and made from fully
managed and sustained forest sources.

A catalogue record for this book is available from the British Library.

Library of Congress Cataloging-in-Publication Data
Globalization and the welfare state / edited by Bo Södersten.
        p. cm.
    Papers presented at a symposium held at Jönköping in May/June 2002.
    Includes bibliographical references and index.
    ISBN 1–4039–1894–5 (cloth)—ISBN 1–4039–3257–3 (pbk.)
      1. International economic relations–Congresses. 2. Globalization–Economic
aspects–Congresses. 3. Globalization–Social aspects–Congresses. 4. Welfare
state–Congresses. 5. Foreign trade and employment–Congresses.
6. Anti–globalization movement–Congresses. 7. Globalization–Economic
aspects–Scandinavia–Congresses. I. Södersten, Bo.
HF1359. G58197 2004
330.12′6–dc22   2003066465

10   9   8   7   6   5   4   3   2   1
13 12 11 10 09 08 07 06 05 04

Printed and bound in Great Britain by
Antony Rowe Ltd, Chippenham and Eastbourne

Contents

List of Figures   vi

List of Tables   vii

Preface   ix

Notes on the Contributors   xi

  Introduction: Globalization and the Welfare State   1
  Bo Södersten

1 Coping with Anti-globalization   24
  Jagdish Bhagwati

2 The Aftermath of Welfare Reform in the USA   45
  Robert M. Solow

3 Among the Believers: The Emerging Threat to Global Society   55
  Mats Lundahl

4 Multinational Enterprises and Their Effect on Labour Markets   74
  Karolina Ekholm

5 The Welfare State as a General Equilibrium System   96
  Bo Södersten

6 What to Make of the Dutch and Danish 'Miracles'?   128
  Christoffer Green-Pedersen

7 An Essay on Welfare State Dynamics   149
  Assar Lindbeck

8 Employment and Non-employment: A Study of the
  Swedish Labour Market   172
  Erik Jonasson and Lars Pettersson

9 Immigrants in the Welfare State   195
  Jan Ekberg

10 The Stability of the Globalized Welfare State   213
  Cynthia Kite

Name Index   239

Subject Index   243

List of Figures

3.1	The principal's striking power	60
3.2	The optimum of the terrorist principal	60
3.3	The agent's utility maximum	65
3.4	The effects of the repression of terrorism	69
3.5	Frequency distribution of terrorists	71
4.1	Total compensation per employee	86
5.1	Current account deficit as percentage of GDP	104
5.2	Exchange rate and employment in the manufacturing and public sectors, 1970–96	107
5.3	Total general government outlays, as a percentage of nominal GDP, 1970–2000	109
5.4	Total tax revenue as a percentage of GDP, 1967–99	110
5.5	Swedish inflation compared to that of Germany, 1970–2000	113
5.6	Average number of days of paid sick leave per person, per year	117
5.7	Export growth per sector	122
5.8	Real export growth	124
6.1	Long-term interest rates in Denmark, Germany and the Netherlands, 1980–2001	138
8.1	Non-employment as a share of the working age population (20–64) in Sweden	177
8.2	Non-employment	
8.2a	Open unemployment as a percentage of the labour force	181
8.2b	Number of people involved in labour market policy programmes	182
8.2c	Students	182
8.2d	People working in their own homes	182
8.2e	People too disabled to work	183
8.2f	Other people outside the labour market	183
A8.1	Non-employment and unemployment, standardized and seasonally adjusted	188
10.1	Economic openness and domestic resistance	216
10.2	Openness–resistance and economic performance	231

List of Tables

4.1	FDI inward stock per capita	84
4.2	Characteristics of foreign affiliates of Swedish manufacturing MNEs	87
4.3	Mean changes in MNE employment and exposure to relocation in different regions	90
5.1	Growth in real GDP, 1870–1970	98
5.2	Manufacturing output per hour, average annual growth rate	100
5.3	Numbers employed in public and private sectors	101
5.4	Public-sector productivity, by sector	102
5.5	Yearly rates of inflation in the EU, Germany and Sweden	105
5.6	Real and nominal annual wages for full-time employees in the private industrial sector	114
5.7	Real and nominal annual wages for full-time employees in the public sector	114
5.8	Nominal and real wage trend for industrial workers, 1970–90	114
5.9	Employment rates, 1976, 1990 and 1998	115
5.10	The effects on the average number of sickness days related to changes in sickness insurance	116
5.11	Percentage shares of total exports	121
6.1	Macroeconomic indicators for Denmark, 1982–2001	136
6.2	Macroeconomic indicators for the Netherlands, 1982–2001	136
8.1	Open unemployment and non-employment in European countries, people aged 15–64 years, 1990 and 2000	177
8.2	The working-age population in Sweden, 1970–2000	180
A8.1	Perron's test for structural break for non-employment in Sweden	189
A8.2	Perron's test for structural break for open unemployment in Sweden	189
A8.3	LR test for cointegration between non-employment and open unemployment in Sweden	190
A8.4	Perron's test for structural break for population outside the labour market in Sweden	190

A8.5 LR test for cointegration between open
      unemployment and the population outside the labour
      market in Sweden   191
9.1   Educational level, ages 16–64, 2002   198
9.2   Index for employment rate at ages 16–64 years,
      foreign born   199
9.3   Index for employment rate at ages 16–64 years,
      foreign born, in different regions   200
9.4   Unemployment rate among foreigners compared
      to natives, average 1999–2000   201
9.5   Employment rate, Bosnians in Sweden, ages
      20–59 1997 and 1999   204
9.6   Index of allowances, benefits and pensions,
      ages 16–64, foreign born   208
10.1 Trade exposure and Quinn scale   219
10.2 Cross-border financial flows   220
10.3 Public spending   222
10.4 Resistance potential   225
10.5 Determinants of public expenditure   228
10.6 Determinants of economic performance   230
A10.1 Domestic variables – political institutions   235

Preface

By the end of 1996 I had retired from my chair in international economics at Lund University in Sweden, and I began to think of starting up a research project combining my two main interests in economics and politics – international economics and economic policy issues. I approached some of my former Ph.D. students from Lund. Two of them, Henrik Braconier and Karolina Ekholm, agreed to take part in the project.

I, then contacted Professor Gunnel Gustafsson at the Department of Political Science in Umeå, as I wanted to have both economists and political scientists involved in the venture. She recommended Cynthia Kite, who had just successfully defended her dissertation 'Scandinavia Faces EU'. Cynthia agreed to take part in our group and brought with her David Feltenius, her Ph.D. student.

We decided to call our project 'Globalization and the Welfare State', and applied for a research grant from the Bank of Sweden Tercentenary Foundation. Our first application in 1997 was turned down. We sent a new application in 1998 and this time we obtained a grant. Great thanks go to the Foundation for its generous grants!

In the meantime, I had moved to Jönköping, where I became a professor at the newly established Jönköping International Business School. The project has been led and administered from Jönköping, and the administration has been handled by Viveca Lageson in an extremely efficient way.

On the academic side, I have had Lars Pettersson and Sara Johansson as excellent and hard-working collaborators in Jönköping. Important support and input to the project have also been given by Kristian Nyberg and Mårten Wallette.

In May/June 2002, we organized a symposium in Jönköping on our main theme. All the chapters in this volume (apart from those by Lundahl and Solow) were presented as papers at the symposium, and commented upon and discussed. We are naturally grateful to the authors of these papers, and special thanks go to all who participated in the symposium, and contributed with comments on the draft versions of the chapters in this volume: Lars Behrenz, Per-Olof Bjuggren, Pontus Braunerhjelm, Jacob Christiansen, Per Davidsson, Alan Duncan, Tore Ellingsen, David Feltenius, Magnus Henrekson,

Carl B. Hamilton, Layna Mosley, Anders Nordlund, Rolf Ohlsson and Victor Pestoff.

We are also most grateful for generous research grants to our project from the Jenz and Carl-Olof Hamrin Foundation and Sparbanksstiftelsen Alfa.

BO SÖDERSTEN

Notes on the Contributors

Jagdish Bhagwati is Professor at Columbia University and Andre Meyer Senior Fellow in International Economics at the Council on Foreign Relations.

Christoffer Green-Pedersen is Assistant Professor in Political Science at the University of Aarhus and a member of the Center for Comparative Welfare Studies at the University of Aalborg.

Jan Ekberg is Professor in Economics at the Centre of Labour Market Policy Research (CAFO), Växjö University.

Karolina Ekholm is Assistant Professor in Economics at the Stockholm School of Economics.

Erik Jonasson is a Ph.D. candidate at the University of California, Riverside.

Cynthia Kite is a Lecturer in Political Science at Umeå University.

Assar Lindbeck is Professor of International Economics at the Institute of International Economic Studies, University of Stockholm.

Mats Lundahl is Professor of Economics at the Center for International Economics and Geography, the Stockholm School of Economics.

Lars Pettersson is a post-doctoral student of economics at Jönköping International Business School.

Bo Södersten is Professor of Economics at Jönköping International Business School since 1998. Professor of International Economics at Lund University, 1977–96. Professor of Economics at Gothenburg University, 1971–7. Visiting professor at the American University, Washington, DC, and at Harvard University, 1974–5. Visiting associate professor at the University of California, Berkeley, 1965–7. Bo Södersten has written and edited some thirty books (most of them in Swedish). He was a member of the Swedish Parliament, 1979–88; and President of the Swedish University Teachers' Association, 1990–6. Bo Södersten is a frequent contributor to Swedish media commenting on political, economic and cultural issues.

Robert M. Solow is Institute Professor at Massachusetts Institute of Technology, Cambridge.

Introduction: Globalization and the Welfare State

Bo Södersten

Both globalization and the welfare state are very important concepts at the start of the twenty-first century. They are also controversial topics. Most economists and economic historians would probably agree that the period of 'Pax Britannica', (the years from 1820 – after the end of the Napoleonic Wars – to the outbreak of the First World War in 1914) was the splendid era of globalization, first and foremost comprising the Western world (Western Europe, North America and Australia) but also having a deep influence on other parts of the world. During that period, there was a great expansion in international trade, and international migration became important when large groups of people emigrated to North America and to parts of Latin America.

It is not by chance that the period 1820–1914 constituted the first great burst of globalization that changed the fate of the world, and not only for those countries more or less directly involved in the globalization process.

In part, this economic progress came about through scientific progress. In 1817, the British economist, David Ricardo, worked out his famous example of the foundation for trade between England and Portugal in wine and cloth. Despite the fact that Portugal had higher productivity than England in both the production of wine and cloth, it would be advantageous to both countries to trade as long as there were productivity differences in both lines of production. This is an assumption that is almost always present, and is part of the reason why the theorem is applied to such a high degree. The theorem of comparative advantage is, however, completely counter-intuitive, making it hard to understand – which, in turn, makes it such a tremendously strong and important theorem. The century following the publication of Ricardo's theorem also came to demonstrate its overwhelming importance.

1

The welfare state hardly existed before 1914, when the first great wave of globalization came to an end. It is basically a construction of the twentieth century, and the states of Western Europe are among those countries that have been pioneers in developing welfare arrangements encompassing the great majority of their populations. In particular, we are concerned here with the situation in Denmark, Sweden and the Netherlands.

These three countries were severely hit by the international crisis of the early 1970s, with the first oil crisis and the breakdown of the inter-national exchange rate system in 1973. It took Sweden about twenty years to emerge from the new pressures of the international system, while Denmark and the Netherlands started to reform their fiscal and exchange rate policies in the early 1980s. As shown by the analysis of these countries, the speed at which policy-makers are able to react to changing international circumstances is of great importance for the efficiency of economic policies as well as the countries' economic performance and the well-being of their citizens.

Returning to the issue of globalization, it is important to remember that the nineteenth century was the great era of globalization. The eighteenth century could be viewed as a necessary prerequisite at the intellectual and organizational levels. It was at that time that important institutions favourable to commerce were established, such as a new legal structure where quarrels between traders and businessmen could be solved within the framework of a reasonably objective legal system. Furthermore, property rights started to be respected, and a monetary system was established, as was a system of insurance.[1]

In order to understand the twenty-first-century world, some elementary historical knowledge as well as the ability to scrutinize various views on globalization are necessary. One of the objectives and ambitions of this book is to provide the reader with such critical insights.

The great era of globalization was the period 1820 to 1914, with Great Britain initially being the leading nation but, the other two leading nations at the 'European core', Germany and France, soon fol-lowed suit. The United States of America were then drawn in to the world trading system. Globalization during the nineteenth century rested on three pillars: free trade in goods and services; free movements of people; and free capital flows. An important year was 1846, when the British Parliament decided to repeal its Corn Laws; that is, to abolish the protection of British agriculture and instead opt for free trade. Thereafter, Britain became one of the leading industrial nations, exporting industrial goods and importing food and agricultural products. This meant a revolution in Britain as people moved into the cities and abandoned the agricultural areas where they had lived and made a meagre living.

The great era of globalization was characterized by very important technical progress such as the use of steam to drive engines and various types of machine, which had a great impact on transport through the building of railways and steamships. The transport system developed rapidly, transport costs fell drastically, and when the telegraph was invented and a transatlantic cable laid between Great Britain and the USA in 1866, the world became united in a way it had never been before. Previously, it had taken weeks for news to travel from one continent to another. Now, it took minutes or seconds for prices in the Chicago meat market, for example, to be known in London and other European capitals.

The improvements in transportation made safe long-distance travel possible for great masses of people. This was a prerequisite for the large mass migration during the nineteenth century from the poorer parts of Europe to North America and, to a lesser extent, to Latin America and Australia.

Another important aspect of the globalization of the nineteenth century was its monetary system and the role of capital movement. The monetary system in this first great phase of globalization was – or rested on – the gold standard, and the British pound was the leading currency. The gold standard implied that exchange rates were fixed with narrow 'gold points', which meant that each currency of the leading nations (and of smaller nations also belonging to the gold standard) had a fixed price *vis-à-vis* each other and the British pound. This system greatly enhanced trade and international capital movements, and created feelings of security in the international economy.

In this introduction, we are painting a picture with a very broad brush. This is because we want to convey the major aspects of economic development during the nineteenth century; a century that revolutionized the world economy as, for the first time in history, the world came to witness a very broad type of economic progress, in particular in what came to be called 'the developed' countries.

An important part of this development was the equalization of factor prices between countries through the process of international trade and international capital movements. By factor prices, we mean the return earned by the two major factors of production – labour and capital. The return to labour we call the real wage (that is, the price an employer will have to pay a worker for his work), and the return to capital is either called just that, or the interest on capital. What happened to the price of labour (that is, the real wage of the workers), is of special interest. The real wage for (unskilled) workers is probably the best existing measure of the well-being of the great masses: it is often a better measure than national income per capita, as workers and ordinary people pay for food and housing themselves with their real wages and not with gross domestic product (GDP) per capita.

The real wages of workers improved greatly during the period 1820 to 1914. This period was a breakthrough for an increase in living standard and ways out of chronic poverty. The leaders in this process were the USA and the core countries of Western Europe (Great Britain, Germany and France), but several other countries were drawn into the process and became parts of the globalized economy. Examples are the Scandinavian countries that grew rapidly and were rather 'over-achievers'. Other Western European countries that did reasonably well were Belgium, the Netherlands, Italy and Ireland, while the countries on the Iberian peninsula – Spain and Portugal – fell behind and remained poor.

The First World War (1914–18) then came as a tremendous blow to Western civilization, from which the world never really recovered. Out of the ruins of that war grew Communism and Nazism, and the world would never again look the same. The period from 1920 to 1950 was characterized by the Great Depression, other misfortunes and another world war. From 1950, a new world started to take shape. This was the era of the Cold War between the USA and Western Europe in one corner and the Soviet Union, its allies and to some extent China in the other, to use a boxing metaphor.

Soon, new forms of globalization started to take shape, this time with the USA in the lead. One important new aspect was that some Asian countries (Japan, South Korea, Singapore, Hong Kong and Malaysia) grew very rapidly from the early 1960s to the late 1990s; they quite rightly became known as 'the miracle economies'.

Another important factor was the emergence of the welfare state. In some countries, especially in Western Europe, the state and various governments started to take on new responsibilities for their citizens, with the idea and the goal that the state had a specific responsibility to provide welfare for all its citizens. Examples of countries with such aspirations are the earlier mentioned 'core countries' of globalization: Germany, France and Great Britain, and in particular the Scandinavian countries of Denmark, Norway and Sweden. The Netherlands had similar ambitions.

The very concept of welfare is surrounded by ambiguities of which any student of economic and social policies will have to be aware. In the European – or Western European or European Union (EU) context – the concept stands for well-developed social arrangements, such as the provision of schooling, health care, and income security for the unemployed, the weak and the elderly.

In the American context, the concept often has a more limited and more precise meaning. Here, 'welfare' most often means some specific type of support given to some of society's neediest groups to encourage their survival; an example might be unmarried mothers with children who simply need societal support to be able to survive. 'To live on welfare' in the American context most of the time simply means that a person or a group of people live on transfer payments from the taxpayers, a condition that is greatly problematic, both because it opposes the work ethic basic to the American creed and because it implies a situation that is untenable in the long run.

We shall return to these issues both in the chapter by Robert M. Solow (Chapter 2) on specific attempts at welfare reform in the USA and the problems these reforms proposals have encountered, and by Assar Lindbeck in Chapter 7 about welfare state dynamics and changing social norms. Both of these chapters deal with principal issues around work, welfare and economic performance that should be of interest to all people interested in broad social and economic issues.

More specific issues of political problems and macroeconomic performance concerning the mature Western European welfare states are then dealt with in Chapter 5, on the Swedish economy, by Bo Södersten, and Chapter 6 on the Danish and Dutch economies by Christoffer Green-Pedersen.

International interconnections between countries play a double part: both as providers of opportunities through the possibilities of increasing welfare through international trade and investments, and through the constraints they place on the autonomy of national economic policies. Jagdish Bhagwati deals in Chapter 1 with the pros and cons of globalization from a more general – and often worldwide – view.

In recent years, globalization has been a much discussed issue all over the world. Many people – economists, sociologists and experts on literature and similar categories – have expressed great concern about this phenomenon and have been greatly critical of the concept and what it stands for.

The first chapter is written by one of the world's leading authorities on international trade, international economics and globalization,

Professor Jagdish Bhagwati of Columbia University, New York. He deals explicitly with various types of argument that have been raised against globalization. His chapter has the fitting title 'Coping with Anti-Globalization'.

Another, more sinister, aspect of globalization that has come to the forefront in recent years concerns international terrorism. The date of 11 September 2001 has for many become the birthdate of a new world. Professor Mats Lundahl deals with this issue in Chapter 3, with the title 'Among the Believers'. The last decades of the twentieth century saw a revival of globalization where the presence and growth of multinational firms played an important role. Karolina Ekholm deals with this issue in the fourth chapter of the book.

Coping with anti-globalization

Globalization is a hot topic and has received a great deal of attention in recent years, and the critical voices are many, strong and articulate. On several occasions, the anti-globalization critique has turned into violent demonstrations. We only have to remember the protest meeting of the World Trade Organization in Seattle in 1999 and the struggles between demonstrators and police which took place at the European Union Council Meeting in Gothenburg and the G8 top meeting in Genoa 2001, which led to considerable damage, and even to the death of at least one demonstrator. In a way, these events demonstrate the seriousness of the issue of globalization.

The critique of globalization comes from several directions. Two groups or attitudes are prevalent. Bhagwati characterizes them as stakeholders in the globalized world, where one wants to drive a stake through the system and the other wants to exercise its stake in the system: 'The first group wants primarily to be heard; the other wants to be listened to.'

The first group of anti-globalizers consists of a wide range of ideological and sociological adherents who, according to Bhagwati, are driven by a trilogy of discontents: anti-capitalism, anti-globalization and anti-corporation. These three views are interlinked, because globalization is seen as the extension of worldwide capitalism, and corporations are viewed as the firing squad of capitalism in its global reach.

The second group of stakeholders shares the view that, while globalization may be economically benign, it is socially malign. That is to say that, when it comes to social objectives and agendas, globalization needs a human face. In the first chapter, Bhagwati argues that in fact it has a human face. He also claims that globalization is part of the solution rather than the cause of social problems. In fact, globalization often leads to poverty reduction, gender equality and democratic order.

Bhagwati criticizes anti-globalizers for being to narrow in their views; globalization has many different dimensions. Anti-globalizers tend to equate word globalization with modern capitalism or modern imperialism, but apart from referring to international trade, foreign direct investments and short-term capital flows, the word must also embrace international migration, which is important and tending to grow. During the 1990s, the USA absorbed ten million legal immigrants searching for a better life. Between these different aspects of globalization there exist parallels, but the differences are also essential. The issues of trade liberalization and free capital flows are a case in point. Short-term capital flows may play a disturbing role, while free trade is most often beneficial. Chile is an example of a country that has used regulations for international investors. Such regulations force them to pay a deposit fee for short-term capital investment in the country, just to avoid short-term movements of capital that might be disturbing to the economy. There have been several international crises caused by short-run 'flight capital', like that in South-East Asia in 1997–8. Unfortunately – as Bhagwati puts it – economists proclaiming free trade are automatically assumed to be 'for free direct investments, for free capital flows, for free immigration, for free love and free everything else!'

In fact, the anti-globalization sentiments of today are more prevalent in the rich countries of the North, while the poor countries of the South often see globalization as a positive force. This is what Jagdish Bhagwati calls the 'ironic reversal', since the situation was exactly the reverse in the 1950s and 1960s. At that time, the rich countries were busy liberalizing their trade, investments and capital flows, while the poor countries were fearful of international integration. Examples of countries using inward-looking policies up until around 1990 are the newly liberated African states, and India. It is now evident that the countries that abstained from using international trade and investment as opportunities for development made the wrong choice.

Two historical examples point strongly in favour of economies being open and growing through trade. The first is the high tide of globalization from 1820 to 1914, to which we have already referred; a period the French often call 'la belle époque' (O'Rourke and Williamson, 1999). The other is the strong growth and development that occurred in some South East Asian countries (Japan, South Korea, Hong Kong and so on, and turned these countries into 'miracle economies'. They achieved their phenomenal growth rates by being open economies, primarily growing by exports to the leading countries in the West such as the USA, Canada and the market economies in Western Europe (see, for example, Young 1994, 1995; Lucas, 2002, Södersten and Ekholm, 2002; and ch. 5). Bhagwati points to the fact that anti-capitalism has turned into anti-globalization among many left-wing students. Already, in the work of the earliest socialists, there are extensive writings on imperialism and its essential links to capitalism. V. I. Lenin's views on imperialism provide an insight into a principal reason why globalization is considered to be following from capitalism by the left wing. Indeed, this notion of globalization as an exploitive force has returned among some of the more militant of the youth.

Both theory and history have proved Lenin to be wrong. When David Ricardo proposed his famous theory of comparative advantage in 1817, he had a much deeper insight into the workings of the international economy than Lenin would ever get.

Bhagwati's main point is that both theory and history have proved that globalization is part of the solution, not part of the problem. Bhagwati claims: 'But we want to go faster. The central question for the globalizers as well as their foes has to be: how do we do it?'

Welfare reform in the USA

Robert M. Solow deals with welfare reform in the USA in Chapter 2. Specifically, he is concerned with the Welfare Reform Act of the US Congress in 1996, and some effects of that legislation. Solow analyses these new efforts of social reform from some principal points of view, and studies how these new attempts at social reform have affected work effort and the labour market.

In this introduction, we shall be concerned primarily with some of the more deep-seated principal aspects of this new legislation, and to some extent contrast it to European approaches to these issues.

Robert Solow makes some interesting remarks on differences in attitudes towards poverty and low-wage work between Europe and America. Europeans seem to be much more concerned with questions of equality, while Americans are more concerned with poverty as such. The American attitude is specifically concerned with absolute standards, with moving people above the so-called poverty line. Therefore, welfare reform in the USA is primarily about work, about increasing employment opportunities for the needy.

The work ethic is strong and unforgiving: 'middle-class Americans think of making do on transfer payments as a morally repugnant state, unacceptable to the body of tax-payers'. The legislation introduced in 1996 with the aim of lowering the case-loads of poverty and dependence on 'welfare payments' seems to have been successful, by and large. The trick has been to get people into jobs, and to make work a requirement for welfare recipients: social policy in the USA builds on work as a requirement for welfare recipients, and a cumulative time limit for the receipt of welfare payments. This means that the system encourages people to be active, either by working or taking part in programmes designed to improve employability.

At most, a person can receive welfare for 60 months, cumulated over his or her lifetime. This is an interesting part of the American system as compared to European countries. The time limit implies that anyone who receives welfare benefits will be motivated to search for employment at once, since they will otherwise reduce their future options to receive support from the system. From European studies, it is known that search activities for a new job increase when the period of receiving unemployment benefits, for example, gets close expiring. In the American system, search activities are likely to produce much earlier effects.

Robert Solow points out that there have been positive experiences from the time that the welfare reform was implemented. The effects of the reform have been investigated in a few studies. They show, for example, that single mothers with children increased their efforts to seek work in the mid-1990s and an accelerating performance could be seen after the reform efforts in 1996. Furthermore, it seems that welfare leavers are performing well in many cases, with a high probability of being employed.

Both of these rather stringent conditions have been important. They are in rather stark contrast to many – if not most – European experiences. Swedish experiences have been different and rather disappointing, as pointed out in the papers by Södersten on general macro policies, and the experiences of labour market policies described in the chapter by Jonasson and Pettersson on labour market conditions and experiences, and the chapter on immigration by Ekberg.

Other interesting points made by Solow is that direct work experiences seem to be essential for getting individuals off 'welfare', and investment in training and education seems to be less relevant. Naturally, the strong US labour market in the latter half of the 1990s also helped to reduce unemployment and take people off 'welfare'.

The conclusion Robert Solow presents stresses that it is important that politicians are clear concerning the policy goals, and that any policy initiatives should be evaluated by designed evaluation research. Furthermore, dramatic effects should not be expected. Instead, small, incremental improvements should be evoked for. It is also important to understand that a welfare population responds to incentives as does everyone else. There is one problem with the absolute time limit in that it leaves no room for people who can live their lives in a responsible way if they are able to combine welfare and work.

Among the believers: the emerging threat to global society

Many people and groups around the world object to what they see as the negative sides of globalization and a world order dominated by the West, where the USA is the only superpower.

Globalization has encouraged counter-forces. One such force is terrorism, which might be called the dark side of globalization. From a historical perspective, terrorism is not a new phenomenon, and we have seen many examples of 'state terrorism', where dictators use the state apparatus to suppress their people. Violent anarchist groups in the nineteenth century constitute one example, the Stern and Irgun gangs in connection with the creation of Israel, and the Irish Republican Army and the separatist groups in Spain are others.

Lundahl's Chapter 3 discussing terrorism is concerned especially with Muslim types of terrorism, often directed against, and viewed as a protest against, the forces of globalization, in particular against the USA. The events of 11 September 2001, with the bombing of the twin towers of World Trade Center in New York are often regarded as a watershed in modern history. In this book, we are not concerned primarily with modern terrorism as a political, historical or moral subject. Instead, we analyse it from an economic point of view and try to deal with the question of whether it can have rational grounds. We come to the conclusion that – as a matter of fact – it has at least some rational roots. For anyone concerned with modern politics, such an approach can be of interest and need not to be further defended.

Lundahl points out that the events of September 11 proved that terrorism is a highly organized and, in that sense, rational phenomenon that may be analysed with tools from economic theory. Under certain circumstances, terrorism is an extremely efficient instrument, but the efficacity is still dependent on the objectives of the actions. The purpose of Chapter 2 is to answer two very relevant questions in the light of the emerging threat of terrorism to global society: how does terrorism work as an instrument; and what motivates terrorism?

Regarded as a rational phenomenon, terrorism may be translated into a classical principal – agent problem. The principal has a goal, and in order to achieve it he needs to recruit agents willing to sacrifice their own lives. The principal maximizes his utility by maximizing his striking power. This power (the capacity to hit a specific target) increases with the terrorist's number of agents, although diminishing returns to scale most probably exist. However, as the terrorist organization grows, the more visible it becomes, and the more likely it is to be combated actively by legitimate forces. Thus, the more the principal terrorist spends, the larger becomes the risk of retaliation. The optimal size of the organization is an equilibrium point, determined by the strike power and the risk of retaliation, and this optimum corresponds to a point where the marginal benefits equal the marginal costs. The real problem comes when dealing with the agent: how can anybody be willing to sacrifice her or his life, however good a cause may be?

To cast light on this question and thereby on modern terrorism, we must take religion into account, especially the possibility of consumption in Paradise. This may be a part of some religions, and it is definitely a part of the Muslim faith. Once the consumption of heavenly goods is taken into account, the recruitment of terrorist agents can be analysed with simple consumer theory. Given agents' preferences, the relative price of terrestrial and heavenly goods, and the budget restriction, the agents' maximization problem will define the optimal time for the agent to leave this world for Paradise.

The preferences for consumption in the next world can be reinforced systematically by suitable indoctrination. The indoctrinated terrorist is satisfied with fever worldly goods and is therefore easy to recruit. Moreover, Muslim tradition teaches that martyrs are distinguished and privileged compared to others in life after death.

Furthermore, the repression of terrorism may enhance the possibility of terrorist recruitment. The vast majority of members of the community from which terrorists are recruited normally consider themselves to be poor, and when they perceive that their poverty in this life is increasing, their preferences for consumption in Paradise may also increase. Consequently, the recruitment of terrorists is likely to be easier than before, and the repression of terrorism in the real world may just serve to increase the number of suicide bombers.

An economic analysis of the motives of terrorism thus leads to the conclusion that a strategy of building on improvements in the economic and social conditions of the groups from which terrorists are recruited may be the key in combating terrorism.

The role of multinationals in the globalization process

One important aspect of current globalization is the increased importance of multinational enterprises. The expansion and relocation of firms across national borders have several implications for both the world economy and individual home and host countries. In Chapter 4, Karolina Ekholm discusses the effects of foreign direct investment (FDI) and the activities of multinational enterprises (MNEs) on labour markets. The ability of firms to relocate their activities is seen by some groups as a threat to workers in the home countries, in so far that jobs may be lost. Workers in host countries may, however, be worse off, as multinationals may exploit foreign workers in terms of working conditions and wages. Furthermore, the mobility of firms may affect the sustainability of the welfare state by undermining the tax base if, indeed, the mobility of firms leads to a downward pressure of wages through unemployment. Ekholm argues that there is, in fact, very little empirical evidence in support of this, which implies that the fear of a race to the bottom is exaggerated. One reason for this seems to be the tendency for MNEs to expand into other high-wage countries, rather than into low-wage countries. Moreover, an expansion into low-wage countries is likely to have both negative and positive effects on the demand for labour in the parent firms. The relocation of activities constitutes a negative effect, while an overall expansion of the firm as a consequence of increased competitiveness constitutes a positive effect. Thus, whether the net effect tends to be positive or negative is essentially an empirical question. Ekholm reviews the growing empirical literature in this area, and concludes that the evidence suggests that, while there is a tendency for parent employment to decrease as MNEs expand in other high-wage countries, there is no such tendency associated with their expansion in low-wage countries. The most plausible interpretation of this result is that firms treat similar types of locations as alternatives.

Ekholm argues that the closer integration between Eastern and Western Europe is a particularly interesting case to study in this context. Eastern Europe is a low-wage region in geographical proximity to the high-wage countries of Western Europe. Eastern European countries will thus become potential points of location for firms producing for the large European consumer markets. She draws on her own work on the Swedish MNEs' expansion in Central and Eastern Europe to discuss the effects on demand for labour in other parts of Europe. Ekholm claims that there is basically no evidence of this expansion leading to reduced employment in the parent firms in Sweden, or in their affiliates in other high-wage countries in Western Europe. However, she does present some evidence suggesting that the expansion in Central and Eastern Europe has been associated with reduced affiliate employment in other European low-wage countries, such as Greece, Portugal and Spain.

Ekholm's chapter also contains a discussion of the welfare effects of foreign direct investment. Any positive effects in the host countries are likely to stem from a transfer of technology from the parent firms to foreign affiliates, and possibly to other local firms. There seems to be a substantial amount of evidence that technology transfer is important. MNEs usually pay higher wages than do domestic firms, not only in their host countries but also in their home countries. The fact that they do so suggests that they tend to have lower costs and/or tend to be able to charge higher prices than purely domestic firms. This fits in well with the view that MNEs tend to be found among the most profitable and efficient firms in any economy.

The picture Ekholm paints of the impact of the activities of MNEs is thus relatively rosy. At least, it is very far from that conveyed by advocates of the anti-globalization movement.

The Swedish welfare state

The next two chapters, Chapters 5 and 6, deal with three advanced welfare states in Western Europe and their development since the early 1970s. The objective is to make a comparison of how the welfare states fared during the quite turbulent years of the last three decades of the twentieth century.

The 1970s were a period of turmoil and crisis in the world economy. The first oil crisis, with price increases in oil of around 300–400 per cent, during 1973–4 sent a shock wave through the world economy. There was a large increase in the balance of current accounts and the overall savings of oil-producing countries (the OPEC countries), while the industrial countries (the OECD countries) tended to have deficits in their trade balances. Overall, growth rates decreased, at the same time as the oil price hike put inflationary pressure on most industrial economies. The Western world had no previous experience of such a situation, and a new era of stagflation was ushered in. The 1970s can be said to have been the first period of test and trial for these advanced welfare states and how well they stood up in the new globalized world of which they were an integral part. To examine how they fared during the last three decades of the twentieth century is of definite interest.

After a hundred years of uninterrupted growth from 1870 to 1970, Sweden was the most advanced of the three welfare states – Sweden, Denmark and the Netherlands. The remarkably strong Swedish economic performance from 1870 to 1970 had fostered an attitude that the Swedish economy would not falter. However, this attitude only aggravated the problems of the 1970s, since neither politicians nor economists realized that the 'golden years' had come to an end (Södersten, 1991).

From the early 1970s until 1982, economic policies were expansionary in the three welfare states. In all three countries, they led to high rates of inflation, large budget deficits and large increases in government spending. But in 1982, Denmark and the Netherlands changed course. Part of this change was related to political forces and part to changed economic policies. The political change in these two countries – to which we will soon return – depended on new forms of coalitions, where two social democratic parties became more willing to co-operate and accept the conditions imposed by the international financial markets.

In Sweden, the Social Democrats held a strong position, and the country had many more of the characteristics of a one-party regime.[2] There was a slow-down in productivity growth in its international sectors and, in order to avoid unemployment, the government sectors grew rapidly, especially local and county governments.

In order to increase the competitiveness of Swedish industry, the Swedish krona was devalued several times with, for example, a 10 per cent devaluation by the non-socialist government of Torbjörn Fälldin in 1981, and a further 16 per cent devaluation by the new social democratic government led by Olof Palme in October 1982.

These policies turned out to be failures, though, as is carefully described by Bo Södersten in Chapter 5. The devaluation policies were handled ineptly and reached a crossroad with welfare state objectives, which fostered a rapid increase in government sectors. These policies had deep ideological roots in egalitarianism, feminism and aversion to market solutions.

This strategy came to an end with the deep recession that struck the Swedish economy at the beginning of 1990s when, by coincidence, a new non-socialist government had come into power. This crisis led to some unexpected, but very positive, results. The Swedish krona was untied from the ecu on 20 November 1992. The krona then started to float and was depreciated rapidly by some 20 per cent, which led to a strong and rapid expansion of exports. The crisis also turned out to be a blessing in disguise, as it flushed the years of endemic inflation out of the Swedish economy.

Another important factor is that, from 1974 to 1994, Sweden had had continuous deficits in its balance of payments, despite the series of devaluations of the krona that took place during the 1970s and 1980s. Sweden also had large budget deficits financed by foreign borrowing. Consequently, government debt increased from 19 per cent of GDP in 1970 to 68 per cent of GDP in the year 2000.

However, this situation changed completely with the introduction of more restrictive policies in the wake of the crisis of 1992–4. Exports expanded by some 20 per cent in 1993, the year after the depreciation of the krona. The export industries could now expand because labour supply was much more elastic as a result of the prevailing unemployment. The internationally competitive sectors of the economy also expanded, in contrast to the case in the 1980s, when there was a labour shortage caused to a great extent by the expansion of government sectors that absorbed all available labour.

The Danish and Dutch 'miracles'

As we learned from the preceding chapter, the performance of the Swedish economy between 1970 and 1992 was not very good. Inflation was high, the growth rate low, and macroeconomic policies were inefficient. The performances of the Danish and Dutch economies were also quite dismal, as the two oil crises hit these and many other countries in 1973–4 and again in 1979.

Denmark and the Netherlands came to develop in a quite different way from Sweden. The major change in the Danish and Dutch cases came in 1982. There were two important 'turn-arounds' in both countries, one of a political and the other of an economic kind.

In both countries, social-democratic parties had been influential and had also been government parties. Moreover, they had also pursued left-wing policies. This implied loose fiscal policies of a traditional Keynesian kind, which led to high government expenditure, and with high rates of inflation and large budget deficits in their wake.

In the early 1980s, the situation started to become untenable, not least because of negative reactions from the international financial markets, as the interest rates in the two countries began to rise. In 1982, both countries were in a crisis and new governments were formed, signalling a farewell to the old-style Keynesian policies that worked well in the 1950s and 1960s, but proved inefficient in dealing with the crisis years in the 1970s. Two important changes occurred, one on the political and the other on the economic scene.

In Denmark, the Social Democrats lost power in 1982 and a new government was formed. Welfare-state arrangements, such as the - automatic indexation of wages and social benefits, were abandoned, and a more stringent fiscal policy introduced. In contrast to the situation in Sweden, there was no devaluation in 1982; instead, a decision was taken to peg the Danish krona to the German mark; a very strong currency at the time.

A parallel development occurred in the Netherlands. Here, a new type of coalition was formed between the Social Democrats on the one hand and Liberal and Christian Democrats on the other. An important agreement was the so-called Wassenaar agreement, formed between the government and the trade unions in 1982, which led to a moderation in the wage claims of the unions.

More stringent social policies were pursued, with fewer possibilities of opting out from the labour market, and decreases in social benefits. Instead, employment increased, especially in the Netherlands, even though it often took the form of part-time work. There was a sharp increase in female employment. During the crisis years, interest rates were high, and Denmark in particular had to pay a high premium in terms of high interest rates, which peaked at 21.9 per cent in 1982, compared to interest rates of 8.9 per cent in Germany.

The co-operation over party lines in Denmark and the Netherlands – which had not occurred in Sweden – proved to be fruitful. So did the introduction of economic policies in line with those demanded from international markets, which initially required low rates of inflation and a balanced state budget.

Sweden, however, lost another decade, not being able to stem its inflation during the 1980s. Not until the deep crisis of 1992–3 were new policies introduced and the state budget and current account brought into balance after twenty years of continuous deficits. The reforms were also made necessary by Sweden's attempt to live up to the Maastricht criteria.

Further aspects of the welfare state are discussed and analysed in Chapter 7, by Assar Lindbeck, and Chapter 8 on the Swedish labour market written jointly by Erik Jonasson and Lars Pettersson.

Welfare state dynamics – lags and social norms

In a historical context, the welfare state is a quite recent phenomenon, dating back to around the 1950s. Welfare state arrangements were meant to enhance income security and provide social services for broad groups – certainly the majority of people. That welfare state policies have contributed to income security for a majority of people in several welfare states is to a large extent correct. The growth of the welfare state may also have created 'good circles' among people, since better health and improved education for the broad masses imply a growth in a country's human capital, thereby increasing productivity and incomes.

Building up a welfare state is costly, however, as more and more resources are used for various types of welfare arrangements. This means increased taxes and higher tax wedges that may reduce the incentive to work and, in the long run, reduce efficiency and growth rates. In the even longer run, peoples' motives and norms may change in ways that undermine the very foundations of the welfare state.

How social norms change with development and growth is a very important, but poorly researched, area to which Professor Assar Lindbeck devotes Chapter 7, on welfare state dynamics. This is a chapter that – from a rather new perspective – throws light on the description of the three welfare states discussed in the two preceding chapters. Lindbeck conducts an in-depth analysis of some of the central problems of both incentives and motivation, as well as the possibilities of pitfalls, shirking and cheating, which may also be parts of the citizens' reactions to the benefits offered by various welfare arrangements.

Lindbeck makes the distinction between cheating and moral hazard. The meaning of the first term is plain enough, while the second refers to situations difficult or impossible to control – for example, by an employer. If I report sick on a Monday morning because I have been drinking the night before, it is a case of moral hazard, but if I instead travel from Birmingham to London to enjoy myself – and report sick – it is a case of cheating. Acts of moral hazard are characterized by their being difficult to observe directly or control. The concept of moral hazard is as old as is scientific economics; and it may undermine the welfare state arrangements more than cheating. Adam Smith observed in his classic work *The Wealth of Nations* in 1776 that directors managing other peoples' money cannot be expected to show 'the same vigilance with which they watch over their own money' (Smith, 1937 [1776], p. 700).

In the eighteenth century, economists were concerned about the behaviour of directors, and at the start of the twenty-first century we are concerned about the behaviour of the unemployed; 'plus ça change, plus c'est la même chose'. It is fairly obvious that social norms evolve and change over time. The analysis of sick leave in Södersten's chapter showed that there was a clear upward trend in this type of absenteeism that could not be explained in medical terms but was related to the evolving norms making absenteeism from work more acceptable than it used to be. Lindbeck argues that individual adjustments to changes in economic incentives are constrained by social norms for some time, but that the welfare state, with its generous benefits and high taxes, will eventually take its toll. Therefore, we would expect such disincentive effects to be stronger in the longer term than in the short run.

Lindbeck takes unemployment benefits as an example. The more generous these are and the longer they can be accessed, the more people will be unemployed at any specific point in time. Referring to English studies, he points to the fact that psychological factors may be involved: the more 'relevant others' are unemployed, the less unemployed workers may suffer psychologically.

Lindbeck's chapter deals in a thorough and interesting way with problems that are becoming increasingly important, relevant to the developed world in general and to the welfare states in particular.

There are various mechanisms through which welfare states and welfare arrangements may get into trouble. We may have an 'overshooting' of welfare state arrangements, because various social benefits are added haphazardly, resulting from a piecemeal decision-making process. Politicians and voters alike tend to become myopic and cannot weigh and calculate the overall effects and performance of all the arrangements at a single point in time. Such overshooting is more likely to occur in the 'universal' welfare states of a Scandinavian or central European type, than in Anglo-Saxon countries.

Unemployment in the welfare state: the case of Sweden

From the earlier chapters, we have learned that the first half of the 1970s, or more precisely the year 1973, was an important time of demarcation in the development of the Western economies. The decades between the Second World War and the beginning of the 1970s were 'the golden years', with a rapid development of the Western economies, from the USA to the frontiers of the Soviet Union.

There were several reasons for the rapid development of the economies of the core Western countries (USA, Canada and Western Europe). One was that the rebuilding of war-torn countries created an investment boom that lasted for almost a quarter of a century. Another reason was that many people (not least economists) thought that the riddle of depressions had been solved. The solution consisted of applying Keynesian policies of demand management. By pursuing such policies, full employment and a rapid economic growth were maintained for almost a quarter of a century.

Unemployment hovered at around 2–3 per cent in the Western European economies in the 1950s and 1960s. It was slightly higher in the USA, but also there fell from 6 per cent to 4 per cent. This situation was in stark contrast to the inter-war years from 1920 to 1939: when the British prime minister, Harold Macmillan, told his voters before the general election in 1954: 'You've never had it so good', they knew exactly what he was talking about.

But a collapse of full employment occurred during the crisis of 1973–4. As well as the oil crisis, the so-called Bretton Woods system of stable exchange rates – with the US dollar as the reserve currency – broke down. Both the leading countries in Western Europe and the USA had distinct higher unemployment rates in the 1970s compared to 'the golden years'.

Sweden is a special case that may be of interest to study. The country was an exception to the general rule in the 1970s, and was able to maintain a low rate of unemployment at this time. In Chapter 8, by Jonasson and Pettersson, the authors take a close look at the Swedish labour market and find that, until 1990, Sweden had a labour force participation rate that was almost 90 per cent for the adult population aged 20–64. The authors are, however, not only (or not even mainly) interested in the traditional concept of unemployment. Instead, they use the concept of 'non-employment', which – as the word indicates – gives a measure of how large a share of the population aged 20–64 does not engage in paid work. This measure also includes those outside the regular labour market.

It is important to realize that unemployment and non-employment do not measure the same phenomenon. A major finding of their chapter is that the number of 'non-employed' has risen sharply during the 1990s, and roughly doubled in number in Sweden. During the heyday of the Swedish welfare state – which ended around 1990 – the share of non-employed amounted to around 16 per cent of the total population of working age. That number almost doubled during the

1990s, which has made the number of people dependent on various welfare measures larger than it used to be.

The reasons for this development of the Swedish welfare state can be explained both in terms of inefficient and misguided macro policies as they are analysed and described in the chapter by Bo Södersten (Chapter 5), and in changing social norms as they are scrutinized in the chapter by Assar Lindbeck (Chapter 6). Sweden and Finland are the only countries in Europe where there has been a sharp increase in 'non-employment' during the 1990s.

Immigrants in the welfare state

International movements of factors of production – that is, labour and capital – have played a very important part in the globalization process. The classic period of migration was the time between 1820 and 1914. During this period, Sweden imported around 50 per cent of its capital stock from abroad, mainly from the European core countries (France and Great Britain). About 25 per cent of the labour force emigrated from Sweden between the years 1850 and 1910, almost all to the USA. This migration from Sweden had a very large effect on the Swedish economy. It led to factor price equalization as wages rose both in the USA (because of its rich resources of land and capital) and in Sweden because of increased productivity and an increase in the capital stock.

Thus migration was essential to Sweden's economic development up to the First World War (O'Rourke and Williamson, 1999; Södersten, 1991). From the beginning of the First World War (1914) to the end of the Second World War (1945), migration was negligible. Since then, and up to the time of writing immigration has grown and started to become a central issue, both in quantitative and political terms, and in terms of the functioning of the Swedish welfare state.

Before the Second World War, the Swedish population was homogeneous and there were very few immigrants. The numbers of individuals born outside Sweden amounted to less than 1 per cent of the population. But this figure increased to 7 per cent by 1970, and 11 per cent by the year 2000. If second-generation immigrants are also included, the figure amounts to 1.8 million individuals, or 20 per cent of the total population.

In order to understand the effects of immigration on welfare state arrangements, it is important to realize that immigration to Sweden came in two great waves. The first wave – lasting from the late 1940s to the early 1970s – came for labour-market reasons: Sweden was a country of full employment at this time, and it was easy for immigrants to find a job. Furthermore, most immigrants were of European descent and were integrated easily in Swedish society.

After around 1970 and up to the early twenty-first century, there was a change in the character of immigration. The immigration of labour declined and instead turned into the immigration of refugees, originating from more distant parts of the world, such as African countries and parts of the Middle East. These refugees have had great problems in finding work and becoming integrated into Swedish society.

The early immigrants made net contributions to the Swedish economy, but with the latest wave of immigrants, it is the reverse. They are also strongly over-represented in the use of social welfare allowances (ten times more than the average), and the use of housing allowances (around four times the average). The basic reason for this is their lack of success in finding jobs.

Swedish authorities and politicians have had difficulty in dealing with the problems of immigration. A key issue will be how the second generation of immigrants belonging to this second wave (that is, those coming into the country after 1970) integrates into the labour market.

Whether the 'good circles' to which Assar Lindbeck refers in his chapter on changing norms in the welfare state will prevail remains to be seen. So far, the domestic Swedish political debate has not dealt very much with the issues surrounding immigration. The integration of immigrants was not successful during the 1980s and 1990s. In the future, the immigration question might therefore have a large effect on Swedish society and the Swedish welfare state.

Will the globalized welfare states survive?

The final chapter of the book (Chapter 10) is written by Cynthia Kite, who analyses the stability of the globalized welfare state from a political scientist's point of view. Kite takes a comparative approach where she uses databases from OECD to make comparisons of nineteen OECD countries concerning globalization and social spending.

One question she is concerned with is: does globalization and international competition force the welfare states to 'retrench'? Or, put somewhat differently: do they have to forsake social objectives in order to be competitive internationally?

It turns out that the answer to this question rather seems to be no. But the answer (or answers) are more complex and have to be surrounded by exceptions and qualifications. There seems, however, to be little or no validity in the argument that globalization threatens the well-being of the citizens of the welfare states. On the contrary, one significant relationship Kite finds in the statistical tests is that between levels of exposure to international trade and levels of social spending: the more trade, the more social spending. This is an interconnection that has also been recognized and discussed in the literature. It is commonly explained by the fact that, in order to gain support for openness, it is necessary to provide workers with various kinds social insurance against the dislocations and so on that may be incurred by taking part in an open economy competition.

Kite's analysis of concepts such as retrenchment and resistance to this shows that the interconnections between these differ and to a large extent depend on the domestic institutions of each country, possibilities of collaboration between various political forces, and the constitutional conditions characterizing different countries.

The strength of Kite's chapter is that it gives us an overview involving many countries and the ways in which they have been influenced by the evolving international economic conditions since the 1970s. By and large, her findings broaden our perspective on globalization, but also underline some of our earlier findings in the country-specific chapters. In Table 10.3 in Chapter 10, for example, we find that Sweden is second to the Republic of Ireland as the country where exports have grown most rapidly between 1980–3 and 1994–7. In the same vein, we find that the Netherlands has reduced its share of government spending of GDP by 6.4 per cent between 1980–3 and 1994–7, which is by far the largest reduction of spending of any of the countries in the OECD sample.

We shall end this introduction by saying that the interrelationships between globalization and the welfare state are far from simple. But, if anything, globalization promises more, and its features are much more benign than malign.

Notes

1 For the development of these 'good institutions' and their importance for economic development, see North (1990) and Rosenberg and Birdzell (1986).
2 For a more thorough discussion of the one-party regime, see Pempel (1990).

References

Lucas, R. E., Jr. (2002) *Lectures on Economic Growth*, Cambridge, Mass.: Harvard University Press.

North, D. C. (1990) *Institutions, Institutional Change, and Economic Performance*, Cambridge University Press.

O'Rourke, K. H. and Williamson J. G. (1999) *Globalization and History: The Evolution of a Nineteenth-century Atlantic Economy*, Cambridge, Mass.: MIT.

Pempel, T. J. (1990) *Uncommon Democracies: The One-Party Dominant Regimes*, New York: Cornell University Press.

Rosenberg, N. and Birdzell, L. E. (1986) *How the West Grew Rich*, London: I. B. Tauris.

Smith, A. (1937[1776]) *An Inquiry into the Nature and the Causes of the Wealth of Nations*, (ed. E. Cannan), New York: Modern Library.

Södersten, B. (1991) 'One Hundred Years of Swedish Economic Development', in M. Blomström and P. Meller (eds), *Diverging Paths: Comparing a Century of Scandinavian and Latin American Economic Development*, Washington, DC: Inter-American Development Bank.

Södersten, B. and Ekholm K. (2002) 'Growth and Trade vs. Trade and Growth', *Small Business Economics*, vol. 19, pp. 147–62.

Young, A. (1994) 'Lessons from the East Asian NICs: A Contrarian View', *European Economic Review*, vol. 38, pp. 964–73.

Young, A. (1995) 'The Tyranny of Numbers: Confronting the Statistical Realities of the East Asian Growth Experience', *Quarterly Journal of Economics*, vol. 110, pp. 641–80.

1
Coping with Anti-globalization

Jagdish Bhagwati

Globalization first became a buzz word, Davos and Thomas Friedman celebrated its virtues, and its inevitability. But then came the anti-globalizers, Globalization then became a more conventional four-letter word. The Ruckus Society and Pierre Bourdieu proclaimed its vices its vincibility.

As this dialectic has unfolded, it is tempting to think that there is a primeval curse on the phenomenon; after all, if one cares to count, globalization is a thirteen-letter word. But, seriously, globalization has now become a phenomenon that is doomed to unending controversy, the focal point of always-hostile passions and sometimes-violent protests. It is surely a defining issue as we enter a new century. The reasons why this has happened cry out for comprehension. Without such understanding, and then informed refutation of the fears and follies that animate the anti-globalizers, we cannot adequately defend the globalization that many of us seek to sustain, and even deepen.

Though there are many who are upset with globalization, they come from many directions. Basically, there are two types of objector, each claiming to be the new stakeholders in the globalizing world: those who wish to drive a stake through the system, as in the Dracula movies, and those who wish to exercise their stake in the system. The former wish only to be heard, but the latter want to be listened to. Many among the first set have different ideological and sociological factors animating them; and I will address these while focusing more systematically on what I think is the principal driving force: what I call a linked trilogy of discontents that take the form successively of an ethos composed of an anti-capitalist, anti-globalization and acute anti-corporation mindset. These views are interlinked because globalization is seen as the extension worldwide of capitalism, whereas corporations

24

are seen as the B-52s of capitalism and its global reach. But then I address the second set of stakeholders who wish to sit down with us, offer 'policy briefs' and transact changes that they believe are necessary in the global economy.

These latter groups, which are now visible at international meetings such as those of the World Economic Forum, are characterized for the most part by a worldview that, while economic globalization may be *economically benign* (in the sense of increased efficiency and a larger pie), it is *socially malign*. That is to say, when it comes to social objectives and agendas such as the reduction of gender equality, removal of poverty, preservation of culture, and the democratic functioning of a society or nation, globalization fails.[1] In the fashionable language of today's politicians, globalization needs a human face. But I shall contend below that globalization already *has* a human face, and that (economic) globalization is also generally socially benign. In short, if one is interested in improving social outcomes, (economic) globalization is part of the solution, not part of the problem.

What I propose to argue is therefore very different from what even the serious critics of globalization typically believe and propose. It has serious implications also for policy. If it is believed that globalization needs a human face – that is, that it lacks one at present – then one's mind would turn to policy interventions to stop it or to reshape it in constrictive ways. But if it is thought that globalization has a human face, then one would think of policy interventions to supplement and accelerate the good outcomes. The policy prescriptions would thus tend to be dramatically different! I shall therefore conclude with a sketch of which policy prescriptions would improve the outcomes that globalization generates.

Two fallacies of aggregation

But two questions must be faced immediately, or confusion will prevail, as it indeed does in the raging debate on globalization. What does one mean by globalization? And are attitudes towards its virtues and, more emphatically, its vices, as monolithic as the street theatre and the fascination of the media with it suggests? In fact, the answers to both questions are marred by what can only be characterized as *fallacies of aggregation*.

Different aspects of globalization

Globalization, even in its economic aspects (as focused on in this book) has many dimensions. It evidently embraces trade and direct foreign investment or multinationals, and short-term capital flows whose rapidity and size have caused havoc in places ranging from Bangkok to Buenos Aires.[2] But it must also include now-sizeable migrations, legal and often illegal, across borders. And it extends to the diffusion and transfer of technology (such as AIDS-fighting drugs) among producing and consuming nations.

Yet the popular discourse on globalization has tended to blur the lines between these different dimensions, and to speak of globalization and to evaluate its merits and demerits as if it were a homogeneous, undifferentiated phenomenon. Indeed, recent years have seen many polls on attitudes towards 'globalization', one of which I discuss below, and practically all of them are marred by a failure to specify which aspect of (even economic) globalization the respondent is being polled about. So we have no way of finding out what exactly the respondent has in mind when he or she says that globalization is good for him/herself or for the poor or for his/her country.

In fact, the rot goes even deeper. In particular, in the many popular debates I have had with Ralph Nader and other opponents of freer trade before, during and after Seattle, the critics have invariably strayed into the financial crisis that devastated East Asia in the latter half of 1990s, arguing as if the case for freer trade had also been exposed as illusory by this financial crisis.[3] But that is a *non sequitur*.

The case for free trade and the argument for free capital flows have important parallels. But the differences are yet more pointed.[4] The freeing of capital flows in haste, without putting in place monitoring and regulatory mechanisms and banking reforms, amounts to a rash 'gung-ho' financial capitalism that can put nation-states at serious risk from the possibility of panic-fed and rapid reversals of massive short-term capital funds that will drive the economy into a tailspin.

The freeing of trade can hardly do this. If I exchange some of my toothpaste for one of your toothbrushes, we shall both have white teeth; and the risk that we shall have our teeth knocked by this exchange is negligible. By contrast, the proper analogy for capital flows is playing with fire. When Tarzan uses the fire to roast his kill, he feeds himself and has little to fear: a forest on fire is hard to start. But when he returns to England as the long-lost earl, he can carelessly and easily set his ancestral home on fire.

Yet, manifest as this asymmetry is to any but the most ideological economists, it is a common affliction of the untutored. Indeed, they assume that if one is for free trade, one must also be for free direct investment, free capital flows, free immigration, free love, free everything else!

I must confess that, while the case for free trade suffers from this fallacy, and it makes our business of defending the merits of free trade more precarious, I myself have profited from it. Thus, when I wrote of this asymmetry between free trade and free capital flows in 1998 in *Foreign Affairs*, just after the East Asian financial crisis had broken out, alerting all to it, I became a front-rank celebrity. That I, widely complimented and condemned, depending on your viewpoint, as the 'world's foremost free trader' had 'admitted' that unfettered capital flows could be dangerous was considered to be a heresy worthy of the greatest attention. While a few others such as my new (Columbia) colleague Joseph Stiglitz and my old (MIT) student Paul Krugman had also registered their reservations in their own way, I became the poster boy for many who were fearful of 'globalization'. And yet, in truth, I had thought that I was stating the obvious: I had, in fact, never thought otherwise!

The North–South divide: an ironic reversal

The debate on globalization is overlaid and overwhelmed by yet another fallacy, which asserts that the disillusionment with globalization, typified by the street theatre and the campus protests, is *everywhere*. But this belief is simply not true.

In fact, the anti-globalization sentiments are more prevalent in the rich countries of the North while pluralities of the policy-makers and public in the poor countries of the South see globalization instead as a positive force. This was the finding of the World Economic Forum's (WEF's) extensive poll on Global Public Opinion on Globalization, carried out by the Canadian polling firm, Environics International, with 25,000 urban respondents in twenty-five different countries, and presented at the WEF's annual meetings in New York in January 2002.[5]

I call this the 'ironic reversal', since the situation was exactly the other way around in the 1950s and 1960s. At that time, the rich countries were busy liberalizing their trade, investments and capital flows. They saw international integration as the magic bullet that would bring them prosperity; and it did produce the golden age of rising tides that lifted all boats until the OPEC-led explosion of oil prices unsettled the world economy from the late 1970s. But the poor countries were fearful of international integration.

Raul Prebisch, the Argentinian economist, talked then of the dangers to the 'periphery' from the 'centre' in international interactions. The sociologist Henrique Fernando Cardoso of Brazil invented the 'dependencia' thesis, arguing how the poor countries would wind up in the international economy with a dependent status. The Chilean sociologist Osvaldo Sunkel used a striking phrase: integration into the international economy leads to disintegration of the national economy. President Kwame Nkrumah of Ghana, whom the CIA helped to dislodge, wrote of 'neo-colonialism': the embrace by the former colonial powers through innocent-looking instruments such as aid that would intentionally create a crypto-colonialism.

I characterized these fearful attitudes at the time as 'malign impact' and 'malign intent' paradigms, contrasting with the economists' conventional thinking that international integration would benefit all, rich and poor, and was therefore a 'benign impact' phenomenon, whereas aid and other assistance were 'benign intent' policies.[6]

It turned out that many poor countries, which bought into these fearful ideas and turned away from using international trade and investment flows as opportunities to be seized, turned out to have made the wrong choices. Their failures, and the example of the success of the countries of the Far East that used international opportunities to great advantage instead, have proved salutary. The result has been a turn by the South towards more globalization. The sociologist Cardoso who warned of 'dependencia' then became President Cardoso of Brazil, seeking to take Brazil into more, rather than less, globalization. The WEF poll on globalization was simply recording this swing of sentiment.

By contrast, the fearful 'malign impact' ideas have come to haunt several groups, among them the labour unions, in the rich nations. And this reversal, this contrast with the poor countries, is exactly what the WEF poll was picking up. The rich tapestry of reasons why this has happened is of both interest and concern; and it is what I address here.

But before doing that, it is worth noting that the recent polls also show a waning, rather than an enhancement, of the acute anti-globalization of the 1990s. The WEF poll found, for example, that the positive views of globalization (as an omnibus and ill-defined phenomenon) had become more positive in North America and Europe, even while they remained lower than those in the countries of the South, large pluralities of whom continued to express high expectations from globalization. This is also the finding from the polls conducted by the Center on Policy Attitudes of the University of Maryland. Its Americans and the World website, reported on 12 April 2002 that 'Overall, Americans tend to see globalization as somewhat more positive than negative and appear to be growing familiar with the concept and more positive about it. A large majority favours moving with the process of globalization and only a small minority favours resisting it.'[7]

But is too optimistic to go by these polls, which must also reflect changing circumstances in national economic performance. Good times dampen anti-globalization attitudes; while bad times deepen them. The WEF poll is revealing on this: the lowest pluralities in favour of globalization among the poorer nations are Indonesia, Turkey and Argentina, where economies have been through turmoil. And so the task of understanding the anti-globalization sentiments, and responding to them if globalization is to be maintained and managed successfully, remains pressing. To this task I now turn, beginning with what I call a 'trilogy of discontents'.

A trilogy of discontents

Anti-capitalism

As the twentieth century ended, capitalism seemed to have vanquished its rivals. Francis Fukuyama's triumphalism in his celebrated work. *The End of History and The Last Man* (1990), was like a primeval scream of joy by a warrior with a foot atop his fallen victim. It was not just the collapse of communism in Europe, and China's decisive turn away from it. As the energetic anti-globalization NGO, Fifty Years Is Enough, laments, even the Swedish model had lost its appeal. The much-advertised model of 'alternative development' in the Indian state of Kerala had also run into difficulties, much as President Julius Nyerere's celebrated socialist experiment in Tanzania had run the economy into the ground. This vanishing of different possibilities has led to what I have earlier called 'The Tyranny of the Missing Alternative, 'provoking a sense of anguished anti-capitalist reactions from both the old and the young.

The old are fewer, and they matter less, than the young. They could be the generals in the war on capitalism, but the young today are happy to be foot soldiers, fighting on their own. But they can make noise, and these days almost anyone who screams is likely to get, not just heard, but sometimes even listened to.

The old are, of course, the anti-capitalists of the post-war years, ranging from socialists to revolutionaries. They are the ones who, especially when communists or Marxists, are captive to a nostalgia for their vanished dreams.

When the Davos meeting was held by the World Economic Forum in February 2001, there was an Anti-Davos meeting held in Brazil at the same time.[8] (How many know that there is even an Alternative Nobel Prize?) The rhetoric in Brazil was of revolution. I recall George Soros, who properly considers himself to be a radical thinker, a progressive financier, going into a debate from Davos on the video monitor with some of the Anti-Davos participants. I recall his frustration, and indeed astonishment, when he realized that he was the enemy, not a friend, much as the Democrats were chagrined that Ralph Nader thought during the most recent US election that they were not really different from the Republicans.

Soros, who had not interacted with these groups, just did not get it: as far as these anti-capitalist revolutionaries are concerned, anyone who is into stocks and bonds should be put *in* stocks and bonds. Indeed, these groups, who were memorializing Che Guevara and listening to Ben Bella, were the exact antitheses of the Arthur Koestlers of the world who wrote of 'The God That Failed'. They were working from a script – titled 'The God That Failed but Will Rise Again'; they only had to keep the faith.

But the globalizers must also confront the young. And if one has seen images of the streets of Seattle, Washington, Prague, Quebec and Genoa, where the anti-globalizers have congregated with increasing militancy, or seen their impassioned protests on the campuses as I have watched the Anti-Sweatshop Coalition's activities at my own university (Columbia), there can be no doubt that we have here a phenomenon that is truly important in the public space and also more potent: the nostalgia of the fading generation cannot compete with the passions of the rising generation.

So, how is the discontent of the young to be explained? Of course, a rare few among them are like the old. Consider Global Exchange, an NGO that likes to describe itself as a Human Rights group – this is the 'in' phrase much as socialism was in the 1970s, and its moral resonance immediately gets participants on to higher ground and gives them a free pass with the media and the unsuspecting public. It professes politics that is unmistakably in the old revolutionary corner and gets endorsements from the great linguist and activist Noam Chomsky, among other left-wing intellectuals. Quite stereotypically, it describes Israel as 'an exclusionary state' that 'trains other undemocratic, abusive regimes' around the world, and complains that US aid to Israel 'maintains the military-industrial complex here in the US' Its pronouncements on the World Trade Organization (WTO) are no less dramatic and drastic: the WTO 'only serves the interests of multinational corporations' and 'the WTO is killing people'.

But Global Exchange and its radical chic are really a fringe phenomenon. There are several other explanations of what animates the young in particular; each may explain part of the reality, while collectively they provide a more complete explanation.

1 Far too many among the young see capitalism as a system that cannot address meaningfully questions of social justice. To my generation, and that of the British left-leaning intellectuals such as George Bernard Shaw that preceded it, the Soviet model was a beguiling alternative. Indeed, my much-translated 1966 book, *The Economics of Underdeveloped Countries*, contains a distinct not towards the Soviet Union: 'The imagination of many . . . nations has been fired, perhaps most of all, by the remarkable way in which the Soviet Union has raised itself to the status of a Great Power by its own bootstraps and in a short span of time.' How appalling a misjudgement this view of the Soviet alternative seems today, and how commonplace it was then!

That capitalism may be viewed instead as a system that paradoxically can destroy privilege and open up economic opportunity to the many is a thought that is still uncommon. I often wonder, for example, how many of the young sceptics of capitalism are aware that socialist planning in countries such as India, by replacing markets system-wide with quantitative allocations, worsened rather than improved unequal access because socialism meant queues that the well-connected and the well-endowed could jump, whereas markets allowed a larger number to access their targets.

2 But the anti-capitalist sentiments are particularly virulent among the young, who arrive at their social awakening on campuses in fields other than economics. English and comparative literature and sociology are fertile breeding grounds.

Thus deconstructionism, espoused by the French philosopher Jacques Derrida, has left the typical student of literature without an anchor, because of its advocacy of an 'endless horizon of meanings'. Terry Eagleton (2001, p. 128), the sympathetic chronicler of modern literary theory, has written:

> Derrida is clearly out to do more than develop new techniques of reading: deconstruction is for him an ultimately *political* practice, an attempt to dismantle the logic by which a particular system of thought, and behind that a whole system of political structures and social institutions, maintains its force.

True, the Derrida technique will deconstruct any political ideology, including Marxist. Typically, however, it is focused on deconstructing and devaluing capitalism rather than Marxism, often with nihilistic overtones which create the paradox that many now turn to anarchy, not from Bakunin but from Derrida!

The heavy hand of Marxist texts on students of literature, on the other hand, has been beautifully captured by V. S. Naipaul (1998) in his compelling portrait of the Pakistani guerrilla Shabaz, who went from studying English literature in England to starting a revolution (which failed) in Baluchistan:

> There were close Pakistani friends at the university. Many of them were doing English literature, like Shabaz; it was one of the lighter courses, possibly the lightest, and at this time it was very political and restricted. It was encouraging Marxism and revolution rather than wide reading. So Shabaz and his Pakistani friends in their Marxist study group read the standard (and short) revolutionary texts, Frantz Fanon, Che Guevara. And while they read certain approved Russian writers, they didn't read or get to know about the Turgenev novels, *Fathers and Sons* (1862) and *Virgin Soil* (1877), which dealt with conditions not unlike those in feudal Pakistan, but questioned the simplicities of revolution.

As for sociology, many of its students are influenced equally by the new literary theory and the old Marxism. They stand in contempt of economic argumentation that would refute their rejectionist beliefs about capitalism by asserting that economics is about value, whereas sociology is about values. But they are wrong today on both counts.

Economists will retort that, as citizens, they choose ends, but as economists, they choose the (best) means. Moreover, accused of indulging the profit motive, they respond with the legendary Cambridge economist, Sir Dennis Robertson, that economics is addressed heroically to show how 'man's basest instincts', rather than his noblest, can be harnessed through appropriate institutional design to produce public good. Adam Smith would surely have died an unsung hero if he had peddled the pedestrian argument that altruism led to public good.

And, indeed, economists' policy analysis necessarily requires the use of criteria that enable one to say that one policy is 'better' than another. This takes them straight into moral philosophy, of course. One could thus argue that the input of the philosopher, John Rawls, into economic theory has been as profound as that in philosophy; in fact, he drew on the economist Nobel Laureate William Vickrey's concept of the 'veil of ignorance' and gave economists back the maximin principle: a fair trade, I should say!

The presumption that sociology is a better guide to ethics than economics is also misplaced. Certainly, its related discipline, social anthropology, whose many adherents now find their voice in some NGOs, foundations and in the World Bank, traditionally leans towards *preserving* cultures, whereas economics is a tool for *change*. Fascinated by social anthropology, and buried deeply in the writings of the legendary A. R. Radcliffe-Brown and many others, when I studied in England, I still wound up preferring economics for my vocation. What other choice could really have been made by a young student from a country afflicted by economic misery? If reducing poverty by using economic analysis to accelerate growth and thereby pull people up into gainful employment and dignified sustenance is not moral, and indeed a compelling imperative, what *is*?

3. But I should add that many of these students are also susceptible to the bitingly critical view of economics brilliantly propounded by Rosa Luxemburg in her classic essay 'What Is Economics?', the first chapter of a proposed ten-chapter work, only six of which being found in her apartment after her murder. She had argued that 'the new science of economics', which had reached the status of an academic discipline in Germany, was tantamount to an attempted legitimation of the 'anarchy of capitalist production' and was essentially 'one of the most important ideological weapons of the bourgeoisie as it struggles with the medieval state and for a modern capitalist state'. The 'invisible hand', with its rationalization of markets, had a hidden agenda, hence it lacked veracity; a *non sequitur*, of course.

4. But I also think that an altogether new factor on the scene that propels the young into anti-capitalist attitudes comes from a different, technological source in a rather curious fashion. This is the dissonance that now exists between empathy for others elsewhere in their misery, and the inadequate intellectual grasp of what can be done to ameliorate that distress. The resulting tension spills over into unhappiness with the capitalist system (in varying forms) within which the young activists live, and hence anger at it for its apparent callousness.

Today, thanks to television, we have what I call the paradox of inversion of the philosopher David Hume's concentric circles of reducing loyalty and empathy. Each of us owes diminishing empathy as we go from our nuclear family, to the extended family, to our local community, to our county or state (say, Lancashire or Montana), to our nation, to our geographical region (say, Europe or the Americas), and then the world. What the Internet and the media have done is to take the outermost circle and turn it into the innermost, while the same technology, as Robert Putnam has told us, has accelerated our moving to 'bowling alone', glued to our TV sets and moving us steadily out of civic participation, so that the innermost circle has become the outermost one.

So, the young see and are anguished by the poverty, the civil wars and the famines in remote areas of the world but have no intellectual way of coping with it rationally in terms of appropriate action. Thus, as I watched the kids dressed as turtles at Seattle, during the riotous 1999 WTO Ministerial meeting, protesting against the WTO and the Appellate Body's decision in the Shrimp-Turtle case, I wondered how many knew that the environmentalists had won that decision, not lost it! When asked, of course, none knew what they were really protesting; and, when I asked some mischievously if they had read Roald Dahl's famous story about the boy who had freed the giant turtle and sailed away on it into the far ocean, they shook their turtle heads![9] It has become fashionable to assert that the demonstrating youth know a great deal about the policies they protest; but that is only a sentiment of solidarity with little basis in fact. True, there are several serious NGOs with real knowledge and serious policy critiques; but they are not the ones agitating in the streets.

5. Overlaying the entire scene, of course, is the general presumption that defines many recent assertions by intellectuals that in some way the proponents of capitalism, and of its recent manifestations with regard to economic reforms such as the moves to privatization and to market liberalization (including trade liberalization), are engaged, as Edward Said claims, in a 'dominant discourse [whose goal] is to fashion the merciless logic of corporate profit-making and political power into a normal state of affairs'.[10] Following Pierre Bourdieu, Said endorses the view that 'Clinton–Blair neoliberalism, which built on the conservative dismantling of the great social achievements in health, education, labour and security) of the welfare state during the Thatcher–Reagan period, has constructed a paradoxical *doxa*, a symbolic counterrevolution'. In Bourdieu's own words, this is

> conservative but presents itself as progressive; it seeks the restoration of the past order in some of its most archaic aspects (especially as regards economic relations), yet it passes off regressions, reversals,

surrenders, as forward-looking reforms or revolutions leading to a whole new age of abundance and liberty). (Said, 2001)

Frankly, this view stands reality on its head. Of course, we have known since George Orwell that words do matter; and the smart duellists in the controversies over public policy will often seize the high ground by appropriating for themselves, before their adversaries do, beguiling words such as 'progressive' for their own causes. Thus, believe it or not, protectionists in trade have been known to ask for 'tariff reform'; today, they ask for 'fair trade', which no one can deny except for the informed few who see that it is used in truth to justify unfair trade practices. Phrases such as 'corporate profit-making' and 'trickle down' policies do the same for the friends of Bourdieu, creating and fostering a pejorative perception of the market-using policy changes that they reject.

It is therefore not surprising that today's reformers turn to the same linguistic weapons as the anti-capitalist forces of yesterday. But let us also ask: is it 'conservative' or 'radical' to seek to correct, in the light of decades of experience and in the teeth of entrenched forces, the mistakes and the excesses of past policies, no matter how well motivated? In fact, as reformers know only too well, it takes courage and elan to challenge orthodoxies, especially those that are associated conventionally with 'progressive' forces.

As for the policies themselves, the fierce binary contrast drawn by Bourdieu is an abstraction that misses the central issues today. The debate is really not about conservative counter-revolution and the enlightened past order. It is rather about shifting the centre of gravity in public action, more towards the use of markets and less towards *dirigisme*. It is not about 'whether markets'; it is about where the 'limits to markets' must be drawn.

The present-day turn towards reforms in the developing countries is also prompted by excessive and knee-jerk *dirigisme*. As I have often said, the problem with many of these countries was that Adam Smith's Invisible Hand was nowhere to be seen! Their turn to economic reforms is to be attributed, not to the rise of 'conservatism', but to a pragmatic reaction of many to the failure of what many considered once to be 'progressive' policies that would lift people out of poverty, illiteracy and many other ills. As John Kenneth Galbraith once said about Milton Friedman, and here I take only the witticism and not sides, 'Milton's misfortune is that his policies have been tried'!

Anti-globalization

Anti-capitalism has turned into anti-globalization among left-wing students, for reasons that are easy to see but difficult to accept. After all, Lenin wrote extensively about imperialism and its essential links to capitalism; and present-day writers such as Immanuel Wallerstein have seen the growing integration of the world economy in related ways as the organic extension of national capitalism.

Lenin's views on imperialism provide an insight into a principal reason why anti-globalization is seen by those on the left so readily as following from anti-capitalism. In his famous work, *Imperialism: The Highest Stage of Capitalism* (Lenin, 1996) Lenin stated that the 'distinctive characteristics of imperialism' in the form of monopolies, oligarchy and the exploitation of the weak by the strong nations 'compel us to define it as parasitic or decaying capitalism'. Nikolai Bukharin, for whose work *Imperialism and the World Economy* (1915), Lenin wrote a Preface, considered that imperialism with its attendant globalization of the world economy is little more than capitalism's '[attempt] to tame the working class and to subdue social contradictions by decreasing the steam pressure through the aid of a colonial valve'; that 'having eliminated [through monopolies] competition within the state, [capitalism has] let loose all the devils of a world scuffle'.

This notion, therefore, that globalization is merely an external attenuation of the internal struggles that doom capitalism, and that globalization is also in essence capitalist exploitation of the weak nations, does not only provide an inherent link between capitalism and globalization. It also makes globalization an instrument for the exploitation of the weak nations. And this certainly has resonance again among the idealist young on the left: capitalism seeks globalization to benefit itself, but harms others abroad. The Lenin–Bukharin argument then leads, as certainly as a heat-seeking missile, to anti-capitalist sentiments.

Anti-corporations

But central to that perspective is the notion, of course, that it is the 'monopolies' (for that is indeed how the multinationals are often described even today in much of the anti-globalization literature) that are at the heart of the problem: they do not benefit the people abroad; they exploit them instead. Indeed, this notion of globalization as an exploitative force that delays the doomsday for capitalism at home and harms those abroad has captured some of the more militant among the naïve youth of today.

Anti-corporation attitudes come to many others, who are not aficionados of left-wing literature, also from the obvious sense that multinationals, as the B-52s of capitalism and of globalization, that are the object of concern. Their proliferation has been substantial, and unprecedented in history. But their strength is grossly exaggerated because few understand that they, even when huge, undercut one another in economic power because they compete against one another – economists describe this as markets being contestable – and their political power is similarly stifled by economic and national competition in many instances.

Yet others find it plausible that multinationals must necessarily be bad in a global economy because global integration without globally shared regulations must surely amount to a playing field for multinationals that seek profits by searching for the most likely locations to exploit workers and nations, thereby putting intolerable pressure on their home states to abandon their own gains in social legislation in what is feared to be a 'race to the bottom'. Indeed, this view is so credible that even a shrewd and perceptive intellectual such as Alan Wolfe, who sees through cant better than most, has written disapprovingly and casually of the 'policies of increasingly rapacious global corporations' (Wolfe, 2001).

But appealing as this scenario may appear, it will not withstand scrutiny. Much recent empirical work shows that the evidence for a race to the bottom is practically non-existent. The political scientist, Daniel Drezner, has written extensively, showing that we have here much rhetoric by both opponents and supporters of globalization; but no empirical support. Econometricians have also found little to report. This may sound contrary to common sense; surely, these social scientists must be consultants to the corporations? But they are not. There are plenty of reasons why corporations do not rush in to pollute rivers and the air simply because there are no regulations. I suspect that, aside from economic reasons for not choosing, say, environmentally-unfriendly technology, the main check is provided by reputational consequences: in today's world of CNN, civil society and democracy proliferation, the multinationals and the host governments cannot afford to do things beyond the pale.

So the 'obvious' truth of the race to the bottom in an unregulated world turns out to be not so obvious. Economists are indeed a nuisance: they complicate analysis by telling people that their gut feelings are too simplistic. This makes them particularly unpopular with the young, who want to believe what seems perfectly plain but is rarely so in truth.

And so, many of the young zero in, with a 'gotcha' mentality, seizing on every misdeed of a multinational they can find, seeking to validate their anti-corporation biases. This surely accounts for the return of Ralph Nader: the great scourge of misdeeds by corporations. It has also magically transformed Julia Roberts, the passable actress whose early triumph was in *a Pretty Woman*, into an acclaimed actress in *Erin Brockowich*; and introduced the gifted actor Russell Crowe to celebrity on the screen in *The Insider*: both films where a David takes on a Goliath in shape of a venal corporation.

The anti-corporation militancy that is on the rise among the young anti-globalizers is also strategic, of course. We have witnessed the brilliant way in which the anti-globalizers have managed to use the meetings of the international agencies such as the World Bank, the IMF and particularly the World Trade Organization (originally the GATT), the pride of progressive architectural design regarding the management of the world economy and the permanent legacy of legendary men of vision, to protest and profess their anti-globalization sentiments. After all, these meetings were where the world's media gathered. What better place to create mayhem and get attention from the vast multitude of reporters looking for a story? So, where the old guerrillas struck where you *least* expected them, these new guerrillas strike where you *most* expect them: at these meetings!

The same strategic sense has been displayed in attacking the corporations as well. Nike and Gap, two fine multinationals, now have a permanent set of critics, with newsletters and websites worldwide. With Nike and Gap being household names and having gigantic overseas operations that cannot possibly avoid lapses from whatever is defined as good behaviour (for example, that Nike does not pay a 'living wage', as Global Exchange would define it, they represent obvious targets in a propaganda war that is stacked against them. Naomi Klein, the Canadian writer, admitted it frankly in a recent article in *The Nation* (2002): faced with the amorphous but overwhelming globalization phenomenon, the only way to get at it is to latch on to something concrete and targetable. So, they go after the corporations that spread and constitute the globalization that is reprehensible. Teenagers are then seen carrying placards outside Staples and demonstrating in front of Starbucks while their more militant adult friends throw stones through the coffee chain's windows in Seattle. I talk with them at every opportunity; I find enthusiasm, even idealism, but never any ability to engage concretely with the issues they take a stand on. But then the Kleins of the anti-globalization movement are not fazed; it is all strategic, it is in a good cause.

Political alliances

But the recent successes of the anti-globalization forces can also be assigned to the fortuitous alliance struck between the young agitationists and the conventional organized lobbies such as the labour unions, the new pressure groups such as the environmentalists, and movements such as those for human rights.

Seattle saw these groups merge and emerge as a set of coalitions. 'Teamsters and turtles' joined the unions with the students and the environmentalists. 'Green and blue' joined the environmentalists with the blue-collar unions. 'Labour standards' became 'labour rights', heralding the alliance of human rights activists and the unions. The Anti-Sweatshop movement on the campuses signified the return of several union-trained summer interns who would ally themselves, and align their views, with the unions.

While these alliances have made the anti-globalizers more effective to date, the alliances themselves are fragile. Thus, after Black Tuesday's attack on the World Trade Center, the alliance between the unions and the students has turned brittle as the campuses have turned against war, and the unions for it. The turn to violence by the students in Seattle, Quebec and Genoa has also prompted union misgivings: the rank and file of the unions is not sympathetic to such tactics.

The Teamsters have broken with the environmentalists over the Bush Administration's decision on drilling for oil in the Alaska Wildlife Refuge. At the WTO, the environmentalists got their agenda, in some form, on to the Doha Development Round of trade negotiations; but unions did not have their way on a Social Clause, so the blue-and-green alliance is likely to have a parting of the ways similar to the way that there is today no unified bloc of underdeveloped nations in international economic negotiations, but only coalitions around different interests that often cut across the conventional North–South divide. The fissures are therefore many; and, in particular, the negative agenda of anti-globalization is unlikely to be sufficient glue when the disparate groups start on different trajectories of positive achievements.

Confronting anti-globalization: why globalization is socially benign but good is not good enough

But that does raise the broader question: will anti-globalization then collapse? Do not count on it. It cannot happen unless we engage the anti-globalizers on many fronts. Let me sketch some of the principal ways we must do this.

At the outset, we need to use reason and knowledge, in the public policy arena, to controvert the many false and damning assumptions about capitalism, globalization and corporations that I have only sketched, and that cannot be allowed to fester and turn to gangrene. It is truly astonishing how widespread is the ready assumption (endemic by now even in some international institutions) that, if capitalism has prospered and if economic globalization has increased while some social ills have worsened, then the former phenomena must have caused the latter! It has almost reached a farcical level where, if one's girlfriend walks out, it must be a result of globalization – after all, she may have left for Buenos Aires!

Perhaps the chief task facing those who consider globalization favourably is to confront the notion, implicit in varying ways in many of the intellectual and other reasons for the growth of anti-globalization sentiments, that while globalization may be *economically benign* (in the sense of increasing the pie), it is *socially malign* (that is, in terms of its impact on poverty, literacy, gender questions, cultural autonomy and diversity and so on).

That globalization is often the friend of social agendas and not their enemy is not that difficult to argue, once we get down to thinking about the matter deeply and empirically. Take the corporations again. Have they hurt women, as some claim? I would say, far from it. Consider three examples: two from the North, the other from the South. In the first example, Japanese multinationals, as they spread through the world during the years of Japanese prosperity, took their workers with them, and they brought their wives, to New York, Paris, London, cities where the Japanese housewives saw for themselves how women could lead a better life. And that, among other channels of diffusion of ideas and values, has turned them into feminist agents of change. In the second example the economists Elizabeth Brainerd and Sandra Black have shown how wage differentials against women have reduced faster in internationally competing industries, since they can least afford to indulge their biases in favour of men. And, in the third example, women in poor countries also benefit when they find jobs in the globalized industries in export-processing zones. Some feminists complain that young girls are exploited and sent back to where they came from as soon as they are ready for marriage: that they therefore pick up no skills, for example. But ask the girls themselves and one finds the ability to get away from home for work a liberating experience, and the money they earn gives them the 'empowerment' that will not come from being confined to their homes.

Indeed, the jaundiced view of corporations prevents an appreciation of their often beneficial role: familiarity breeds contempt, but contempt does not breed familiarity. Thus the young campus activists against sweatshops accuse the corporations of exploitation of foreign workers. But the available empirical evidence for some developing countries, in studies such as that by Ann Harrison of Columbia School of Business, shows that, in their own factories (as distinct from those of subcontractors or suppliers of components and parts, who probably pay the going wage instead) the multinationals tend to pay what the economics literature calls a 'wage premium' of the order of 10 per cent over the going rate. Is this exploitation? Yes, but only if one is smart enough to know that the English dictionary defines exploiting labour as either using or abusing it!

In fact, even as we continue to teach in the classroom about the nefarious activities of ITT in destroying Salvador Allende's elected Chilean regime, or the sordid story of Union Meuniere in Katanga, we must come to terms with the fact that these examples, and more minor atrocities, have become less likely in a world where democracy – admittedly not always liberal or otherwise pleasing – has broken out in several developing nations, and where again civil society and the media make retribution for misdeeds more likely.

But if common apprehensions about globalization's social impact are in the main mistaken, we cannot retreat into the notion that 'by and large', 'more or less', globalization is helpful. The occasional downside needs to be addressed. This requires imaginative institutional and policy innovation. For example, the insecurity that freer trade seems to inculcate in many, even if not justified by the economists' objective documentation of increased volatility of employment, needs to be accommodated through provision of adjustment assistance. For poor countries that lack resources, such a programme must be supported by World Bank aid focused on lubricating the globalization that this institution praises and promotes.

But we also need to recognize that, particularly with the growth of civil society, there is legitimate impatience with the speed at which globalization will deliver the social agendas. Thus, child labour will certainly diminish over time as growth occurs, partly as a result of globalization. Globalization is part of the solution, not of the problem. But we want to go *faster*. The central question before the globalizers and their foes has to be: how do we do it?

The answer has to be one that is different from the obsession of several lobbies and the US Congress with trade sanctions, a remedy that threatens globalization by using disruption of market access, and hence is fraught with temptation for the protectionists around us. In rare cases of huge moral outrage, a widespread resort to trade sanctions can work. But otherwise, suasion, especially for social agendas that appeal to our moral sense, surely has a better chance. This is particularly true now that we have both CNN and the NGOs.

Indeed, I find it ironic that many among the several serious and thoughtful NGOs at the time of writing, who after all must believe that public action will follow their advocacy, are the ones who are often sceptical of moral suasion. As they search for 'teeth' (in the shape of sanctions), I tell them: God gave us not just teeth but also a tongue; and today a good tongue-lashing is more likely to be effective in advancing the social agendas that we espouse and share. Indeed, teeth may not just be unproductive; they may even be counter-productive. Thus, the sheer threat to exports embodied in the proposed Harkin Child Deterrence Bill led to children being laid off in Bangladeshi textile factories, and female children wound up in worse employment: prostitution! Contrast this with the International Programme for the Eradication of Child Labour at the ILO, which eschews sanctions but does the heavy lifting required to reduce child labour by working with local NGOs, interested aid donors and co-operative host governments, and ensuring that schools are available that children go to the schools, and that impoverished parents who lose the child's income are assisted financially where necessary.

Indeed, a great upside of the use of moral suasion to accelerate the social good being done by economic globalization is that it joins for common good the two great forces that increasingly characterize the twenty-first century: expanding globalization and growing civil society. Partnership, rather than confrontation, can lead to shared success. It is worth the hassle.

A final thought. We need to defend the corporations against ignorant, ideological or strategic assault. They generally do good, not harm. Again, the question has to be: can they help us to do even more good? The purists say that the shareholders must do the social good, not the corporations. But we are well past that, certainly in the USA, when it comes to what they do at home. Non-profit organizations such as Columbia use their student and faculty resources to assist Harlem; Microsoft and IBM assist the communities in which they function, and others too.

In fact, this policy of 'social responsibility' has traditionally made capitalism attractive, giving an added lie to the anti-capitalist and anti-business sentiments. When there were no modern-style corporations but substantial fortunes made by individuals and their families, successful capitalism was characterized precisely by such behaviour. Recall Simon Schama's Dutch burghers with their 'embarrassment of riches', the Calvinists, and the Jains and Vaishnavs of Gujerat in India, Mahatma Gandhi's home state, who accumulated fortunes but spent them, not on personal indulgence but on social causes.

Corporations today need to do just that, each in its own way. Pluralism here is of the essence: no NGO, or government, has the wisdom or the right to lay down what corporations *everywhere* must do. Social good is multi-dimensional, and different corporations may and must define social responsibility, quite legitimately, in different ways in the global economy. A hundred flowers must be allowed to bloom, so that they constitute a rich tapestry of social action that lends more colour to globalization's human face.

Notes

1 The effect of economic globalization on these social agendas is discussed, and a benign conclusion reached, in my earlier-cited book, *In Defense of Globalization* (2004).
2 The recent financial crises have been analysed splendidly in Desai (2003).
3 In fact, this confusion can also be laid at the door of a fine economist such as Dani Rodrik.
4 These differences were noted in Bhagwati (1998). Interestingly, the arguments in that essay have been adopted bodily and endorsed in a remarkable editorial in *The Economist*, 'A Place for Capital Controls', 3 May 2003, p. 15.
5 The distinguished Swedish economist and Member of Parliament, Carl Hamilton, has analysed this and other polls in discussing and rejecting the notion, advanced by NGOs, that in someway trade liberalization has been 'undemocratic'. His paper is available from the Stockholm School of Economics.
6 Cf. Bhagwati (1978), ch. 1.
7 Cf. *http://www.americans-world.org.*
8 That meeting has now been annualized and will run parallel to the Davos meeting each year in Porto Alegre, Brazil. Whereas Davos is organized by the World Economic Forum, the Porto Alegre organizers call themselves the World Social Forum, as if they are concerned with social issues and people, while Davos is concerned with profits and corporations.
9 Roald Dahl (1988).
10 Edward Said (2001), p. 32. The following quote from Bourdieu, the French sociologist, is also from Said's essay.

References

Bhagwati, Jagdish (1966) *The Economics of Underdeveloped Countries*, London: Weidenfeld & Nicolson (World University Library Series).

Bhagwati, Jagdish (ed.) (1977) *The New International Economic Order: The North–South Debate*, Cambridge, Mass.: MIT Press.

Bhagwati, Jagdish (1998) 'The Capital Myth: The Difference between Trade in Widgets and Dollars', *Foreign Affairs*, vol. 77, no. 3, May/June, pp. 7–12.

Bhagwati, Jagdish (2000a) 'Globalization in Your Face', *Foreign Affairs*, vol. 79, no. 4, July/August, pp. 134–9.

Bhagwati, Jagdish (2000b) *Globalization and Appropriate Governance*, WIDER Annual Lecture 4, November, United Nations University, Helsinki.

Bhagwati, Jagdish (2004) *In Defense of Globalization*, New York: Oxford University Press.

Bukharin, Nikolai (1973) *Imperialism and the World Economy*, (first published in English 1929), New York: Monthly Review Press.

Dahl, Roald (1988) 'The Boy Who Talked With Animals', lead story in Dahl's collection, *The Wonderful Story of Henry Sugar*, New York: Puffin.

Desai, Padma (2003) *Financial Crisis, Contagion and Containment: From Asia to Argentina*, Princeton, NJ: Princeton University Press.

Eagleton, Terry, (2001) *Literary Theory: An Introduction*, 2nd edn, Minneapolis: University of Minnesota Press, p. 128.

Fukuyama, Francis (1990) *The End of History and the Last Man*, Penguin.

Klein, Naomi (2002) 'No Logo: No Space, No Choice, No Jobs', *The Nation*, April.

Lenin, V. I. (1969) *Imperialism: The Highest Stage of Capitalism*, New York: International.

Luxemburg, Rosa ( ) 'What is Economics?'

Naipaul, V. S. (1999) *Beyond Belief: Islamic Excursions among the Converted People*, New York: Vintage.

Putnam, Robert (2000) *Bowling Alone: The Collapse and Revival of American Community*, New York: Simon & Schuster.

Said, Edward (2001) 'The Public Role of Writers and Intellectuals', *The Nation*, September 17, no. 8, vol. 273, p. 27.

Wolfe, Alan (2001) 'The Snake: Globalization, America and the Wretched Earth', *The New Republic*, October 1.

2
The Aftermath of Welfare Reform in the USA

Robert M. Solow

The 1996 welfare reform act is now in the normal course of revision and renewal, a process called 'reauthorization' in the American system. Its proper name is the 'Personal Responsibility and Work Opportunity Reconciliation Act' (PRWORA) but this sort of verbal inflation is typical of the US Congress. It cannot be said that either the Administration or the Congress is basing its decisions on any serious analysis of the working of the 1996 Act, and that is an interesting fact by itself. This brief note cannot fill that gap, but it will make some selected inferences, and at least point to the relevant academic literature.

If there are any useful lessons for European countries to be found in the American experience, they will have to take into account the basic motivations of the American legislation and the background presumptions that conditioned its form. The motivations and presumptions are not necessarily the same in Europe and America. For example, there is little or no interest in the USA in redistributional policy intended primarily to diminish existing inequality. I have come upon an indicator of this difference in a separate, but closely related, context. When the OECD discusses 'low-wage work' it usually defines this as work paying less than two-thirds of the median wage. The incidence of low-wage work is then really a measure of wage-compression, not wage-level. A worker in a 'low-wage' job could, in principle, experience a wage-reduction from one year to the next, and simultaneously move out of the low-wage category. American usage would prefer an absolute standard, like the so-called 'poverty line.' The significant point is that welfare policy in the USA is not about redistribution, though of course it will inevitably have redistributional effects.

Analogously, the welfare-reform discussion in the USA is not really about the reduction of poverty either. When the question arises, as it does, typical responses are usually vague references to the long run, sometimes even the intergenerational long run. It is not a strong argument against a proposed provision in the welfare system that its immediate effect may be an increase in the incidence of poverty (although references to child poverty carry much more weight in public and Congressional rhetoric).

So what is welfare reform about? The emphasis is mostly on employment, more or less for its own sake. The work ethic is very strong and unforgiving: middle-class Americans think of making do on transfer payments as a morally repugnant state, unacceptable to the body of taxpayers. (There may be an exception for the physically or mentally disabled.) Welfare recipients themselves feel this stigma strongly, and they internalize it and express it, as I documented some years ago in *Work and Welfare* (Solow, 1998). This is perhaps part of the individualism that is so pervasive in American society. One of its consequences for welfare policy is that it tends automatically to rule out simultaneous dependence on work and welfare as a permanent pattern for some members of society.

Finally, I want to mention another important aspect of the American discussion of welfare policy that may or may not have echoes in some parts of Europe. Most welfare recipients in the USA are single mothers, sometimes very young, and disproportionately African-American. It is not surprising, then, that debate about welfare policy becomes mixed up with attitudes towards race, sex and illegitimacy, topics not generally associated with rational social policy. That is why attempts to promote marriage and reduce non-marital births find their way into welfare legislation. But the whole debate is affected.

Many of the important innovations of the 1996 Act had to do with the allocation of financing and control between the federal government and the states. These will not have much meaning or interest for Europeans, so I shall not bother with details here; they were important in the American context because effectively they ended any federal commitment to universal social assistance.

The two major social-policy provisions of the Act were (a) a work requirement for welfare recipients; and (b) cumulative time limits for the receipt of welfare payments. Under (a), at least half of all recipients in 2002 and after were required to be working or enrolled in other activities designed to improve their employability. States were given a lot of leeway in the definition and design of these programmes. In effect, moreover, the law allowed states to count any reduction in case-loads as an offset to the work requirement. This has proved to be a significant escape hatch, and it plays an important part in current debates over reauthorization.

Under (b), the legislation limited any welfare recipient to, at most, 60 months of benefit cumulated over a lifetime. Welfare could not be 'a way of life'. States were allowed to set shorter limits, but not longer ones, for the use of federal funds; they could, however, exempt up to 20 per cent of their caseloads from this requirement, and could allow longer limits if financed entirely from state funds.

Between them, these two provisions were to mark the 'end of welfare as we knew it'. As you might expect, then, the 'success' of the 1996 Act has been discussed in the political arena mainly in terms of the evolution of caseloads. It is an easily available measure, and, while it provides no information about the number of successful transitions to jobs, it does say something about the speed with which welfare as we knew it is being made to disappear. Unfortunately – for the careful social scientist, though not for the careless politician – it is not clear exactly what the caseload figures are trying to say.

The striking fact is that the aggregate welfare caseload at the end of 2001 had fallen by almost 60 per cent of its previous peak value. That sounds like a clear verdict. But there are at least three reasons to doubt any simplistic interpretation. First, caseload reduction began in 1994, two years before the passage of the Act. It is conceivable that the change in public attitudes that led to welfare reform was already visible enough in 1994 to affect the behaviour of the welfare population, actual and potential; but that seems a little implausible and certainly cannot be taken for granted. It is probably more relevant that many states had launched experimental welfare-to-work programmes in the early 1990s, some of which had experienced modest success in reducing recourse to the welfare system. (There is excellent research on these programmes, much of it by the Manpower Demonstration Research Corporation (MDRC) – see the later reference to a booklet by Gordon Berlin – but they fall outside my main topic in this chapter.)

Second, the peak caseload in 1994 and the 1996 Act came just as the boom of the 1990s was entering its most hectic phase. The number of welfare cases would surely have decreased if there had been no legislation. In all, between 1994 and 2000, 17.5 million net jobs were created. Non-farm employment rose by a little over 15 per cent, with an average increase of 2.4 per cent per year. Some part of the drop in the caseload has to be attributed to sheer prosperity and demand-pull in the labour market; it is not obvious how big that part was, and how much is left to be accounted for by reform legislation.

Third, there was an unusually sharp rise in the caseload between 1990 and 1994; it is possible that part of the post-1994 reduction was an unwinding of that earlier anomaly. There too, the quantitative interpretation cannot be read from the gross figures and needs to be estimated by whatever research methods can be brought to bear.

There has been an enormous amount of econometric research aimed at explaining variations in welfare caseloads in terms of more fundamental economic variables; any such explanation will also provide an estimate of the specific effect of the 1996 Act on the evolution of caseloads after 1996. An important advantage of the US economy as a test-bed for this kind of research is the possibility of extracting information from both interstate and intertemporal variation in caseloads and certain economic variables (such as employment). The main entry point for anyone wishing to identify and study this body of research is the clear and comprehensive survey by Rebecca M. Blank (2002).

This is a hard question, and it is made more difficult by the fact that other policy actions were occurring at the same time as welfare reform, especially changes in the Earned Income Tax Credit. There were several forces operating to change the incentive to seek work. Another complicating factor is worth explicit emphasis, because it rarely plays a part in econometric policy analysis: the effect of a given formal policy usually depends non-trivially on informal details of the way it is administered by local civil servants. It is natural to see this in US-based research, because state bureaucracies have a lot of *de facto* independence, even if formally they are subject to the same rules.

The answers emerging from different studies, using different data and different economic and statistical models, are thus not all the same. But neither are they seriously contradictory. It is no surprise that caseloads are sensitive to both macroeconomic conditions and policy actions. It is a little disconcerting, however, that the degree of sensitivity seems to vary over time – before and after 1996, for example. So extrapolation to future policy actions is not automatically valid. Nevertheless, it is a reasonable conclusion that the 1996 Act was responsible for something between a third and a half of the dramatic fall in welfare caseloads after 1996.

The research that has been reported so far has naturally not had time to make use of data arising from the fairly short recession and considerably longer period of relative stagnation that has characterized the US economy since 2001. When that has been done, one can hope that margins of error will narrow. Between September 2000 and September 2001, the national caseload fell by 7.4 per cent; and between September

2001 and September 2002 it fell by another 6.3 per cent. So the reduction has continued into the period of macroeconomic weakness. States vary in their patterns, with some showing a rising caseload. Some of the differences relate to disparate economic conditions, while others may reflect differences in the way the law is administered. In any case, we can be pretty sure that this particular policy action has had its effect, but that the claims of politically motivated enthusiasts are subject to the usual significant discount.

Merely reducing the caseload is not the ultimate goal of welfare reform, however, except perhaps for a few libertarian extremists. If it were, the caseload could be reduced to zero by abolishing the programme outright. In the US context, though not necessarily elsewhere, the final evaluation of welfare reform depends on what happens to former welfare recipients and potential future welfare recipients, and most particularly on their labour-market experience, and that is a lot harder to measure. Even those who leave the welfare rolls for jobs may lose them soon afterwards, without returning to welfare. Unfortunately, there is no nationwide system for tracking the employment (and other) status of welfare-leavers after they have left the system. There are, as will be seen, some fragmentary research studies.

Rebecca Blank points out that single mothers with children under the age of 18 increased their labour-force participation rate substantially in the mid-1990s. The rise began in 1993–4, and accelerated sharply after 1996. She reports other scattered bits of evidence of increased work effort by women currently and recently on welfare. But she notes too that there were other influences besides welfare reform working in the same direction at that time. And, of course, there is the besetting obstacle to unambiguous inference that the strong labour market of the late 1990s would have siphoned many women off welfare in the absence of any legislation.

I will mention the results of one study, just to give the flavour of what has been done. It was carried out in New Jersey, Washington and Wisconsin among early TANF recipients (Cancian *et al.*, 2003) (TANF stands for Temporary Assistance to Needy Families, the name given in 1996 to the welfare system that replaced the old AFDC – Aid to Families with Dependent Children.)

It happens that these three states, though they differ in terms of social and economic characteristics, in the nature of their TANF programmes, and in the ethnic and other composition of their client populations, have tracked substantial samples of current and former welfare participants (about 2000 in New Jersey; and 3000 in

Washington and Wisconsin). One problem for the researchers is to compile comparable answers to interesting questions, despite the difficulties arising because the individual states draw on different mixes of administrative data and answers to differently-stated survey questions, and cover slightly different time periods during 1999–2001. One lesson for any European country that wants to understand the consequences of its own policy actions is the importance of setting up a uniform system for tracking and acquiring well-designed data about a sample of those who pass through the welfare apparatus (and, *nota bene*, a demographically reasonable control group or comparison group).

Here is a sample of conclusions from three years of observation in these three states. In all three, the fraction of the sample that had at least some earnings and no TANF payments rose over the three periods to 58 per cent in Wisconsin (which seems to have provided the most extensive support apparatus for welfare-leavers), 44 per cent in Washington, and 40 per cent in New Jersey. The fraction with neither earnings nor TANF also rises over time, to about 30 per cent in Washington, a little more than that in New Jersey, and a little less in Wisconsin. (The subgroups that decrease are those with both earnings and TANF – very small – and those remaining on TANF, with no earnings.) There are obvious complications in interpreting these figures.

The survey data include some figures on income from a variety of sources in addition to TANF payments and earnings (for example, food stamps, the earnings of a spouse or partner, transfers from the federal government and so on). Again, there are questions of interpretation, including those that arise from the extraordinary national prosperity of those years; in any case, mean income from all sources seems to have increased for these women, although with wide dispersion.

The researchers make an interesting estimate for the probability of being employed and off TANF in Year 2, for each state and for various demographic subgroups. For example, a woman aged 20–29, white, with a high-school education, never married, with two children and the youngest under age three, and some work experience in the two years before entry into TANF, the probability is close to 50 per cent in New Jersey and Washington, and 80 per cent in Wisconsin. These proportions drop to one-third in the first two states and two-thirds in Wisconsin for those who have less than a high-school education. (The proportion of all welfare clients without a high-school education is 39 per cent in New Jersey, 21 per cent in Washington, and 46 per cent in Wisconsin.) It is fairly certain that these projected probabilities would be less favourable in a period with a softer labour market. These estimates are consistent with other studies of welfare-leavers – for example, Loprest (2001). I would have to agree with the conclusion arrived at by Cancian *et al.* (2003), that 'the challenge of designing programs that can move single-parent families from difficult circumstances to modest levels of economic success remains unresolved'.

A serious assessment of the success of welfare reform will turn ultimately on the extent to which it moves the relevant population out of poverty, at least absolute poverty. Perhaps something, but certainly not much, can be said for a policy that moves a fraction of the welfare population into jobs, but leaves them worse off than before. Only the punitive-minded would be satisfied with that outcome. The evidence on this question is fragmentary. Blank (2002) surveys the available studies. Once again, it must be kept in mind that the years immediately following 1996 were a time when pervasive macroeconomic forces were improving the labour-market status of unskilled workers.

The three-state study by Cancian *et al.* (2003) shows that poverty rates decreased in all three state samples during the years covered. (Interestingly, the fraction with income of less than half the poverty line increased slightly in Washington and Wisconsin, but this was more than offset by the fall in the fraction between half the poverty line and the line itself.) Not much can be inferred from this fact. These were boom years, after all, for reasons that had nothing to do with welfare reform. And there is no explicit comparison group in the study, though surely poverty rates must also have fallen in the non-TANF population.

For the USA, the consequences of this particular 1996 legislation are naturally of special interest. For other countries contemplating their own welfare-reform decisions, there is an equally interesting body of research that studies the effects of state-designed and state-operated welfare-to-work programmes in the years just before 1996 (and, in some cases, after that). Because these experiments were not the result of national legislation, they could be designed with random-assignment control groups, to allow careful estimation of programme effects. Much of this work was pioneered by the Manpower Demonstration Research Corporation, and elaborate detail is available in their project-by-project reports. For overviews, see Gueron and Pauly (1991) and Berlin (2000).

Here is a bird's-eye view of the general conclusions to be drawn from this extensive and excellent work, as they seem to me. Welfare-to-work schemes more often than not generated statistically significant favourable differences between experimentals and controls: those in the programme were more frequently employed, and often at higher average wages, than the controls. But the differences were usually quite small, and often not enough to compensate for the loss of welfare payments. Those in the programmes may not have been better off for the experience, especially considering that there are child-care and other costs associated with working.

It is possible that the long-run gains from work experience will be substantial and long-lasting enough to enable the welfare-to-work experience to create a clear lifetime gain for those involved. One of the truly important aspects of the MDRC studies is that data collection through follow-up interviews with experimentals and controls were usually continued for several years after experimentals had left the programme. The results varied: in some cases the programme effect seemed to attenuate after a couple of years, while in others it persisted, and sometimes appeared to widen. The important residue is that the programmes do improve employment and earnings prospects for those involved, but definitely not dramatically.

A second general conclusion is interesting and provocative, and perhaps not yet fully understood. Most of the state welfare-to-work programmes included a 'work-first' option and a 'human-capital' option. In the first, the initial and main emphasis was on organized job-search, the details of job-readiness, and, if all else failed, some sort of public or semi-public employment experience. The idea was to get the welfare recipient into some form of paid employment as quickly as possible. In the second option, the initial emphasis was on some sort of educational supplementation, usually at a fairly low level; many welfare recipients had not completed secondary school. The idea, of course, was to increase later employability. Most programmes had some system for selecting and changing these options.

It is perhaps surprising that the work-first participants seem on the whole to have had better success in the job market than those exposed initially to an educational experience. There are several possible interpretations of this result. It may only mean that the particular educational supplements tried were generally inadequate, providing little or nothing in the way of improved employability. Or it may mean that work experience, or even just job-seeking experience, adds more to employability and earning power than the educational option. Or, alternatively, while the work-first advantage seemed to persist over the follow-up period, it is possible that still further down the road the advantage of the educational option will show itself. But that is pure optimism, as far as the current evidence is concerned.

Some more recent experiments suggest a further generalization (Berlin, 2000). What they have in common is that those experimental subjects (all drawn from the welfare rolls) who found jobs and worked at them for a substantial number of hours per week (say 35 hours) were provided with very large wage supplements, generally enough to lift them above the conventional poverty line. They also had access to health, child-care and similar services. The results were very promising; not only were labour-market outcomes favourable, but also were self-reported family and behavioural tendencies. These more expensive programmes apparently led to considerably deeper changes in the welfare of participants.

There is a generic uncertainty about all these local experimental programmes: one does not know if they could be scaled up successfully to the national level and made universal. To take an obvious difficulty, they usually require skilled and dedicated administrators, and they are in short supply. Outcomes may depend on the quality of the support staff. A less obvious uncertainty is the so-called 'displacement' issue. When welfare recipients in substantial numbers make successful transitions to jobs, to what extent is there a net increase in unskilled employment, and to what extent do they merely displace formerly-employed (non-welfare) workers? There is no convincing answer to that question, and it is hard to see how a practical test could be constructed. The key here is to realize that the total amount of employment, including – though to a lesser extent – unskilled employment, is in large part a macroeconomic fact. The creation of an incremental supply of unskilled workers has to be accompanied by appropriate demand-side policies, or else the net burden may simply fall on the working poor.

In addition to the fundamental MDRC reports referred to earlier, a brief tabular survey of the relative advantages and disadvantages of alternative welfare-to-work policies can be found in the paper by Grogger *et al.* (2000), published by the Rand Corporation. This contains a reference to the full Rand Report.

What might a European learn from the American experience with welfare reform? I would suggest just a few broad conclusions:

1. One needs to be clear about the goals: reducing the incidence of welfare, increasing employment, diminishing inequality, improving the lives of the unskilled.
2. Any policy initiatives should be accompanied from the start by carefully designed evaluation research; there is no other way to distinguish policy effects from good or bad coincidences.

3. Dramatic effects are very unlikely. It is better to start with the expectation that success consists of small incremental improvements in the status of the welfare population, however that is to be measured.
4. The welfare population responds to incentives, like anyone else. If it is desired to move part of the welfare population into the world of work, what is needed are policies that are complementary to work rather than substitutes for work. The Earned Income Tax Credit is the important example in the US. It amounts to a wage subsidy, payable through the tax system, to low-wage workers and it phases out as earnings rise beyond a certain point. (On this point, see the note by Haveman (2002/3).
5. My own view is that one of the major mistakes in US policy is the absolute time limit. (In practice, some states find ways to circumvent the federal five-year time limit, because they find it counter-productive.) Room should be found for those in the population who can have reasonable lives only with a combination of welfare and work.

References

Berlin, Gordon (2000) *Encouraging Work, Reducing Poverty: The Impact of Work Incentive Programs*, New York: MDRC.

Blank, Rebecca M. (2002) 'Evaluating Welfare Reform in the United States', *Journal of Economic Perspectives*, December, pp. 1105–1166.

Cancian, Maria; Klawitter, Manika M., Meyer, Daniel R., Rangarajan, Anu, Wallace, Geoffrey and Wood, Robert G. (2003) 'Income and Program Participation Among Early TANF Recipients: The Evidence from New Jersey, Washington and Wisconsin', *Focus*, vol. 22, no. 3, Summer (Institute for Research on Poverty of the University of Wisconsin).

Grogger Jeffrey, Karoly Lynn, and Klerman, Jacob Alex (2000) 'Conflicting Benefits: Trade-Offs in Welfare Reform', *Rand Review*, vol. 26, no. 3, Fall (Rand Corporation).

Gueron, Judith and Pauly, Mark (1991). *From Welfare to Work*, New York: Russell Foundation.

Haveman, Robert (2002/3) 'When Work Alone is Not Enough', *La Follette Policy Report*, vol. 13, no. 2, Fall Winter Robert M. La Follette School of Public Affairs, University of Wisconsin.

Loprest, Pamela (2001) *How Are Families that Left Welfare Doing?*, Assessing the New Federalism Project, Urban Institute, Washington, DC.

Solow, R. M. and Gutmann, A. (eds) (1998) *Work and Welfare*, Princeton, N. J.: Princeton University Press.

3
Among the Believers: The Emerging Threat to Global Society*

Mats Lundahl

Globalization is usually thought of in economic terms as consisting of trade flows, factor movements, spread of information and technology, and financial flows. To this may also be added the increasing independence and harmonization of economic policies across wide areas, ranging from stabilization policies to income and welfare policies. This view is shared both by those who advocate globalization as a means for increasing living standards and welfare levels, and by those who contend that its impact is wholly or partly negative.

The present chapter deals with a 'different' negative aspect of globalization: its tendency to call forth violent responses from extreme groups who, in their frustration over global trends, do not hesitate to resort to outright terrorism to further whatever 'alternative' cause they may deem worthy. This is the 'dark' side of globalization. In their attempts to prevent globalization on what is perceived as 'Western', 'American, "capitalist" or other derogatory terms, terror groups set up their own mulitinational networks, make use of modern, global communication facilities and strike against any target of their fancy in the world.

The actions of these groups are amenable to economic analysis. On the occasion of the centennial of the Nobel Prize in 2001, the Stockholm School of Economics organized a series of seminars with former Laureates in economics, who were invited to talk on some topic related to their work's and to answer questions from the audience. One of the speakers was Gary Becker, who was asked the question, among others, of whether he thought that what had happened on September 11 was susceptible to rational analysis, with tools drawn from economics. The answer was an unconditional 'Yes'. I agree, and the present chapter constitutes an effort in this direction.

In a recent book, written in the wake of September 11, military historian Caleb Carr (2002) has suggested that terror is an inefficient strategy that sooner or later bounces back on the perpetrators: it does not work. In the end, the group or regime practising it will be beaten or deposed, precisely because the very act of practising terrorism will ensure its defeat by mobilizing resistance to it. I think that this is, if not fundamentally wrong, at least a truth with very strong modifications. Chinggis Khan lasted for over twenty years, Joseph Stalin for almost twenty-five, Rafael Trujillo in the Dominican Republic for over thirty, and the empires set up by the Mongols and the Soviets for considerably longer. Empires and great powers rise and fall, and in the long run we are all dead, even the most ruthless of rulers, with or without the help of others, but whether this eventual outcome is the result of their terrorism is a completely different matter. While the murder of Trujillo may indeed be linked to his liberal administration of terror to the Dominican people, arguing that the collapse of the Soviet Union was due primarily to the same cause, or that there was a direct link between the dissolution of the Mongol empire and the atrocities committed by its armies amounts to stretching the thesis far beyond what is reasonable.

Under certain circumstances terrorism is an extremely efficient instrument. It all depends on what you want to achieve. The relevant question to ask must be: what purposes does terrorism serve? We will not argue that terrorism serves all kinds of purposes: it does not – and while it is very versatile, there is a limit to what terrorism may achieve, and this is where I think Carr goes wrong. Terrorism is just one of many instruments used to conquer and keep power, territory, people and wealth, and it is not possible to establish any direct links between the use of terror and the causes of the collapse of empires. In what follows we will focus on precisely this: terrorism as an instrument on the one hand, and what motivates terrorism on the other.

Little has been done, not only to look at terrorism but also to incorporate conflicts in general into the main body of the economic literature.[1] In his recent collection of papers on conflict, Jack Hirschleifer (2001, p. 1) begins by quoting Vilfredo Pareto (1971, p. 341): 'The efforts of men are utilized in two different ways: they are directed to the production and transformation of economic goods, or else to the appropriation of goods produced by others', and then goes on to note that traditional economics has been devoted almost exclusively to the analysis of the former of these ways. This in no way implies that no conflict theories exist – on the contrary – but indeed that these theories have 'developed as separate fields with no recognition of their common foundation in the microeconomics of production and exchange' and even more that 'a unified theory' that allows 'for *both* of the two main forms of social interaction: on the one hand exchange and contract, and on the other hand struggle and contention' is lacking (Hirschleifer, 2001, p. 2). But of course, as George Stigler (1984) has reminded us, economics is the 'imperial science'. Can we use it for an analysis of terrorism as well? Let us begin with a look at our object of study: the events of September 11.

September 11

On 11 September 2001, at 8.45 a.m., American Airlines Flight 011, a Boeing 767, crashed into the northern Twin Tower at the World Trade Center in New York City, where 50,000 people were working in some 450 companies. The world was stunned. Was it an accident? At 9.03 a.m. United Airlines Flight 175, also a Boeing 767, hit the southern Twin Tower, which collapsed less than an hour later. After another half-hour the northern tower was converted to debris as well. By then it was completely clear: this was no mere accident. Shortly after the second hit, American Airlines Flight 077, a Boeing 757, ripped a 61-metre-wide hole in the Pentagon building in Washington, DC, killing 189 people. The three planes had been hijacked in the air. A fourth plane – United Airlines Flight 093, also a Boeing 757 – obviously aimed at the White House, or possibly Camp David – crashed into a field south-east of Pittsburgh, Pennsylvania, with 44 people on board, after a violent struggle between passengers and terrorists. The four aircraft – full of fuel and scheduled for transcontinental flights – had been hijacked more or less simultaneously in the air after take-offs from the airports of Newark, Boston (two) and Washington, DC. As the world would later learn, at the end of the day, more than 3,000 people had lost their lives – 2,823 of them at the World Trade Center. The calculations of the economic costs of September 11 run high, not for the terrorists, who may have spent as little as US$200,000, but for the US economy: possibly as much as US$2 trillion (Navarro and Spencer, 2001).

The evidence was strong that the deeds were the work of a terrorist network known as al-Qaeda ('The Base') believed to span as many as forty to sixty countries, established in 1989, collaborating with the Hizbollah guerillas in Lebanon and possibly also with the Islamic regime in Iran. It had a record of setting up training camps for terrorists and warriors from a number of Islamic countries in the Sudan, after the Islamic coup there in 1989, and, since 1996, also in Afghanistan. Its leader was the enigmatic Osama bin Laden (Bodansky, 2001; Bergen, 2002); a super-rich Saudi constructor, a one-time favourite of the royal family, heading a consortium that every year turned over tens of billions of dollars, but who had lost his Saudi passport in 1994. Bin Laden was suspected of involvement in the previous attack on the World Trade Center in February 1993, and of being behind the bombings of the US embassies in Nairobi and Dar es Salaam in August 1998 (Reeve, 1999; Bodansky, 2001). He had been in hiding in Afghanistan since 1991, protected by the Taliban and their leader, the notorious Mullah Muhammad Omar, and from there he masterminded the events of 11 September.

The events proved that terrorism is a highly organized, and in that sense, rational, phenomenon. The al-Qaeda organization had managed to carry out a co-ordinated attack against some of the main symbols of a hated enemy. There was no question. The world changed on 11 September. Terrorism and its repression made it into the living rooms of the world, and people are increasingly running the risk of seeing it as a recurrent feature of their lives. The year 2002 was marked by an escalation of the struggle between Palestinian suicide bombers and the Israeli army, repeating the experience of New York and Washington, DC, only on a smaller, but almost daily, scale.

Unfortunately, the phenomenon of terrorism is not new in Western society. Violent anarchism emerged as a feature of the extremist political scene in the late nineteenth century (Woodcock, 1962). The Stern and Irgun gangs figured prominently in the events that led to the creation of the modern state of Israel. Sundry Palestinian organizations have subsequently proved that they have learnt the same game. The Irish Republican Army (IRA) has been active since 1969. Euskadi ta Askatasuna (ETA) regularly makes its detonations heard in Spain. The Italian Brigate Rosse (Red Brigades) had their day, as did the Baader–Meinhof gang (the Rote Armee-Fraktion) in Germany, and the Sendero Luminoso (Shining Path) began to spread death and despair in Peru in the 'People's War' it initiated in 1980. Examples abound (see Kumm, 2002).

Among the believers I: the principal

One way of looking at the rationality behind the events of September 11 is as a principal–agent problem. The principal has a goal, and in order to achieve it needs to recruit agents who are willing to sacrifice their own lives. Let us begin with the former.

As far as the terrorist principal is concerned, we may assume that his goal is to maximize what he thinks of as his striking power; that is, his capacity to hit a given target – for example, buildings or civilians at home or abroad. Björn Kumm (2002, pp. 253–4) has pointed to the possible logic behind September 11:

> the thought may be that . . . a spectacular action would inspire, galvanize the believers and make the Muslim masses of the entire world go into a holy war in defense of Islam – and this defense would be even more efficient if the attack against New York and Washington would make the Great Satan, the USA, strike blindly, indiscriminately, against all Muslims.

In order to make the hit, the terrorist must recruit agents to carry out the terrorist actions. We may furthermore assume that the more agents there are, the higher will be, *ceteris paribus*, the capacity to hit. In Figure 3.1 this is captured in the striking power (*SP*) curve. Like everything else, however, terrorist activity is likely to be subject to diminishing returns, so the SP curve will become gradually flatter as spending increases:

$$SP = S_P(M) \tag{3.1}$$

where M is the number of agents and $S_P^M > 0$ and $S_P^{MM} < 0$.

Figure 3.1 also contains a second curve: the risk for retaliation or repression (*RR*) from the intended targets or their governments – something that will weaken the terrorists') power to strike. We assume that the more the terrorist principal spends, the more visible he becomes, and the more likely it will be that his adversaries opt for a pre- emptive strike against him. Thus,

$$RR = R_R(M) \tag{3.2}$$

and $R_R^M > 0$ and $R_R^{MM} > 0$.

The maximum striking power, M_m, is found when

$$S_P^M = R_R^M \tag{3.3}$$

In the case of what Rathbone and Rowley (2002, p. 7) call non-stationary or roving terrorists who operate via a network of cells in

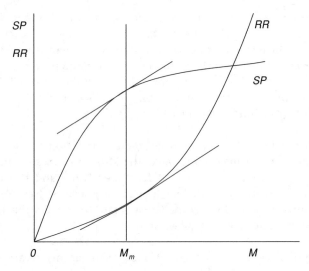

Figure 3.1 The principal's striking power

many countries, without being in the middle of a population or population segment with whom they identify, are difficult to detect, and the risk of major retaliation against them is low. This moves M_m in Figure 3.1 towards the right and increases the net striking power for any M.

The two curves of Figure 3.1 can be merged into a single one – $NSP = SP - RR$, as in Figure 3.2, showing the net benefit to the terrorist principal of spending on recruitment of agents (the distance between SP and

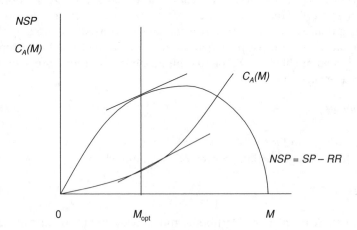

Figure 3.2 The optimum of the terrorist principal

RR). This curve rises first and peaks at M_{opt}, and thereafter falls again. Figure 3.2 also contains a recruitment cost curve. We may use the standard assumption that terrorist agents can be recruited only at an increasing marginal cost, so that

$$CA = C_A (M), \ C_A{}^M > 0, \ C_A{}^{MM} > 0 \tag{3.4}$$

The principal finds the optimum number of agents by equating the marginal benefits and costs of recruiting, at M_{opt}.

Among the believers II: the agents

Next we have to model the situation of the agent. What does *his* cost–benefit calculation look like? For this we may use the framework developed by Gordon Tullock (1974) to deal with the economics of revolution. This focuses on both collective and private benefits. If we assume that the prospective agents sympathize with 'the cause' they are likely to regard the strength of the organization as a collective good. When the organization strikes it does so for all the members. A hit makes all members feel 'better', because they feel that the cause has been furthered by the terror action. However, this benefit accrues to all prospective members regardless of whether or not they join the terrorist organization. They cannot be excluded from it. Thus there is a benefit (B_p) from remaining passive, equal to the public good (P_g) generated, multiplied by the likelihood (L_v) that the attack will succeed:

$$B_p = P_g L_v \tag{3.5}$$

If the individual chooses to be a terrorist agent, the calculation changes:

$$B_t = P_g (L_v + L_i) + R_i (L_v + L_i) - P_i [1 - (L_v + L_i)] - I_t L_w \tag{3.6}$$

Equation (3.6) shows the benefit of the prospective agent if he in fact enters the service of the principal. L_i is the *increase* in the likelihood that the attack will succeed that is related to the entry of the agent. This increases the expected public benefit. Entry into active service also brings some private rewards (R_i), say, a 'salary'. Against these public and private benefits the agent has to put two cost items. The first is the likelihood that he will be punished if for some reason the attack fails (P_i). This happens with probability $[1 - (L_v + L_i)]$. The last term is the physical injury (I_t) that the agent may suffer multiplied by the probability of an injury (L_w).

If we get rid of the term common to both inaction and participation we arrive at the net benefit to the agent of participating in the terror attack:

$$NB_t = P_g L_i + R_i(L_v + L_i) - P_i[1 - (L_v + L_i)] - I_t L_w \qquad (3.7)$$

What about the magnitudes of the variables in expression (3.7)? Tullock argues that, in the case of a revolution, the increase in the likelihood that the revolution will succeed precisely because the individual in question joins is low: 'It is likely that any individual joining in the revolution as opposed to remaining at home and cheering will normally make only a tiny change in the likelihood of success, perhaps improving the likelihood of success from .53278 to .53279' (Tullock, 1987, p. 63).

That would make the first term small. Tullock also claims that the private benefit accruing to someone fighting as a common soldier is low. However, neither statement seems to hold true in the case of terrorism. Revolutions should be thought of as large-scale wars in comparison to terrorist actions, and the performance of a single individual may make a lot of difference in the latter case. Also, the private rewards may be substantial, but let us save that for the time being. We will come back to this issue below. Instead, we may proceed to look at the cost terms, none of them can be neglected. Should the attack fail (for example, because the agents carrying it out are caught before they can do what they have planned), punishments may be hard indeed, and if the terrorist network is ill-prepared or under strong surveillance the probability of success may also not be high. Finally, there is the likelihood of injury. For a suicide bomber, this likelihood is equal to one and the injury will be fatal. This, in turn, means that all terms of Equation (3.7) except the last one (which will equal – I_T) will vanish. The cost–benefit calculation will be unambiguously negative. The principal will never be able to recruit any agent, unless, of course, he can force people to become suicide bombers or brainwash them. Both of these possibilities are real see, for example, Reuter, 2003), but we will disregard them in the following.

Still, agents abound. It is obvious that, as formulated in Equation (3.7) the Tullock model does not capture the core feature: that terrorists are willing to sacrifice their own lives. Clearly, people in general will never do so if they can avoid it. What we are dealing with is a principal–agent problem that goes far beyond the normal, and the difficult part is, of course, how the self-sacrifice should be modelled. A very simple way is the following. We may conceive of the agent as having a two-period utility function:

$$U = (C_W, C_\infty) \tag{3.8}$$

The agent can consume goods in the present world (W) but he can also consume goods in Paradise (∞). The utility function, in other words, extends beyond death. If this formulation is accepted we can analyse the agent's behaviour with the aid of standard consumer theory.

There is no question for the believer about the reality of the Islamic Paradise and its desirability (Farah, 1987, p. 117):

> The Qur'ān goes into considerable detail to portray the nature of . . . rewards. The righteous will gain eternal peace and joy in the garden of Allah, studded with trees, flowing water, and all the niceties which the desert Arabian considered the chief attractions of his ideal of paradise.

> And hath awarded them for all that they endured, a Garden and silk attire.
> Reclining therein upon couches, they will find there neither (heat of) a sun nor bitter cold.
> The shade thereof is close upon them and the clustered fruits thereof bow down.
> Goblets of silver are brought round for them, and beakers (as) glass.
> There serve them youth, whom, when thou seest, thou wouldst take for scattered pearls.
> Their raiment will be fine green silk and gold embroidery.
> Bracelets of silver they will wear. Their Lord will slake their thirst with a pure drink.
> (And it will be said unto them): Lo! This is a reward for you. Your endeavour (upon earth) hath found acceptance.

> . . . The rewards of Paradise . . . vary in degree, depending on earned merits . . . as seen in the verses of the Qur'ān, if taken literally . . . [these] rewards are depicted in sensual and material terms with body and soul together being subjected to them.

The preferences for consumption in the next world can be reinforced systematically by suitable indoctrination, (for example, in a Qur'ān school), as witnessed in recent television interviews from the primitive *madrasas* in Pakistan during the war in Afghanistan. Indoctrination also lowers the cost curve in Figure 3.2. The indoctrinated terrorist is satisfied with fewer worldly goods, which in turn makes it possible for the principal to recruit more agents. Kumm (2002, p. 255) quotes Sayid Hassan Nasrallah, the leader of the Lebanese Hizbollah:

> Imagine that you are in a sauna . . . It is tremendously hot, but you know that in the next room there is air conditioning, a comfortable chair, classical music and a cocktail. Then it is easy to enter the next room. This is how I would like to explain to a Westerner how a martyr thinks.

What is the price of the pleasures of Paradise? The Qur'ān regulates what a good Muslim has to do in order to get in. He has to pray five times a day, he has to fast during Ramadān, and go to Mecca on pilgrimage (*hajj*) at least once in his lifetime if he can afford it. He has to pay poor tax (*zakāh*) (Farah, 1987, p. 141):

> Invariably referred to as the 'poor tax' or 'poor-due' and 'almsgiving', the *zakāh* literally means giving back to Allah a portion of His bounty as a means of avoiding the sufferings of the next life, and as an 'expiation' or 'purification' of what the Muslim retains for himself of material possessions.

> While the *zakāh* may be regarded as an act of beneficence, a precept of right-doing and a charitable act in a moral sense, *zakāh* is less of a voluntary and more of a required religious observance; indeed it is a fundamental of the faith.
> Establish worship and pay the poor-due and obey the messenger, that haply ye may find mercy.

The believer has to spend in the way of Allah; that is, he has to give assistance to the needy: 'righteous is he who . . . giveth his wealth, for love of Him, to kinsfolk and to orphans and the needy and the wayfarer' (Farah, 1987, p. 126). This imposes a number of obligations:

> To be beneficent is . . . [a] duty of each Muslim who respects the commandments of his religion. In its broader application beneficence (*birr*) obligates the faithful to act rightly in all

circumstances: comfort the poor with material gifts, be truthful in transactions, good in his communal relations, and constantly mindful of God's will in every aspect of his dealings, all of which must conform to the principle of right-doing. It is the duty of and the privilege of the one who has to give to him who has not. 'And in their wealth the needy and the deprived have due share', states the Qur'ān. (ibid., p. 129)

Thus, given his preferences, the relative price of terrestrial and heavenly goods as well as his budget restriction, Figure 3.3 depicts how the agent maximizes his utility by choosing OA units of the former and OB units of the latter. These amounts also define the optimum time to leave this world for the other: when you have consumed OA of worldly goods. For a normal Muslim the optimum may be impossible to attain, not least because the Qur'ān prohibits suicide, but it is of course not impossible for a terrorist agent. He is involved in a holy war and can choose the time e.g. by carrying out an act of suicidal bombing.

Choosing to become a terrorist has a definite advantage from the economic point of view. It shifts the budget line outwards, since, once the agent has joined the terrorist organization he will be subsidized by it, and so will his family, especially in the event of his death. The families of dead Palestinian suicide bombers receive economic compensation and pensions via the fundamentalist organizations, out of funds that have been collected throughout the Muslim world (*El País*, 2002;

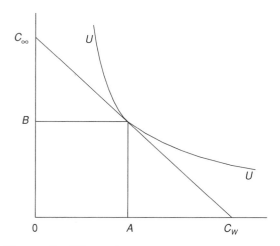

Figure 3.3 The agent's utility maximum

Reuter, 2003, p. 93). As far as the dead terrorist himself is concerned, his status in Paradise will also increase, because he will enter as a *mujāhid* who has died in the holy war (*jihād*) against the infidels. In the extreme version that concerns us here, the 'classic Islamic belief in jihad as a defense of Islam and the Muslim community against aggressions was transformed into a militant jihad culture and worldview that targets unbelievers, including Muslims and non-Muslims alike' (Esposito, 2002, p. 16). Intimately connected with the concept of holy war is martyrdom (ibid. pp. 33–4):

> Martyrs who sacrifice their lives to establish Islamic ideals or to defend those ideals hold a special place in Islam. The Quran has many passages that support the notion of martyrdom and that comfort those left behind. For example, 'Were you to be killed or die in the way of God, forgiveness and mercy from God are far better than what they amass' (3:157); and, 'Never think that those who are killed in the way of God are dead. They are alive with their Lord, well provided for' (3:169). Both Sunni and Shii traditions, value and esteem martyrdom in their beliefs and devotions.
>
> . . . Muslim tradition teaches that martyrs are distinguished from others in life after death in several ways: their self-sacrifice and meritorious act render them free of sin and therefore they are not subject to the post-mortem interrogation of the angels Nakir and Munkar; they bypass 'purgatory' and proceed to one of the highest locations in heaven near the Throne of God; as a result of their purity, they are buried in the clothes in which they died and do not need to be washed before burial.

The organization of a terrorist coup has to contend with the problem of collective action as analysed by Mancur Olson (1965, 1982). Organization is not easy, especially not in the case of large groups. The free rider problem is tremendous, so selective incentives are needed: 'Senior members who actively plan or execute terrorist attacks are provided with affluent life-styles and international travel that are unattainable through ordinary market transactions' (Rathbone and Rowley, 2002, p. 2), and those lower down receive their share, but frequently not until they are in Paradise. The glorification of martyrdom plays an important part here.

The best breeding ground for terrorism is found in impoverished communities where gloom has carried the day. Life is hopeless. Every thing has been tried, but nothing works. In this situation it is easy to fall prey to messages about a better life, be it here and now, or be it in Paradise. Frequently the promises made come from what Eric Hobsbawm (1959) has called 'primitive rebels' – 'pre-political' people who have not yet found any specific language they can use to express their aspirations – and the setting is one of modernization in the Western sense, often (but not necessarily) the advent of capitalism. This triggers a conservative reaction among the losers: a primitive rebellion that aims at going back to the circumstances at hand during some distant or not so distant 'golden age'. The change (Hobsbawm, 1959; p. 3):

> comes to them from the outside insidiously by the operation of economic forces they do not understand and over which they have no control . . . They do not grow with or into modern society: they are broken into it . . . Their problem is how to adapt themselves to its life and its struggles.

In this situation, new religious movements frequently spring up. As Avinash Dixit and Gene Grossman (1984, pp. 1087–8) have remarked, 'free entry into the religion business . . . [is] an assumption that seems well supported by casual empirical observation'. Then the typical cycle unfolds: once the movement has begun, the prophet or Messiah and his followers go into the middle of nowhere and found a holy place or city that arouses the suspicions of the powerful in society. In the end the military move in, wipe out the holy city and its inhabitants, and the movement is destroyed. History abounds with examples (see, for example, Hobsbawm, 1959; Pereira de Queiroz, 1965; Lundius and Lundahl, 2000, esp. ch. 10).

Much better, of course, is when an organized religious movement is already around, particularly if it is organized on a mass basis – and this is precisely where the fundamentalist version of Islam comes into the picture. Esposito (2002, p. 83) has pointed to some of the main characteristics of the societies where Islam, including violent Islam, experienced a revival during the last decades of the twentieth century:

> The causes of the resurgence vary by country and region but there are common threads: widespread feelings of failure and loss of identity in many Muslim societies, as well as failed political systems and economies. Overcrowded cities with insufficient social support systems, high unemployment rates, government corruption, a

growing gap between rich and poor, and the breakdown of traditional religious and social values plagued many nations.

As Bernard Lewis has demonstrated in a couple of recent books (Lewis, 2002, 2003), the history of Islam for centuries has been one of economic stagnation and decline in comparison to the industrialized West and more recently also the East Asian nations. And the fruits of whatever economic progress has taken place have not been shared by the masses but have been concentrated in the hands of the few. This comparative decline and degradation has been capitalized on by ideologues of different shades and intensities making their own use of history to reproach Western values, influences and Western-style globalization. They advocate an active embrace of the traditional values, customs and laws of Islam, as well as a firm commitment to their spread on the one hand, and the active use of violence against those perceived as being responsible for the negative influences, on the other.

The extreme interpretations of Islam are often to be found on the other side of the modernizing coin (Bodansky, 2001, pp. xiv–xv):

> The Muslim world has found itself at a historical crossroads. Its encounter with Western civilization seems to have failed despite the unprecedented wealth accumulated by the elite. Attempts to consolidate modern regimes brought about widespread repression and impoverishment of the masses, creating popular tension for which the state system has no solutions and that further modernization can only exacerbate. And the Islamist intellectuals – popularly called 'fundamentalists' – could not transform their alluring theories into practical solutions . . . And so, starting in the late 1970s, Islamist thinkers could see no way out of the crisis of Islam except for an all-out confrontation with the West that would be incited once an excuse legitimizing the outbreak of violence was provided.

They share the conviction of Samuel Huntington (1998) that there is a clash between the Western and Islamic civilizations, and the 'solution' they advocate is violent confrontation. Not least in Palestine, the sufficient conditions for this exist (Esposito, 2002, p. 99):

> What drives young Muslims to become suicide bombers? . . . The increased use of force under the Ariel Sharon government sparked the second intifada, which began in September 2000. Growing up

oppressed and under siege, facing a future with little hope, high unemployment, and endemic poverty can produce an anger and desire for revenge against those responsible. Just as among inner city youth in the United States, some of those young people lose all hope: For others, religion holds the answer. For a small minority suicide bombing seems a proud and powerful response.

Repression of terrorism, especially when it takes the form of bulldozing living quarters and destroying the means of subsistence for the community from which the terrorists and recruited, will shift the budget line inwards, as shown in Figure 3.4, but not only that. It is likely to have at least two more effects. In the first place it will change the relative price of the two goods. Destruction of the means of subsistence makes terrestrial goods relatively more expensive; that is, forgoing a given amount of heavenly goods will now buy fewer terrestrial commodities than before. Also, preferences may be affected, both among those who are already terrorists, and among those who are not. The former may now choose to leave this world earlier, that is, they will want to increase their consumption of heavenly goods and reduce that of worldly ones at given prices and incomes. For example, if

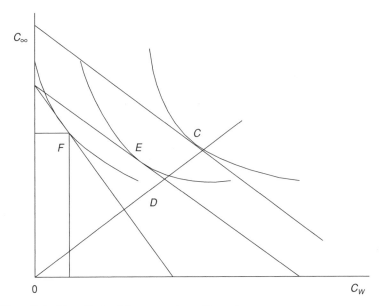

Figure 3.4   The effects of the repression of terrorism

preferences are homothetic, instead of moving from C to D at given relative prices the terrorists would end up at a point north-west of the CDO line – for example, E. Since the relative price of heavenly goods has fallen, the new equilibrium will, however, be in F instead.

Also, those who are not terrorists are likely to be affected by the repression in the same way. Their incomes are reduced, they face a higher price on worldly goods than before, relatively speaking, and the despair in their lives is likely to increase, shifting their preferences in favour of Paradise. According to the standard Fisherian theory of time preference, when people get poorer their consumption preferences tend to shift in favour of more present and less future consumption, and the same is true for people who approach the end of their life (Fisher, 1930, ch. 4). Once we allow for the possibility of consuming in the afterlife as well, however, this may no longer be true. The vast majority of members of the community from which terrorists are recruited may consider themselves collectively to be 'poor' (Hobsbawm, 1959, p. 4). Christoph Reuter (2003) has argued that suicide bombers are not recruited exclusively, and not even mainly, from among the poorest groups,[2] but that is not necessary. What matters is rather that they perceive that their poverty increases, or that of the society in which they live, with which they sympathize, and where their worldly consumption must take place. Under these circumstances, their preferences for consumption in Paradise may well increase, and the more massive the repression and the more widespread the destruction, the more likely is a general feeling that life is poorer than before, both economically and otherwise. Recruitment of terrorists is then likely to be easier than before. The income level in the community has fallen, and prices and preferences have shifted in such a way as to further the interests of the terrorist organization.

This is also likely to produce a ratchet effect (see Andvig and Moene, 1990). We may assume that different people require different amounts of money to join a terrorist organization, and that the population in the community from which terrorists are recruited display a more or less normal distribution in this respect. In Figure 3.5 the prospective terrorists are ordered from left to right with respect to the amount they require to join the terrorist organization, in ascending order of payment ($). As payment increases, more and more people choose to join the organization, and once we approach the point where the curve starts bending sharply upwards numbers increase rapidly. In this way we may move from a situation with very few terrorists to one with many. Let us now go backwards instead; for example, by reducing the income of terrorist principals, or by reducing their numbers, so as to decrease the size of payments as well. But then we will not come back to the same equilibrium as where we started, since in the meantime preferences have changed because incomes have fallen, as a result of the repression, and this has changed the normal distribution as well. On average, smaller payments than before are required to induce people to become terrorists. Society may be stuck in a high-terror equilibrium even though terrorist agents are being paid less than they used to be.

The ideological variety of terrorism lends itself to economic analysis as much as the other two varieties we have been concerned with in this chapter. What is needed is a principal–agent setting. The principal wants to maximize his striking power and to this end must hire agents capable of carrying out the terror deeds. The agents in turn appear to have nothing to gain by becoming terrorists – at least in the cases that involve committing suicide for the cause. At first sight, the free-rider problem appears so formidable that recruitment of agents seems impossible. Once we are open to the possibility of consumption not only in the present world but also in the next one, however, the situation changes, and recruitment can be explained with the aid of simple standard consumer theory.

The explanation also has an important corollary: the type of repression of terrorism we are presently witnessing in Israel is not efficient, unless carried to extremes, and then only in the short-run perspective. On the contrary: it may serve just to increase the number of potential suicide bombers. What is needed is a strategy that builds on improvement of the economic and social conditions of the groups from where the terrorists are recruited. The higher your income and living standard, the less likely you are to perform acts likely to produce retaliation that

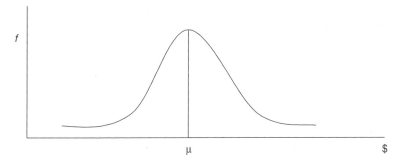

Figure 3.5 Frequency distribution of terrorists

destroys your standard of living. To argue that the money spent may simply be used to finance more terrorism would be to miss the point, since doing nothing about the conditions that produced terrorism in the first case will simply perpetuate them, and the alternative, retaliation, will make them deteriorate even more. Clearly, something else is needed. If President George W. Bush wants to proclaim in the future that he rid Afghanistan and Iraq of terrorists, he must begin by ensuring that the economic and social conditions likely to breed the phenomenon disappear, and in the case of Israel and the Palestinians nothing can be achieved without going back to the negotiation table.

Notes

* Thanks are due to Kai Konrad and Steffen Huck for constructive criticism, and to Kerstin Ankerst and Lilian Öberg for bibliographical assistance.
1 Cf., however, Enders and Sandler (1995), for a survey of the existing economic literature on terrorism.
2 Reuter's conclusion that it is the specific circumstances of each case that determine whether people become suicide bombers or not is not very helpful. It simply substitutes pure 'ad hockery' for attempts at generalization or classification.

References

Andvig, Jens Chr. and Moene, Karl Ove (1990) 'How Corruption May Corrupt', *Journal of Economic Behavior and Organization*, vol. 13 pp. 63–76.
Bergen, Peter L. (2002) *Holy War, Inc. Inside the Secret World of Osama bin Laden*. London: Phoenix.
Bodansky, Yossef (2001), *Bin Laden: The Man who Declared war on America*. Roseville, CA: Prima Publishing.
Carr, Caleb (2002) *The Lessons of Terror. A History of Warfare against Civilians: Why It Has Always Failed and Why It Will Fail Again*, New York: Random House.
Dixit, Avinash and Grossman, Gene (1984) 'Directly Unproductive Prophet-Seeking Activities', *American Economic Review*, vol. 74, pp. 1087–8.
Enders, Walter and Sandler, Todd (1995) 'Terrorism: Theory and Applications', in Keith Hartley and Todd Sandler (eds), *Handbook of Defense Economics, Vol. 1*, Amsterdam: North-Holland.
Esposito, John L. (2001), *Unholy war: Terror in the Name of Islam*. Oxford: Oxford University Press.
Farah, Caesar E. (1987), *Islam: Beliefs and Observances*. 4th edn, New York: Barron's.
Fisher, Irving (1930) *The Theory of Interest. As Determined by Impatience to Spend Income and Opportunity to Invest It*, New York: Macmillan.
Hirschleifer, Jack (2001) *The Dark Side of the Force: Economic Foundations of Conflict Theory*, Cambridge University Press.

Hobsbawm, Eric (1959) *Primitive Rebels: Studies in Archaic Forms of Social Movement in the 19th and 20th Centuries*, Manchester: Manchester University Press.

Huntington, Samuel P. (1998) *The Clash of Civilizations and the Remaking of World Order*, London: Touchstone Books.

Kumm, Björn (2002) *Terrorismens historia*, 2nd edn, Lund: Historiska Media.

Lewis, Bernard (2002) *What Went Wrong? Western Impact and Middle Eastern Response*, New York: Oxford University Press.

Lewis, Bernard (2003) *The Crisis of Islam: Holy War and Unholy Terror*, New York: The Modern Library.

Lundius, Jan and Lundahl, Mats (2000) *Peasants and Religion: A Socioeconomic Study of Dios Olivorio and the Palma Sola Movement in the Dominican Republic*, London New York: Routledge.

McGuire, Martin C. and Olson, Mancur, Jr (1996) 'The Economics of Autocracy and Majority Rule: The Invisible Hand and the Use of Force', *Journal of Economic Literature*, vol. 34, pp. 72–96.

Navarro, Peter and Spencer, Aron (2001), 'September 11, 2001: Assessing the Costs of Terrorism', *Milken Institute Review*, vol. 2, pp. 16–31.

Olson, Mancur (1965) *The Logic of Collective Action: Public Goods and the Theory of Groups*. Cambridge, MA and London: Harvard University Press.

Olson, Mancur (1982) *The Rise and Decline of Nations: Economic Growth, Stagflation and Social Rigidities*. New Haven and London: Yale University Press.

País, El (2002) 'Las ventajas de ser padres de un "mártir" ', 20 July.

Pareto, Vilfredo (1971) *Manual of Political Economy*, New York: Augustus M. Kelley.

Pereira de Queiroz, Maria Isaura (1965) 'Messiahs in Brazil', *Past and Present*, no. 31, July, pp. 62–86.

Rathbone, Anne and Rowley, Charles K. (2002) 'Terrorism', *Public Choice*, vol. 111, pp. 1–10.

Reuter, Christoph (2003) *Med livet som insats: En bok om självmordsbombare*, Lund: Historiska Media.

Schelling, Thomas C. (1984) *Choice and Consequence: Perspectives of an Errant Economist*, Cambridge Mass. London: Harvard University Press.

Stigler, George J. (1984) 'Economics – the Imperial Science', *Scandinavian Journal of Economics*, vol. 86, pp. 301–13.

Tullock, Gordon (1974) *The Social Dilemma: The Economics of War and Revolution*, Blacksburg, Va.: University Publications.

Tullock, Gordon (1987) *Autocracy*, Dordrecht: Kluwer.

Woodcock, George (1962) *Anarchism*, Cleveland, Ohio: The World Publishing Company.

4
Multinational Enterprises and Their Effect on Labour Markets*

Karolina Ekholm

Introduction

The most distinctive feature of the current globalization process is perhaps the increased importance of multinational enterprises (see, for example, Bordo *et al.*, 2000). Foreign direct investments (FDI), the main channel by which multinationals expand abroad, have exhibited very high growth – even higher than the growth in world trade in goods and services. During the late 1980s and early 1990s, the yearly rate of growth in total FDI flows was around 20–25 per cent, and during the late 1990s it was as high as around 40 per cent (UNCTAD, 2001)[1].

The expansion of firms national boundaries raises many issues about how it affects the world economy and the individual countries involved, as home and host countries of multinational firms. We often hear fears being expressed that the expansion of multinationals has adverse effects on workers in both the home and host countries: in the home countries because the expansion abroad may lead to a loss of jobs, and in the host countries because multinationals may be able to exploit foreign workers in terms of working conditions and wages. There are especially important issues at stake for the welfare state. The mobility of firms has implications for the mobility of the tax base. If the existence of tax differentials is a strong motive for firms' expansion abroad, a high degree of firm mobility is likely to limit the ability of governments to finance the welfare state out of corporate taxes.[2] Moreover, if the ability of firms to relocate activities does indeed lead to unemployment and downward pressure on wages in high-wage countries, the effect will be to reduce the tax base while increasing expenditure on unemployment benefits, thereby implicitly threatening the sustainability of the welfare state.

This chapter discusses what economic research has contributed to our knowledge about whether these fears are justified. It starts out with a brief account of the theory of the multinational enterprise (MNE) and its implications for the effect of an expansion of MNEs on labour in both home and host economies. It then discusses a number of empirical studies that have attempted to estimate the effects based on detailed data over the foreign operations of MNEs. It also discusses a few recent attempts to study whether an expansion of Western European firms into Central and Eastern Europe can be expected to have negative effects on employment and wages in Western Europe. The focus on Central and Eastern Europe is motivated by the fact that it constitutes a low-wage region in geographical proximity to the large welfare states in Western Europe. With the recent closer integration between the different European regions, Central and Eastern Europe has become an obvious potential location for firms producing for the European market, thereby also potentially reducing wages in Western Europe. Finally, in the last section we discuss what conclusions can be drawn from these studies.

The theory of the multinational enterprise

There is a long-standing theoretical literature on the multinational enterprise, focusing on various aspects of the international operations of firms. It was, however, not until the mid-1980s that the multinational enterprise was fully integrated in the theory of international trade (Helpman, 1984; Markusen, 1984). At the time of writing, there is well-established theory that is set in general equilibrium, but incorporates elements from industrial organization, such as scale economies and imperfect competition.[3] The literature based on this theory usually distinguishes between *horizontal* and *vertical* FDI. The former occurs when the firm invests in similar types of activities to those it carries out at home, whereas the latter occurs when the firm fragments its production geographically and locates different stages of production in different countries. According to the theory, horizontal FDI is driven mainly by market-seeking motives, such as the desire to supply large markets without having to incur trade costs associated with exporting from the home country (Horstmann and Markusen, 1992; Brainard, 1993; Markusen and Venables, 1998, 2000). Vertical FDI, on the other hand, is driven by production-cost motives. According to theory, the firm reduces overall production costs by locating labour-intensive stages in low-wage countries, and stages that require intensive input of capital and highly skilled labour in countries in which these input factors are relatively cheap (Helpman, 1984; Helpman and Krugman, 1985).

In the public debate about the operations of multinationals, it is often taken for granted that their foreign operations are of the vertical type, in so far as they are assumed to be motivated by low production costs. However, empirical studies of the determinants of FDI find that horizontal-type (or market-seeking) FDI seem to dominate in the aggregate (see, for example, Carr *et al.*, 2001; Markusen and Maskus, 2002). The fact that most FDI takes place within the industrialized countries is indicative of the relative importance of horizontal FDI.

In a synthesized model, which is often referred to as the knowledge capital model, both motives for investing abroad co-exist (Markusen, 1997, 2002). In this model, firms can separate geographically two different activities: a skill-intensive headquarters activity, and a less skill-intensive production activity (but the production activity is still more skill-intensive than the production of other goods in the economy). Whether one motive will be dominant over the other depends on the characteristics of the home and host countries. If one country is relatively small and skilled labour abundant, and the other is large and skilled labour is scarce, there will be vertical MNEs with headquarters in the small country and production in the large country. In this case, the small country specializes in skill-intensive headquarters activities, while some or all of the firms headquartered in the small country will find it advantageous to supply the consumers in the large country through affiliate production. An example of this would be when a firm based in a small and peripheral country such as Sweden, Norway or Denmark mainly keeps headquarters activities such as R&D, management and marketing at home, while most of the production takes place abroad.

If, instead, the two countries are relatively similar in both size and relative factor endowments, horizontal FDI will predominate, since there are no advantages for either country to specialize in headquarters activities (although there are still advantages to be gained from supplying customers from local plants). An example of this case would be when a US firm decides to supply the European market from a plant located within the European Union (EU).

One way of drawing out the implications of this theory for labour is to think about what happens when there is investment liberalization, moving from an initial situation without any FDI to a new situation where FDI may occur. It turns out that the effects from vertical and horizontal FDI are fairly similar: there will be two opposing effects on the demand for labour in the home country, one stemming from a *relocation* of activities and the other from *increased competitiveness* of the firm. In the following we shall go through the effects in the horizontal and vertical cases separately.

With vertical FDI, the firm is able to reduce per-unit costs by exploiting international differences in factor prices so that, for example, skill-intensive headquarters are located in a high-wage country, while less skill-intensive production plants are located in a low-wage one. We can see two effects from this. First, as a firm goes from being a national firm to a multinational one, there will be a relocation of production activities from the high-wage to the low-wage country. Second, the reduction in per-unit production costs will make the firm more competitive, which will enable the firm to capture a larger market share and expand its overall activities. Since the increase in home-country employment resulting from the increase in firm competitiveness will involve more highly skilled labour than the labour originally employed in the relocated activities, both effects of a vertical FDI will contribute to an increase in the relative demand for skilled labour compared to unskilled labour. The long-run effect of this type of FDI is therefore to shift the demand for labour towards skilled labour, and to put upward pressure on the relative wage between skilled and unskilled labour in the home country.

In the host country, the effect may also be to increase the relative demand for skilled labour. Although the activity relocated from the high-wage country is relatively intensive in unskilled labour from the perspective of the home country, it may still be relatively intensive in skilled labour from the perspective of the host country – that is, it may be skill-intensive relative to other sectors in the host country. This means that an increased specialization in affiliate production might lead to an increase in the relative demand for skilled labour in the host country as well.

The short-run effect of vertical FDI for home-country labour is less clear. This effect, defined as the change in the parent firm's demand for labour, will depend on whether the negative effect on employment from a relocation of activities outweighs the positive effect on employment from increased competitiveness.

Now let us consider the case of horizontal FDI. In this case, the firm will go from being a national exporting firm to being a multinational serving foreign consumers from a foreign affiliate. Again, there will be a relocation of activity, in this case of export production. Again, the ability to serve foreign consumers more cheaply from a foreign affiliate will make the firm more competitive, thus potentially leading to an increased market share and an expansion of overall activities. In this case, however, it is less clear that there will be long-run effects on labour demand stemming from a changed composition of skilled and unskilled labour. The relocated activity is likely to use skilled and unskilled labour in similar proportions to the ones remaining in the home country, although the existence of a skill-intensive headquarters may make overall activities in the parent firm somewhat more skill-intensive compared to the case with a national exporting firm. The short-run effect on firm employment will again be determined by the net effect from the decrease stemming from the relocation of exports production, and the increase stemming from an overall expansion of the firm's activities as it becomes more competitive.

What about the effects on labour in the host countries, apart from a possible long-run change in the skill composition of labour demand? In general, the effects on the host country's economy can be divided into effects related to *technology transfers*, effects related to technological *spillovers*, effects related to changes in the degree of *competition*, and effects related to *repatriation of profits*. Foreign firms often have an informational disadvantage compared to domestic firms, because of poorer access to information about local institutions, demand conditions and business practices. This implies that, in order to enter a foreign market, a foreign firm usually has to have some advantage that compensates for this informational disadvantage. Superior technology and know-how is one such advantage. When a foreign affiliate of an MNE with superior technology compared to domestic firms employs local workers, these workers will be more productive than if domestic firms had employed them. In such a case, the superior technology of the MNE has been transferred to the foreign affiliate, and this technology transfer makes local resources employed by the affiliate more productive than if domestic firms had employed them.

The superior technology and know-how brought by the foreign firm may also spill over to domestic firms. That is, by observing and/or interacting with MNEs operating in the country, domestic firms may be able to improve their productivity. If such spillovers occur, it will raise the productivity of workers employed in domestic firms as well. Productivity of domestic firms may also increase, but for a different reason – namely that the entry of foreign firms leads to stronger competition in the domestic market. In particular, the entry of foreign firms may break up local monopolies, or make collusion between local firms less feasible. However, the effect of entry of MNEs on the degree of competition does not necessarily have to be positive; if a highly productive MNE were to drive local competitors completely out of business, the degree of competition would be likely to decrease instead.

A final point regarding the host-country effects of MNE activity is that, if the MNE operates in a market that allows it to generate pure profits, these profits will not be included in the host country's national income but will be repatriated and added to the national income of the home country instead. Compared to a situation with only domestic firms operating in this market – a situation in which all the profits generated would be included in the host country's national income – this causes a potentially negative effect on host-country welfare. However, at the same time, it should be noted that if the MNE enters a country by acquiring a domestic firm, expected future profits will be at least partly reflected in the acquisition price – which means that the host country may capture part of the rents generated by MNEs through this mechanism.

Out of the four possible effects on host country welfare, there are thus two positive and one negative effect, and one whose direction cannot be determined *a priori*. The net effect on host-country welfare will be determined by the relative strength of these effects. For host-country labour, the most important effects are technology transfer and technology spillovers. Both effects would generate an upward pressure on wages, and thereby be beneficial for labour.

Empirical evidence on home country effects

Long-run effects

We now turn to the empirical evidence on labour market effects of the expansion of MNEs, and start by considering evidence relevant to assessing the effects on labour in the home country of a multinational.

Some researchers have studied whether a foreign expansion of MNEs has led to a change in the composition of labour demand. For example, Feenstra and Hanson (1996, 1999) have studied the contribution of *international outsourcing* to the observed increase in the skill premium in the USA.[4] The outsourcing focused on by Feenstra and Hanson does not only relate to the activities of multinationals, but also of subcontracted independent foreign firms producing intermediate inputs used by US companies. They find that outsourcing is indeed an important source of an increase in the relative demand for skilled labour in the USA. Whether this is mainly a result of vertical FDI, or of arm's-length trade in intermediate inputs between US firms and foreign producers, however, is not assessed.

A study that also uses US data but focuses directly on the effect of the foreign operations of MNEs is Slaughter (2000). M. Slaughter examines whether a foreign expansion by MNEs has contributed to an increase in the relative demand for skilled labour in the USA. He finds basically no such effect. However, in a similar study based on Swedish data, Hansson (2001) finds some evidence that a foreign expansion in non-OECD economies led to an increase in the relative demand for skilled labour in Sweden. A foreign expansion in OECD economies, on the other hand, had no effect. This result fits in nicely with the predictions from theory, which say that, whereas vertical FDI from a skill-abundant country should lead to an increase in the relative demand for skilled labour, there is no strong reason for horizontal FDI to affect the relative demand for skilled labour at all.

Taken together, this evidence suggests that there are only small, or even negligible, effects of FDI on the relative demand for skilled and unskilled labour, although outsourcing in a broader sense, encompassing arm's-length trade in intermediate inputs, does seem to have a significant effect. One might ask what determines the choice between FDI and arm's-length imports of intermediate inputs in this context. That is, given that the firm has decided that the best location for production of its intermed iate inputs is abroad, what determines whether production takes place in a foreign affiliate or in an independent firm subcontracted by the importing firm? This question relates to what determines the boundaries of the firm, an issue that has been researched extensively but is not yet fully understood. There are, however, reasons to expect that if the technology required for producing the intermediate input is relatively advanced and proprietary of the producer of the final good, FDI will be chosen over subcontracting. Subcontracting would in this case entail licensing technology, and it may be difficult for the final producer to get a licensing fee that matches the return the firm would have as the owner of the intermediate input producer.[5] Moreover, producing intermediate inputs with sophisticated technology may entail investment in very specific machinery, and this creates potential incentive problems if the upstream and downstream producers are organized into separate firms.[6] This implies that subcontracting would tend to involve technology that is less advanced than FDI. The empirical results discussed here are consistent with this prediction in so far as subcontracting seems to be associated with a stronger international specialization in high- and low-skilled activities than FDI.

Short-run effects

Whereas the long-run effects on the home country's labour market of the expansion of multinationals abroad are most likely to affect relative wages, the short-run impact is likely to take place through levels of employment. If a foreign expansion leads to a reduction in the level of employment of the parent firm, there will be temporary unemployment associated with adjustment costs for the society as a whole, and for the unemployed individual in particular. A number of studies have tried to assess empirically whether a foreign expansion is associated with a reduction in parent-firm employment.

Based on data about US multinationals, Brainard and Riker (1997a, 1997b) find a substitution relationship between employees in *similar* locations (for example, high-wage countries). This means that similar countries seem to be engaged in wage-competition for MNE employment. However, the relationship between employees in different locations seems mainly to be complementary, meaning that employment in a high-wage country increases when employment in a low-wage country increases. The implication of this for the effect of a foreign expansion on parent-firm employment is that a negative effect would be expected when the expansion took place in other high-wage countries, but a positive effect would occur when the expansion takes place in low-wage countries.

Braconier and Ekholm (2000) carried out a similar study based on Swedish data. Their findings include weak evidence that an expansion of affiliate activities in high-wage countries has a negative effect on parent employment in Sweden, as would be expected based on the results from the US studies. With respect to an expansion of activities in low-wage countries, they do not find any effects at all. Moreover, Konings and Murphy (2001), who use data on a large number of European MNEs, find very little evidence of employment shifting between low-wage and high-wage countries. Consequently, the only source of potential wage-competition seems to be other high-wage countries, which is consistent with the idea that similar countries are viewed as alternative locations for similar types of activities by firms. This conclusion is reinforced by evidence on how the discrete choice of setting up a foreign plant is affected by wage costs in the different locations presented. For example, Braconier and Ekholm (2002b) find that Swedish wage costs have a positive (although weak) effect on the likelihood of an MNE setting up affiliate production in high-wage countries in Europe.

To sum up, there is some evidence that a foreign expansion of MNEs is associated with a reduction in parent-firm employment. However, this effect only seems to occur when the expansion takes place in other high-wage countries. In other words, this effect seems to be related mainly to horizontal FDI, and less so to vertical FDI. Since horizontal FDI seems to be more prevalent than vertical FDI, however, there may be significant consequences of this for labour markets in high-wage countries in the sense that workers in these countries are eventually in stronger wage-competition with one another.

Empirical evidence on host-country effects

In this section we shall discuss the empirical evidence regarding the effect on labour in the host countries of MNEs. Labour in the host country will benefit from technology transfers from the parents to the affiliates and from any productivity spillovers from affiliates on domestically owned firms.

One way of studying whether there is evidence of technology transfer is to examine whether foreign affiliates of MNEs tend to be more productive than domestic firms. Several studies have shown that productivity is indeed higher in foreign-owned firms, and that wages paid by foreign-owned firms are typically higher than those paid by domestic firms (Aitken *et al.*, 1996; Aitken and Harrison, 1999). The difference in productivity and wages between foreign-owned and domestic-owned firms seems to be explained mainly by the fact that foreign-owned firms typically differ from domestic-owned ones along a number of dimensions. For example, they are typically larger and more capital-intensive than their domestic counterparts (Globerman *et al.*, 1994; Howenstine and Zeile, 1994; Feliciano and Lipsey, 1999). It may even be the case that being multinational *per se* is associated with paying higher wages. Doms and Jensen (1998) find that multinational establishments, be they foreign or domestically owned, pay higher wages than purely domestic ones, controlling for other factors. Taken together, there is thus evidence that MNEs have superior technology than domestic firms, and that their superior technology is, at least partly, transferred to their foreign affiliates.

Wages may be higher in foreign-owned firms, either because productivity is higher or because the firms are more profitable and profits are to some extent shared with the employees in the form of higher wages. A study using information on union contracts in Canada finds some evidence of profit-sharing between US MNEs and Canadian workers (Budd and Slaughter, 2002).

A number of studies have tried to assess whether labour productivity is also increased through spillovers. The evidence regarding this issue is, however, rather mixed. A number of early studies concluded that there was substantial evidence of spillovers, whereas a number of studies conducted in the 1990s, using more detailed data and more sophisticated econometric techniques, concluded that there was no such evidence. In fact, an influential study found that the presence of MNEs tended to reduce productivity of local firms (Aitken and Harrison, 1999). A possible interpretation of this result is that the MNEs pushed local firms into less profitable segments of the market, which then had a negative effect on measured productivity. The most recent study in this area is based on detailed data for the USA (Keller and Yeaple, 2003). This study finds significant productivity spillovers from foreign-owned firms in the USA. The authors conclude that such spillovers account for 14 per cent of productivity growth in US firms during 1987–96.

What about the assertion that multinationals exploit labour abroad by offering low wages and poor working conditions? The result that multinationals tend to offer higher wages than domestic firms does not, of course, prevent these wages from being substantially lower than those paid to their workers in the home country. On the contrary, this is what we would expect in the case of vertical FDI, since the primary motive for the foreign investment is to achieve a reduction in production costs. However, it is still the case that, from the point of view of the foreign worker, it may be better to be employed by the multinational than by a purely domestic firm. The studies referred to above find that the multinationals tend to pay higher wages, but whether they offer better or worse working conditions is an issue that has not been explored in a systematic way. However, it seems likely that working conditions could be, on average, better in the multinationals compared to domestic firms, although worse in a foreign affiliate located in a poor country than in the parent firm in an industrialized country.

The expansion of MNEs into Central and Eastern Europe

When discussing potential threats posed by the activities of MNEs to the European welfare states, the recent closer integration between Western and Eastern Europe constitutes a particularly interesting case. The countries in Central and Eastern Europe (CEE) have experienced a rapid transition to market economies and a dismantling of trade barriers. The geographic proximity to Western Europe and the fairly low trade costs for trade with Western Europe make these countries especially suitable locations for production for the European market. The countries in CEE may thus confront Western European labour markets with stronger wage competition than other low-wage countries.

During the first few years of transition, FDI flows into the countries in Central and Eastern Europe (CEE) were relatively small. However, in more recent years, there have been large inflows of FDI into the region. These inflows have been directed mainly towards the relatively large economies in Central Europe, such as Hungary, Poland and the Czech Republic (see Table 4.1)

In the early period of transition, most FDI in CEE seemed to be of the horizontal rather than the vertical type. Surveys conducted in the mid-1990s asking about the motives for Western firms to invest in CEE found that getting access to the local markets was the predominating motive (EBRD, 1994; Lankes and Venables, 1996). However, vertical-type FDI may very well become more important in the CEE region in the future. At the time of writing, there are low formal trade barriers for exports to EU countries. With an Eastern enlargement of the EU, trade barriers will be reduced even further. This means that Western firms may find it advantageous to use affiliates located in CEE as export platforms, carrying out labour-intensive stages of production at low cost and then exporting the output to the large markets in Western Europe. Some studies have also reported an increased importance of factor cost advantages as a motive for FDI in CEE (Szanyi, 2000).

Table 4.1   FDI inward stock per capita (current US$)

	1993	*1994*	*1995*	*1996*	*1997*	*1998*	*1999*	*2000*
World	415	460	521	569	611	722	872	1046
N Europe	2380	2790	3213	3442	3588	4573	5462	7059
S Europe	2179	2560	2810	2819	2651	3100	2667	3194
CEEC	53	73	114	150	204	266	320	393
Albania	24	41	63	92	108	123	136	166
Baltic States	79	157	190	320	455	663	841	977
Bulgaria	29	42	52	66	126	192	290	414
Czech Republic	332	440	712	831	896	1398	1710	2059
Hungary	542	691	979	1181	1435	1568	1915	1979
Poland	68	110	203	297	377	581	683	941
Romania	47	49	51	48	102	193	243	288
Russian Federation	17	22	37	53	100	96	112	131
Slovakia	75	168	237	373	377	518	524	908

Source: UNCTAD (2001).

The obvious location advantage of countries in CEE is the relatively low labour cost. Figure 4.1 shows the development of labour costs during 1990–2000 for Poland, the Czech Republic and Hungary along with the average for the EU and a number of specific EU countries. It is apparent that average levels of compensation per employee are considerably lower in Poland, the Czech Republic and Hungary than in any of the EU countries, even in comparison with the low-wage countries within the EU; Greece, Portugal and Spain. The labour costs in Greece and Portugal, the EU countries with the lowest labour costs, are still almost twice as high as those found in the countries in CEE. Large differences in the level of wage costs between countries do not necessarily reflect large differences in production costs, however – this would only be the case if labour were completely homogenous. In reality, labour is very heterogeneous and differs widely between countries, especially with respect to the skill composition.

Table 4.2 compares affiliates of Swedish MNEs located in CEE with affiliates located in other European regions along a number of dimensions. Western Europe has been divided into Northern Europe, which is taken to consist of all Western European countries apart from Greece, Portugal, Spain and Turkey; and Southern Europe, which is taken to consist of the latter four countries. We are interested in finding out whether data about the actual operations of MNEs support the idea that the relatively low labour costs in CEE mainly reflect relatively low productivity. The first row shows a measure of unit labour costs constructed by dividing labour costs per employee by value added per employee. The reported unit labour costs are substantially lower for CEE than for the high-wage countries in the Northern Europe, but only marginally lower than for the low-wage countries in Southern Europe.[7] According to these figures, then, the difference in productivity is not sufficiently large to offset the difference in wage costs.

However, it still seems likely that the location advantage held by CEE would be in activities intensive in relatively unskilled labour compared to activities intensive in highly-skilled labour. Certainly, compared to many other countries, a relatively large proportion of the population in many of the countries in CEE have a long formal education. Nevertheless, it is unclear to what extent such an education has generated skills that are valued highly in the labour market when firms are operating in market economies. The second row of Table 4.2 shows a crude measure of skill abundance in the different European regions, based on the information given by foreign affiliates of Swedish MNEs. It shows the average wage ratio between white-collar and blue-collar

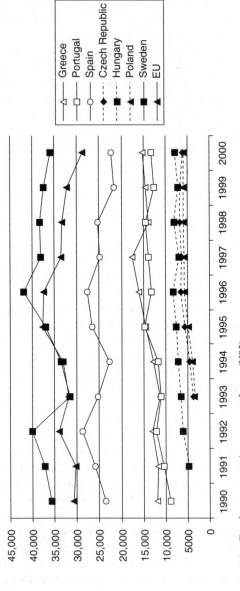

Figure 4.1 Total compensation per employee (US$)
Source: OECD (2000).

Table 4.2 Characteristics of foreign affiliates of Swedish manufacturing MNEs

	Sweden	CEE	Northern Europe	Southern Europe
Unit labour cost (wage costs in SEK per SEK value added)	0.65	0.51	0.62	0.54
Wage ratio white collar/blue collar workers	1.69	2.12	1.62	1.99
Employment ratio white collar/ blue collar workers	0.65	0.29	0.48	0.21
Affiliate exports (share of total sales)	–	0.48	0.38	0.40
Affiliate exports to Sweden (share of total sales)	–	0.04	0.12	0.04
Affiliate imports from Swedish parent (share of total sales)	–	0.16	0.13	0.03
Affiliate imports of intermediates from Swedish parent (share of total sales)	–	0.16	0.10	0.02

Source: Braconier and Ekholm (2002a).

workers in these affiliates. A relatively high wage ratio would indicate a relative scarcity of white-collar workers, which, to the extent that white-collar workers can be associated with relatively high-skilled workers would also indicate a relative scarcity of skills. The average wage ratio is about two for both CEE and Southern Europe, while it is around 1.6–1.7 for Sweden and other Northern European countries. According to this measure, then, CEE looks more similar to the Southern European countries than to the Northern European countries in terms of their skill abundance.

The third row of Table 4.2 shows the ratio between white-collar and blue-collar workers, thus giving information about factor intensities in production. This ratio is the lowest for affiliates in Southern Europe and highest for the Swedish parents. The latter is likely to be partly a reflection of headquarters activities being relatively intensive in white-collar workers. The ratio of white-collar to blue-collar workers is somewhat higher for affiliates in CEE than in Southern Europe, but substantially lower than for affiliates located in Northern Europe. It thus seems to be the case that the firms use production techniques that are less skill-intensive in CEE than in the high-wage countries in Northern Europe.

The last four rows of Table 4.2 show information about intra-firm trade patterns. They show that, on average, affiliates located in CEE have a relatively high propensity to export their output. Although we do not have information about the destination of these exports, it is likely that they are destined mainly for Western European markets. This suggests that there is an element of export platform production by affiliates located in CEE. Still, about half of affiliate sales are sold in the local market, so horizontal-type FDI is evidently also very important.

The table also shows that the average propensity to export back to the Swedish parent is relatively low for affiliates located in CEE (4 per cent of total affiliate sales). It is considerably lower than for affiliates located in Northern Europe, but the same as for affiliates located in Southern Europe. This suggests that there is no strong orientation towards upstream production in relation to the Swedish parents. In other words, the production of components used as inputs in relation to the Swedish parent companies does not seem to be important in CEE.

The propensity to import intermediate inputs from the Swedish parent is, on the other hand, higher than for affiliates located in other European countries. In fact, all the imports from the Swedish parent consist of intermediate inputs (16 per cent of affiliate sales). This suggests that there is a stronger orientation towards downstream production than in other European countries. The picture that emerges from this is that, compared to affiliates located in other European countries, affiliates in CEE are orientated more towards assembly-type activities.

What, then, about the fears that a closer integration between Western and Eastern Europe is going to hurt Western workers as Western firms relocate production to the low-wage economies in CEE? Of course, Western European firms already have the opportunity to locate production in countries with the same low wage level as in CEE. However, the geographical proximity to, and close integration with, Western Europe, and the fact that the workforce is relatively skilled compared to many developing countries make CEE potentially much more attractive as a location for Western European firms. Whether we would expect a negative effect on employment from FDI in CEE depends on whether there is an actual relocation of activities to this region. Relocation to countries in CEE is more likely to occur for those activities that are less costly to carry out in this region. On the basis of the data shown previously, production costs are likely to be lower in CEE for relatively labour-intensive activities rather than for capital-intensive and/or skill-intensive activities. Thus, we would expect primarily a relocation of relatively labour-intensive activities from Western Europe, at least in the short-run. This means that especially labour-intensive industries in the high-wage countries in Northern Europe might be affected along with the countries in Southern Europe, which in the past have constituted the low-wage region in Europe.

There are a few studies that attempt to carry out explicit analyses of the effect of FDI in CEE on employment in Western Europe. These studies focus only on employment effects within firms and do not take into account how overall employment levels are affected when laid-off workers eventually become employed elsewhere in the economy. The previously mentioned study by Konings and Murphy (2001) examines whether labour employed in CEE tends to be price substitutes or price complements to labour employed in the parent companies (which were all located in Western Europe). That is, they analyse whether an increase in wage costs in CEE leads to an increase or decrease in parent employment. If it leads to increased parent employment, parent and affiliate employees are said to be price substitutes (the firm substitutes parent employees for affiliate employees in CEE as they become more expensive). If it leads to decreased parent employment, on the other hand, parent and affiliate employees are said to be price complements (the reduction in the number of workers in the affiliate in CEE also leads to a reduction in the number of workers in the parent). They find evidence of neither of these for firms operating in the manufacturing sector, suggesting that, in this sector, parent employment is unaffected by the wage level in CEE. However, for firms operating in some service sectors, such as wholesale trade and construction, labour employed in CEE and labour employed in the parent companies seem to be price substitutes (that is, a wage increase in CEE has a positive effect on employment in the parent company).

Braconier and Ekholm (2002a) find some evidence that an expansion of Swedish MNEs' activities in CEE has led to a reduction in their employment in Southern Europe. They base their analysis on information about foreign-producing affiliates of Swedish manufacturing MNEs in 1990, 1994 and 1998. Table 4.3 reproduces some of the results from that study. The top part of the table reports *average* changes in employment in different locations according to whether the firms expanded in the CEE region during the time period studied or not. According to the table, average employment in all non-CEE locations decreased over the period studied. However, in all three regions, the decrease was substantially larger in firms that expanded simultaneously in CEE.

The total reduction in employment in Sweden, Northern Europe and Southern Europe 1990–8 by firms expanding in CEE was around 50,000. Around 32,500 (65 per cent) of this reduction can be attributed

Table 4.3 Mean changes in MNE employment and exposure to relocation in different regions

	Sweden	Northern Europe	Southern Europe
Expansion in CEE	−1103	−498	−541
Non-expansion in CEE	−216	−124	−109
Share of relocation	0.65	0.24	0.11
Share of employment, 1990	0.54	0.42	0.03
Exposure to relocation	1.20	0.57	3.67

Source: Braconier and Ekholm (2002a).

to employment in Sweden, whereas around 12,000 (24 per cent) and 5,500 (11 per cent) can be attributed to employment in Northern and Southern Europe, respectively. By comparing each region's share of this employment reduction with its share of MNE employment in 1990, Braconier and Ekholm define a measure of the exposure to relocation resulting from an expansion in CEE. This measure is shown in the lower part of Table 4.3. According to this measure, an employee in Southern Europe was three times as likely to be replaced by workers in CEE as a Swedish employee, and six times as likely as a Northern European employee. On the basis of this analysis, Braconier and Ekholm conclude that the countries in Southern Europe have been the ones most strongly affected by the Swedish MNEs' expansion in CEE.

Braconier and Ekholm (2002a) also report some evidence that firms with operations in Southern Europe are more sensitive to the level of wage costs in CEE when deciding whether to set up affiliate production in CEE compared to firms without operations in Southern Europe. No similar difference is found for firms with and without operations in Northern Europe. This may be interpreted as evidence of MNEs facilitating wage competition between countries in Southern Europe and CEE in the sense that investment decisions become more sensitive to wage costs when the firm has already invested in the other region.

Neither the study by Konings and Murphy (2001), nor the study by Braconier and Ekholm (2002a), thus support the idea that a closer integration between Western and Eastern Europe poses a threat to the welfare states in Europe through a relocation of the activities of Western European firms. Remember that a negative effect on employment because of a relocation of activities should be weighed against a potential positive effect resulting from increased competitiveness of the firm in order to assess the net effect on parent employment. It may very well be the case that an expansion into CEE increases competitiveness of

Western European firms so much that it contributes to an expansion of the tax base, thereby facilitating the financing of a large welfare state.

Concluding remarks

This chapter has discussed what economic research has to say about the effect on labour of the increased importance of multinational firms. While there is little evidence that the foreign expansion of multinationals has any long-run effects on the demand for labour in the home country, there is some evidence of short-run effects. In the short run there seems to be a tendency for parent firm employment to decrease when the MNE expands in other high-wage countries. However, there is no evidence that such an employment decrease occur as a consequence of an expansion into low-wage countries, which is what most of the headline news about the foreign expansion of MNEs seems to imply. Even in the case with an expansion of Western European firms into Central and Eastern Europe, there is no evidence that this has been associated with reduced employment in the home countries of the MNEs. There is some evidence that it has been associated with reduced affiliate employment in other low-wage countries in Europe, however.

In order to assess the welfare consequences of the tendency for parent firm employment to fall as the MNE expands into high-wage countries, we would have to know what happens to those workers who are laid off by the parent firm. Do they move on immediately to another job which pays about the same as the old one, or do they remain unemployed for a long time and perhaps lose human capital before they eventually get another job? These are questions that have as yet not been studied, but are likely to be addressed in the future.

There is evidence that MNEs have positive effects on wages in their host countries. More precisely, there is evidence that firms that are multinational pay higher wages than firms that are purely domestic. The reason for this is most probably that multinationals have better technology and know-how than domestic firms, and that this technology and know-how is transferred throughout the firms' production units. Another reason why MNEs may have a positive effect on wages in the host countries is that their higher productivity partly spills over into purely domestic firms. Labour in the host countries thus seems to be sure to gain from a foreign expansion of MNEs.

Of course, labour in a particular country is likely to be affected by both the foreign expansion of domestic MNEs and the operations of foreign-owned firms in the domestic economy (at least if the country is an industrialized one). What are the net effects on labour in a typical industrialized country? On the basis of the research surveyed in this chapter, we would expect that the MNEs' expansion into other high-wage countries leads on balance to lower employment in the parent firms, with a potentially negative effect on wages. However, at the same time we would expect a counteracting effect stemming from the fact that both domestic MNEs and foreign-owned firms operating in the domestic economy are on balance likely to pay higher wages than purely domestic firms. The net effect is thus difficult to assess. However, if the result that multinational firms tend to pay higher wages than non-multinational ones is true, it seems to be a generally good thing for workers to have multinationals.

Notes

* This chapter is based partly on a paper written jointly with Henrik Braconier for presentation at the Symposium 'Globalization and the Welfare State' in Jönköping, Sweden, 31 May–2 June 2002. I would like to thank Pontus Braunerhjelm and other participants at the symposium for valuable comments. Financial support from the Bank of Sweden Tercentenary Foundation is gratefully acknowledged.

1 A substantial part of these FDI flows relate to cross-border mergers and acquisitions. During recent years, the growth rate has been lower on account of the reduction in merger activity.

2 There is some recent evidence suggesting that firms have become more sensitive to tax differentials in their location decisions (Altshuler *et al.*, 2001).

3 The most comprehensive account of this body of theory can be found in Markusen (2002).

4 See also the survey by Feenstra and Hanson (2003).

5 In order to reveal sufficient information for the licensing firm to be able to fully appreciate the potential profitability of a licensing contract, the final producer would have to give away what it is trying to sell.

6 When the downstream firm has made its investments, the upstream firm has incentives to give as low a price for the intermediate inputs as possible, since the upstream producer at that point has no alternative buyer to sell to.

7 Some caution should be observed when interpreting these figures because of the construction of the measure of productivity. Value added is measured as the total wage costs plus the operating income, which means that, by construction, the measure of unit labour costs is the share of wage costs in value added.

References

Aitken, B. J. and Harrison, A. E. (1999) 'Do Domestic Firms Benefit from Direct Foreign Investment? Evidence from Venezuela', *American Economic Review*, vol. 89, pp. 605–18.

Aitken, B. J, Harrison, A. E. and Lipsey, R. E. (1996) 'Wages and Foreign Ownership: A Comparative Study of Mexico, Venezuela, and the United States', *Journal of International Economics*, vol. 40, pp. 345–71.

Altshuler, R., Grubert, H. and Newlon, T. S. (2001) 'Has U.S. Investment Abroad Become More Sensitive to Tax Rates?', in J. R. Hines (ed.), *International Taxation and Multinational Activity*, Chicago: University of Chicago Press.

Bordo, M., Eichengreen, B. and Irwin, D. (2000) 'Is Globalization Today Really Different to Globalization a Hundred Years Ago? Part I: Commercial Integration', *Wirtschaftspolitische Blätter*, vol. 47, pp. 3–12.

Braconier, H. and Ekholm, K. (2000) 'Swedish Multinationals and Competition from High- and Low-Wage Locations', *Review of International Economics*, vol. 8, pp. 448–61.

Braconier, H. and Ekholm, K. (2002a) 'Foreign Direct Investment in Central and Eastern Europe: Employment Effects in the EU', mimeo, rev. version, Department of Economics, Stockholm School of Economics CEPR Working Paper No. 3052.

Braconier, H. and Ekholm, K. (2002b) 'Competition for Multinational Activity in Europe: The Role Played by Wages and Market Size', mimeo, Department of Economics, Stockholm School of Economics.

Brainard, S. L. (1993) 'A Simple Theory of Multinational Corporations and Trade with a Tradeoff between Proximity and Concentration', NBER Working Paper No. 4269, Cambridge, Mass.: National Bureau of Economic Analysis.

Brainard, S. L. and Riker, D. (1997a) 'Are U.S. Multinationals Exporting U.S. Jobs?', NBER Working Paper No. 5958, Cambridge, Mass.: National Bureau of Economic Analysis.

Brainard, S. L. and Riker, D. (1997b) 'U.S. Multinationals and Competition from Low Wage Countries', NBER Working Paper No. 5959, Cambridge, Mass.: National Bureau of Economic Analysis.

Bruno, G. and Falzoni, A. (2000) 'Multinational Corporations, Wages and Employment: Do Adjustment Costs Matter?', CEPR Discussion Paper No. 2471, Centre for Economic Policy Research, London.

Budd, J. W. and Slaughter, M. J. (2002) 'Are Profits Shared Across Borders? Evidence on International Rent Sharing', *Journal of Labour Economics*, forthcoming.

Carr, D., Markusen, J. R. and Maskus, K. (2001) 'Estimating the Knowledge Capital Model of the Multinational Firm', *American Economic Review*, vol. 91, pp. 693–708.

Doms, M. E. and Jensen, J. B. (1998) 'Comparing Wages, Skills, and Productivity between Domestically and Foreign-Owned Manufacturing Establishments in the United States', in R. E. Baldwin, R. E. Lipsey and J. D. Richardson (eds), *Geography and Ownership as Bases for Economic Accounting*, Chicago: University of Chicago Press.

EBRD (European Bank for Reconstruction and Development) (1994) *Transition Report*, London: EBRD.

Feenstra, R. C. and Hanson, G. H. (1996) 'Globalization, Outsourcing, and Wage Inequality', *American Economic Review*, vol. 86, pp. 240–5.

Feenstra, R. and Hanson, G. (1999), 'The Impact of Outsourcing and High-Technology Capital on Wages: Estimates for the United States, 1979–90', *Quarterly Journal of Economics*, vol. 114, pp. 907–40.

Feenstra, R. and G. Hanson (2003) 'Global Production Sharing and Rising Inequality: A Survey of Trade and Wages', in Choi, K. and J. Harrigan (eds), *The Handbook of International Trade*, Oxford: Basil Blackwell.

Feliciano, Z. and Lipsey, R. E. (1999) 'Foreign Ownership and Wages in the United States, 1987–92', NBER Working Paper No. 6923, Cambridge, Mass.: National Bureau of Economic Analysis.

Globerman, S., Ries, J. S. and Vertinsky, I. (1994) 'The Economic Performance of Foreign Affiliates in Canada', *Canadian Journal of Economics*, vol. 27, pp. 143–56.

Hansson, P. (2001) 'Skill Upgrading and Production Transfer within Swedish Multinationals in the 1990s', FIEF (Trade Union Institute for Economic Research) Working Paper No. 166, Stockholm.

Helpman, E. (1984) 'A Simple Theory of International Trade with Multinational Corporations', *Journal of Political Economy*, vol. 92, pp. 451–71.

Helpman, E. and Krugman P. R. (1985) *Market Structure and Foreign Trade*, Cambridge, Mass.: MIT Press.

Horstmann, I. and Markusen, J. R. (1992) 'Endogenous Market Structure in International Trade', *Journal of International Economics*, vol. 9, pp. 169–89.

Howenstine, N. G. and Zeile, W. J. (1994) 'Characteristics of Foreign-owned U.S. Manufacturing Establishments', *Survey of Current Business*, vol. 74, pp. 34–59.

Keller, W. and Yeaple, S. R. (2003) 'Multinational Enterprises, International Trade and Productivity Growth: Firm-Level Evidence from the US', CEPR Discussion Paper No. 3805, London: Centre for Economic Policy Research.

Konings, J. and Murphy, A. (2001) 'Do Multinational Enterprises Substitute Parent Jobs for Foreign Ones? Evidence from European Firm-level Panel Data', CEPR Working Paper No. 2972, London: Centre for Economic Policy Research.

Lankes, H. P. and Venables, A.. J. (1996) 'Foreign Direct Investment in Economic Transition: The Changing Pattern of Investments', *Economics of Transition*, vol. 4, pp. 331–47.

Markusen, J. R. (1984) 'Multinationals, Multi-plant Economies, and the Gains from Trade', *Journal of International Economics*, vol. 16, pp. 205–26.

Markusen, J. R. (1997) 'Trade versus Investment Liberalization', NBER Working Paper No. 6231, Cambridge, Mass.: National Bureau of Economic Analysis.

Markusen, J. R. (2002) *The Multinational Firm and the Theory of International Trade*, Cambridge, Mass.: MIT Press.

Markusen, J. R. and Venables, A. (1997) 'The Role of Multinational Firms in the Wage-Gap Debate', *Review of International Economics*, vol. 5, pp. 435–51.

Markusen, J. R. and Venables, A. (1998) 'Multinational Firms and the New Trade Theory', *Journal of International Economics*, vol. 46, pp. 183–203.

Markusen, J. R. and Venables, A. J. (2000) 'The Theory of Endowment, Intra-Industry and Multinational Trade', *Journal of International Economics*, vol. 52, pp. 209–34.

Markusen, J. R. and Maskus, K. (2002) 'Discriminating among Alternative Theories of the Multinational Enterprise', *Review of International Economics*, vol. 10, pp. 694–707.

OECD (2000), *Economic Outlook*, no. 67, Paris: OECD.

Slaughter, M. J. (1995) 'Multinational Corporations, Outsourcing, and American Wage Divergence', NBER Working Paper No. 5253, Cambridge, Mass.: National Bureau of Economic Analysis.

Slaughter, M. (2000) 'Production Transfer Within Multinational Enterprises and American Wages', *Journal of International Economics*, vol. 50, pp. 449–72.

Szanyi, M. (2000) 'The Role of FDI in Restructuring and Modernisation: An Overview of Literature', in G. Hunya (ed.), *Integration through Foreign Direct Investment: Making Central European Industries Competitive*, Cheltenham/ Northampton, Mass.: Edward Elgar.

UNCTAD (2001) *World Investment Report 2001: Promoting Linkages*, New York and Geneva: United Nations.

5

The Welfare State as a General Equilibrium System

Bo Södersten

Introduction

During the last quarter of the twentieth century – or at least since the 1970s – the Western European welfare states have been under quite some pressure, including the Nordic welfare states, in particular that of Sweden.

In this chapter, we shall analyse the development of the Swedish welfare state, and in particular the development of the Swedish economy, from a general equilibrium point of view. The reason for taking this approach is that it permits us to see how certain variables are interrelated, and how they influence each other. It will also permit us to take a critical view of various policy stances, and judge economic policy measures from a standpoint of coherence and economic logic.

We shall also touch on the political aspects of this development and how political decisions have both been influenced by economic performance and, in turn, have influenced this development. The analysis will primarily be economic, but policy issues will also be taken into account. The welfare state is, after all, primarily a policy construction. It was – and is still – constructed around certain policy wishes and objectives. The specific solutions used by various countries are only understandable in comparison with the prevailing policy views; but they must be viewed against existing concepts of reality, against the background of what is feasible and what is deemed to be politically possible and desired.

To understand the development of the Swedish welfare state, it is especially important to maintain a policy perspective, since Sweden's political system can most appropriately be described as a one-party regime. Since 1932, Sweden has had social democratic governments almost without interruption, the only exceptions being during the war years from 1939 to 1945, when a coalition government ruled the country, and two short spells (b1976–82 and 1991–4) when a coalition of non-socialist parties formed the government. The only modern democracy that can be compared with Sweden in this respect is probably Japan, where the Liberal Democratic Party (LDP) has been in power since the end of the Second World War (see Pempel, 1990).

Why general equilibrium?

We state in the title of this chapter that a general equilibrium approach will be taken. This concept is central to economic theory and has two distinct features: an economy is usually characterized by some equilibrium conditions, and the variables of which it consists are inter-dependent. The concept in its more applied form is used mainly in international trade theory (for a survey of the concept, see MacKenzie, 1987).

We use this approach as a useful reminder that the Swedish economy consists of sectors that are chronologically, historically and structurally interdependent; the development of the internationally competitive sectors often determines what occurs in the government sectors and welfare arrangements, which then interact with the internationally competitive parts of the economy. The development in one era is often determined by, and can often only be understood against, its historical background. The crisis that occurred in the Swedish economy in the 1990s must be viewed against the inflationary policies of the 1980s. Similarly, the poor growth record of the 1980s must often be explained by the misguided policies of the 1970s. The long run and the short run are connected, and short-run events can at times have implications that might be important in the longer run. But the focus of this chapter is on more fundamental, long-run changes. A broader general equilibrium point of view can be very helpful to gain a firm view of the development of the welfare arrangements and their effects on the real economy.

The legacy of success and the beginning of a new era

Two international events in the 1970s which proved to have important effects on the Swedish economy were the first oil shock in 1973, and the harvest failures in the Soviet Union and other parts of the world that occurred at around the same time. Another important event was the breakdown of the Bretton Woods system with its stable exchange rates among Western countries, and the use of the dollar as a reserve currency.

The ensuing crisis in the world economy led to depressive tendencies with an increase in unemployment, and a monetary inflationary pressure in the USA and Western Europe. Sweden soon started to feel the impact of these events as an era of stagflation was ushered in. The new scenario came as a shock to the Swedish public and Swedish authorities and policy makers, mainly because Sweden had the most outstanding growth record among practically all countries at that time. Table 5.1 shows that, for a hundred years, Swedish GDP had grown by around 3 per cent a year in real terms, practically without interruption.

What was especially striking about the Swedish experience between 1870 and 1970 was its evenness. Sweden's economic development showed no major setbacks, not even during the two world wars and the Great Depression of the 1930s (see Södersten, 1992; Lindbeck, 1999; Schön, 2000). The hundred years from 1870 to 1970 were certainly a striking success story. At the end of the 1960s, many Swedes thought that other countries could be affected by wars, repressive political regimes and economic misfortunes, but could hardly imagine Sweden falling on hard times. Many Swedes, at that time, regarded themselves as the chosen people.

Such attitudes made Sweden particularly unprepared for the economic problems and difficulties of the 1970s. There were several important reasons why Sweden had a specific difficulty in understanding in the 1970s that a new era in the world economy was about to begin. One was simply the legacy of success. Furthermore, almost all Swedish economists believed in interventionist economic policies. They were deeply imbued with their own brand of Keynesianism, and the majority of the profession thought that economic policy was only about 'fine tuning'. It was not easy to see that the 'golden years' had

Table 5.1   Growth in real GDP, 1870–1970

	Average annual growth rate
1870–90	2.6
1890–1910	3.1
1910–30	3.1
1930–50	2.6
1950–70	3.9

Source: Bentzel (1991).

come to an end as the world economy entered a period of worldwide depressive tendencies combined with new inflationary pressures.

Challenges of a new era: downhill all the way

In the early 1970s, many of the developed countries faced the dilemma of whether to pursue expansionary policies to avoid unemployment, or more cautious policies of restraint to combat inflation. Largely because of its strong Keynesian heritage, Sweden chose the former approach.

Sweden had experienced a *de facto* depreciation of the krona against the German mark in 1973–4, providing a short-term boost to exports. Sweden wanted to pursue – single-handedly and apart from the rest of Western Europe – a policy of 'bridge-building'. The theory behind this policy was simple.

The crisis of 1973–4 was viewed as a short-term crisis caused by lack of demand. The Swedish government – and most academic economists – thought that the international economy would soon return to equilibrium and there would soon be an increase in aggregate demand once more. Therefore, the government encouraged private industry – through subsidies and tax concessions – to build up inventories, to be prepared to take advantage of the boom that was expected to be around the corner.

In this way, a domestic boom was created, which is best illustrated by the fact that domestic wages increased by over 40 per cent during 1975–6. This, in turn, caused an increase in inflation, so that the Swedish inflation rate during the latter half of the 1970s was roughly 5–6 percentage points above the German rate of inflation. It was then that Swedish economic policies really started to go wrong, and the famous 'Swedish model' began to be undermined.

The 1970s was a decade of ideological change as well as confusion. At the time, it was difficult to realize that more deep-seated changes had occurred in the world economy. The prosperous years from the late 1940s to the early 1970s were simply over.

Table 5.2 gives a good illustration of what happened to the international economy, as it shows the rate of productivity growth within the Swedish manufacturing sector, and compares it with productivity growth among Sweden's main trading partners (MTP). As we can see, Sweden had a very high growth rate during the 1960s, but it fell drastically in the next two decades and became lower than the rates among its competitors. In particular, the latter halves of the 1970s and in 1980s indicate a remarkably poor performance for Sweden's internationally competitive sector.

Table 5.2   Manufacturing output per hour, average annual growth rate, percentages

	Sweden	Main trading partner[1,] (unweighted average)	Main trading partner[1] (weighted average)[2]
1961–65	7.0	5.4	5.8
1966–70	6.5	6.4	6.0
1971–5	4.5	4.9	4.6
1976–80	2.4	4.1	2.5
1981–5	3.4	4.2	4.0
1986–90	1.9	2.5	2.6
1991–5	5.3	3.1	3.4
1996–2000	4.3	2.8	4.2

Notes: 1. Main trading partners here refers to France, the UK, Norway, Italy, West Germany, Belgium, Netherlands and the USA, since data is not available for Denmark and Finland. (Data for the USA is included from 1977 onwards.); 2 1995-year PPP-adjusted GDP has been used as the weight for all periods.
Source: Bureau of Labor Statistics, US Labor Department and OECD Historical Statistics 1960–95.

We must remember, however, that the manufacturing sector only constituted around 20 per cent of the total economy at the beginning of the twenty-first century. Still, it might be viewed as the engine of the Swedish economy. The development of the sector thus has deep implications for the performance of the whole Swedish economy and understanding this development is absolutely paramount.

The fall in productivity during the 1970s could be explained by these being the years of international crisis. But what about the latter half of the 1980s? These were reasonably good years, in both the USA and most of the EU economies, and productivity in their trading sectors was higher than that in Sweden. These were thus signs that the internationally competitive parts of the Swedish economy were no longer as successful as had been the case during Sweden's long development into a highly successful open economy. We shall return later to the implications of this development for Swedish economic policy.

Changes in employment patterns: the explosion of the government sector

During the 1970s and 1980s, large changes occurred in the Swedish labour market, in terms of both patterns of employment, and productivity. Table 5.3 provides a picture of the development between 1965 and 2001. As we can see, the drop in employment in the competitive private sector amounted to roughly 120,000 people (almost all male) between 1975 and 1985. Practically the entire increase in employment took place in the government sector, especially in the local communes. As shown in Table 5.3, employment in the government sector increased by over a million people, or about 20 per cent of the total labour force.

This increased employment in the government sector had deep ideological roots. Three of the ideological forces were: (i) egalitarianism; (ii) feminism; and (iii) a poor understanding and dislike of market solutions. The expansion of the government sector was part and parcel of the expansion of the welfare state.

As we can see from Table 5.3, both the communal (local communes and counties) and the central government increased their employment by roughly 300 per cent, from 500,000 employees in 1965 to 1.6 million in 1991. This was the year when government employment peaked, as the great crisis hit the Swedish economy and total employment fell by over 10 per cent of the total labour force. The large and rapid growth in official employment had deep and far-reaching effects on the Swedish economy, both on its structure and the framework of policy-making. One of the most important aspects of the large and rapid expansion of the government sectors was its effects on their productivity (see Table 5.4).

The growth of the public sectors and their poor productivity performance had great implications for the performance of the whole Swedish economy. We remember from Table 5.2 that growth in the manufacturing sector weakened, especially in the latter half of the 1970s and in the 1980s. Falling productivity in the public sectors during at least a quarter of a century, from 1965 to 1990, was also added and this had a large impact on the performance of the Swedish

Table 5.3 Numbers employed in public and private sectors

	Public sector	Private sector	Total employment
1965	524,000	–	–
1970	1,014,000	2,419,000	3,433,000
1975	1,253,500	2,461,800	3,715,000
1980	1,508,700	2,348,000	3,856,700
1985	1,643,600	2,342,100	3,985,800
1990	1,652,300	2,419,300	4,073,500
1995	1,368,200	2,170,000	3,539,800
2001	1,301,400	2,507,900	3,815,200

Source: Statistics Sweden.

Table 5.4   Public-sector productivity, by sector (annual percentage change)

	Total public sector	Central government	County councils	Municipalities
1960–5	–3.7	–1.3	–3.8	–4.2
1965–70	–4.3	–2.2	–3.4	–5.9
1970–75	–1.1	–2.1	–1.4	–0.5
1975–80	–1.6	1.1	–2.2	–2.8
1980–85	0.0	0.8	–0.2	–0.2
1985–90	–1.1	–1.2	–1.3	–0.9

Source: Murray (1997), pp. 25–6.

economy. A loss of welfare, at least in comparative terms, was bound to follow. Murray (1997) calculates that, if productivity in the public sector had remained at the level of 1970, the cost of government consumption in 1990 would have been 16 per cent, or SEK70 billion, less than it in fact was in that year. This sum can be viewed as a partial measure of what the fall in productivity cost the Swedish economy. As we shall soon see once more, this implied that the overall performance of the Swedish economy was poor, and that Sweden had started to slide down the ladder of comparison with other OECD countries.

Some policy factors

Thus, the economic crisis hit Sweden hard in the early 1970s. By then, the social democrats had been governing the country since 1932. In 1969, Olof Palme became the new party leader and prime minister, but the Palme government was not very successful in handling the crisis. Their first weapon in their attempt to beat the crisis was by an increase in taxes, with the result that the tax share of GDP increased from 42 per cent to 52 per cent between 1970 and 1976.

In 1976, a new 'bourgeois' or non-socialist party government came into power for the first time in forty-four years. The various non-socialist governments in power between 1976 and 1982 were to a large extent prisoners of the still-predominant social democratic ideology. The main thing they tried to avoid was an increase in unemployment.

It soon became clear, however, that the social democratic government's attempt at bridge building was a failure. In late 1976, Olof Palme, the former prime minister, did try to argue that the non-socialist government came to a 'well-laid-out dinner table', but the true facts behind that remark soon became all too obvious.

International competition increased in the wake of the oil crisis, especially in traditional industries such as mining, steel and shipbuilding, all of which were traditionally very important in Sweden. Some of these industries, especially shipbuilding, relied heavily on state subsidies. Economic difficulties were aggravated by the fact that the declining industries were often concentrated in certain regions. It was thus almost impossible even for non-socialist Members of Parliament coming from shipbuilding regions to vote for a decrease in subsidies that would lead to a closure of shipyards in their own constituencies. Therefore, the necessary changes to the industrial structure became in many cases a long-drawn-out affair.

The devaluation era

In the first years of the 1980s, it became increasingly apparent that Sweden had problems both with its competitiveness and its growth performance (Lindbeck, 1997a). Around 120,000 jobs were lost in the private sector during the international crisis that hit the economy during the latter half of the 1970s.

Sweden also had a continuous deficit in its current account between 1974 and 1985 (see Figure 5.1). There were two reasons for this: first, poor labour productivity growth led to a decline in the competitiveness of the traditional industries; and second, inflationary policies following the objectives of high employment led to overspending.

The devaluation policy approach to these problems suffered from lack of consistency. The left hand simply did not know what the right hand was doing. Or to be somewhat more exact: the governments tried to pursue one line of policy at the macro level, which was completely undone by policies at the micro level.

The ambition of the various governments regarding the krona was to fix its exchange rate to a currency basket consisting of a mix of the currencies of Sweden's major trading partners (where the dollar had a double weight related to its trade importance). It soon turned out, however, that this was difficult to manage, and a depreciation trend was attached to the krona. It was not difficult to understand that this would be the case, as inflation in Sweden tended to be higher than for most of its trading partners – with the most important, Germany, being a case in point.

The first minor depreciations in 1976–7 of around 9 per cent could be seen as an adjustment to the 'basket arrangement' prevailing at the time. These were followed by two large devaluations – in 1981 of 10 per cent

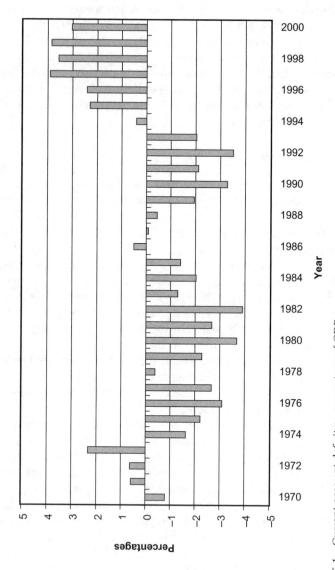

Figure 5.1   Current account deficit as percentage of GDP
Source: SCB *Statistical Yearbook of Sweden* 2001.

during the Fälldin Government, and of 16 per cent in October 1982, when the new Palme Government came into office after its victory in the election of September 1982. The large devaluations of 1981–2 were carried out to initiate a structural change in the economy. These devaluations are often referred to as being 'offensive' and were aimed at strengthening Swedish competitiveness in international markets.

According to the standard theory of devaluation, two criteria must be fulfilled for such a policy to be successful: the overall absorption in the economy must be restrained to give room for an expansion of exports, and some flexibility must exist to allow for a switch of resources from the domestic sectors of the economy to the internationally competitive sectors, to enable the latter to expand at the expense of the domestic sectors.

Immediately after these two large devaluations, relatively stringent demand policies were pursued in 1983 and 1984. This also led to a temporary improvement in the balance of payments by some SEK25 billion over an 18-month period, and the growth of the Swedish economy picked up during 1983 and the first half of 1984.

Soon, however, the gains from the devaluation policies were dissipated, as the government was unable to control inflation. Naturally, we would have expected the large devaluations in the early 1980s to give inflationary impulses to the economy, which was the case, as can be seen from Table 5.5.

An important explanation for the high inflation rates was related to the wage-setting mechanisms. Wages were not set primarily with regard to the conditions of the internationally competitive sectors. Instead, the domestic, low-wage sectors (with large percentages of women in the labour force) tended to lead in wage-setting, because of prevailing egalitarian modes of thought. It was then that the arrangements of the welfare state started to become undermined.

There was also significant policy disagreement within the social democratic government (see Feldt, 1991). When the new Palme

Table 5.5   Yearly rates of inflation in the EU, Germany and Sweden

	EU	*Germany*	*Sweden*
1977–86	9.0	3.5	8.9
1987–95	4.2	2.8	5.5
1996–99	1.8	1.2	0.7

Source: OECD Economic Outlook, 1999.

government took over in 1982, it had been decided that the government sector should not be diminished. Soon, a debate within the government and the social democratic party broke out concerning which economic policy line to follow ('the war of the roses'). After the execution of a fairly stringent line for the expansion of consumption demand in 1983 and early 1984, a more expansionary policy line won the day. This had – as we shall now demonstrate – important implications for the micro side of the Swedish economy.

Micro versus macro

The general policy, especially from 1984 onwards, was to expand the government sector. The interconnections between the competitive sector (represented by manufacturing), the public sector and the exchange rate are illustrated in Figure 5.2.

The devaluation policies were a failure, however, in the sense that they did not succeeded in strengthening the internationally competitive sectors of the economy. Employment in the internationally competitive engineering industry fell, despite the large depreciation of the krona.[1]

The devaluation policies were aimed at improving the competitive situation for Swedish industry, improving the balance of payments and increasing the growth rate. They failed because macro policies were not co-ordinated with micro policies. Economic rationality required the introduction of stringent fiscal and monetary policies, to provide expenditure-reducing effects. At the same time, wages would have to increase in the internationally competitive sectors. Through these mechanisms, resources would have been transferred to exports and there would have been a reduction in imports. At the same time, tight monetary and fiscal policies would have reduced inflation. In this way, the eventual expansion of the government sectors would have occurred in controlled and limited forms, and would have avoided an increase in the tax pressure. The internationally competitive sectors, especially manufacturing, were, however, simply unable to recruit workers at the going rates and could not expand, even though the conditions for international demand were favourable.

Therefore, none of these plans came to fruition. Instead, ideological views and power took over. An equalization of wages and special efforts to increase the wages of low-wage groups became the policy of the trade unions and the social democratic government. Low-skilled assistant nurses and people working in communal day-care centres

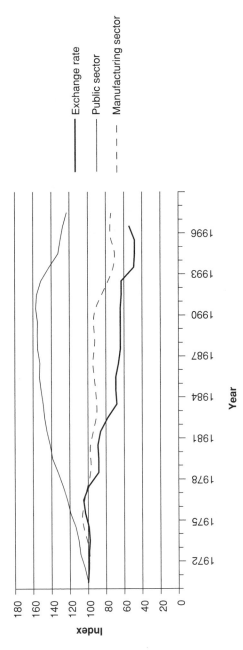

Figure 5.2 Exchange rate and employment in the manufacturing and public sectors, 1970–96; index for 1970 = 100
Source: Pettersson and Södersten, 1999.

were groups the trade unions and the government favoured in particular. This policy eventually had great consequences for taxes, government expenditure and the overall performance of the Swedish economy.

The financing of the welfare state

As we have shown, there were large structural changes in the Swedish economy during the 1970s and 1980s, which had great implications for the financing of the Swedish welfare state.

The reduction in productivity per employee in manufacturing, especially during the latter half of the 1970s and the 1980s, and the continuous fall in productivity per employee in the various government sectors (central, and especially municipal), put a great strain on government finances. The former led to a fall in the growth rate of GDP which, in turn, led to relatively lower government incomes. The productivity fall in the government sectors affected both government expenditure and income, and the county and municipal budgets. As has already been mentioned, government outlays increased because of falling productivity in the public sectors. At the same time, government income decreased – at least in relative terms – as the overall growth rate fell and fewer government revenues were generated.

This put pressure on public finances, and led to both increasing taxes and increased public spending. It also led to periods characterized by large deficits in the government budget, despite a long-run upward pressure on tax rates.

Around 1970, Sweden had a rate of taxation and government spending exceeding the OECD average and slightly above comparable countries such as Denmark and the Netherlands, but the difference was not that large.

Figures 5.3 and 5.4 reveal that Sweden has the highest ratio of government spending and the highest taxes within the OECD area. The differences are huge and amount to 20–25 percentage points of GDP above the OECD average. The first large tax hike came in the early 1970s, when the tax ratio to GDP increased by 10 percentage points of GDP between 1970 and 1976, during the first Palme Government (social democratic). This was, to a large extent, caused by a desire to increase welfare spending and create new jobs within the government sector; the government's ambition was to keep full employment at all costs.

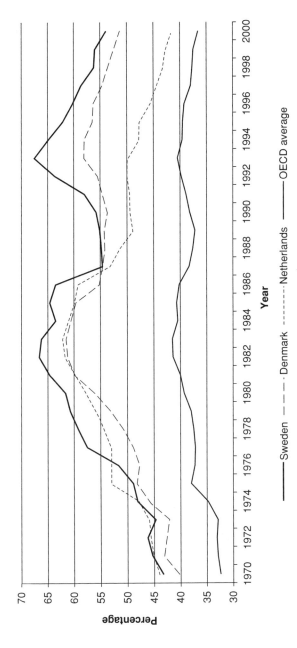

Figure 5.3 Total general government outlays, as a percentage of nominal GDP, 1970–2000
Source: OECD *Economic Outlook* 2000 and 1988.
Note: Because of a change in statistical sources, a downward-shift in the time series occurs in 1987.

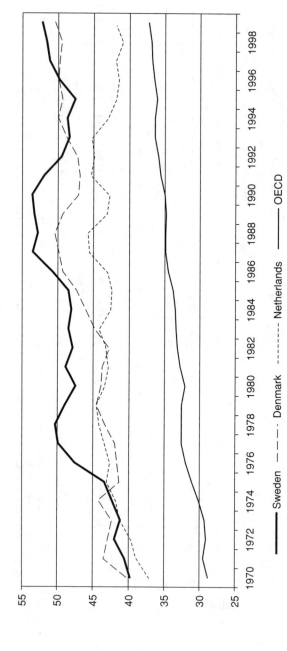

Figure 5.4 Total tax revenue as a percentage of GDP, 1967–99
Source: OECD Revenue Statistics, 2001.

In 1976, a new, non-socialist government came into power, but it was still living under social democratic hegemony and tried to avoid unemployment. Even though taxes remained more-or-less unchanged, general government total outlays increased by 15 percentage points from 50 per cent to 65 per cent of GDP between 1976 and 1982. The resources were used primarily to increase employment in the government sectors, and were financed almost completely by an increase in government debt, which grew at an explosive rate, from 19 per cent of GDP in 1970 to 68 per cent in 2000.

When comparing Sweden to Denmark and the Netherlands, which are also advanced welfare states, we can see that there are some interesting differences. All three countries had great difficulty in coping with the international crisis and the new era characterizing the 1970s. They behaved in a very similar fashion during that decade, and government expenditure increased by some 20 percentage points of GDP in all these countries. Unemployment was quite high, especially in the Netherlands and Denmark, and government debt grew rapidly in all three countries. The political scene changed at the beginning of the 1980s, but in different directions. In Sweden, the social democrats returned to power in 1982. In Denmark, a conservative government instead came into power, and in the Netherlands, a new era of co-operation between conservatives and trade unions started to take shape.

New policies leading to a curtailment in government expenditure were launched in both Denmark and the Netherlands, which led to a fall in government expenditure of 10 percentage points of GDP (OECD Revenue Statistics, 2001) through policies of restraint and hard-currency policies (the Danish krona was tied to the German mark). The coalition governments (basically conservative/liberal) that took over subsequently succeeded in reducing government expenditure and keeping up the growth rate. There was a reduction in government expenditure in Sweden for some time in the 1980s, but there was no basic change in policies, and in the early 1990s there was another peak in government spending.

Weak growth, strains on the welfare state and the crisis of the 1990s

We have already seen that productivity development was weak in the Swedish economy during the 1970s and 1980s. The macroeconomic policies of the 1980s, with a series of devaluations, were also a failure, mainly because they did not – as we have shown – entail either effective expenditure-switching or expenditure-reducing ingredients. The devaluation policies instead induced inflation, as might have been expected. The 1980s also became an era of inflation, as demonstrated in Figure 5.5. As can be seen from the figure, the Swedish rate of inflation was distinctly higher than the German rate between 1973 and 1992. This also had important implications for the real interest rate, which was on average 3–4 per cent higher than in Germany. The wage growth was also dismal, as is shown in Tables 5.6 and 5.7. The tables illustrate that there was a very low increase in real wages for industrial workers and, an even lower one for people employed in the public sector.

During the 1970s and 1980s, Sweden moved in the direction of becoming a work-fare state. Many – or most – of the welfare arrangements of the welfare state such as sickness insurance, early retirement benefits, unemployment insurance and paid parental leave, were tied to employment (Freeman *et al.*, 1997). At the same time, wages were becoming increasingly equalized across various groups of employees, because of solidaristic wage policies and the prevalence of feminist ideology, which called for increases in the wages of women.

The devaluation policies on which we touched earlier also led to high inflation during the second half of the 1970s and the 1980s in Sweden. The high rate of wage inflation and the low rate of increases in real wages are illustrated in Table 5.8. The table implies that the Swedish economy did not develop well during the 1970s and 1980s. We have given the misdirected devaluation policies as one of the reason for the economic policy failure. Another reason is that the welfare policies also started to create clear disincentives for many workers.

For the 1980s, there is little doubt that welfare policies started to induce negative attitudes towards work. Qualifying periods in the insurance system were removed, often as a result of pressure from the labour unions. Various types of allowances, particularly in connection with child-rearing, became increasingly generous, and, over time, spending on family-orientated policies increased. On the one hand, this entailed an increase in government outlays, and on the other, a reduction in the hours worked, which began jointly to undermine the government budget.

The policies we have described and analysed so far, with large increases in government spending, devaluations followed by high degrees of inflation, and a rise in tax pressure, were motivated by employment concerns. They were also successful from this point of

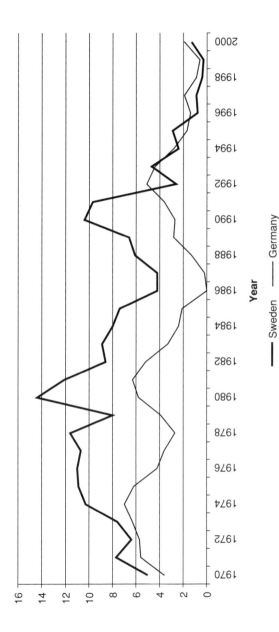

Figure 5.5 Swedish inflation compared to that of Germany, 1970–2000
Source: OECD *Statistics Portal.*

Table 5.6   Real and nominal annual wages for full-time employees in the private industrial sector

| | Blue-collar | | White-collar | |
	Real wage	*Nominal wage*	*Real wage*	*Nominal wage*
1970	25,513	25,513	36,132	36,132
1980	29,695	70,541	40,236	95,580
1990	30,924	152,655	40,536	197,700
2000	36,453	225,773	51,348	318,000

Source: *Statistics Sweden.*

Table 5.7   Real and nominal annual wages for full-time employees in the public sector

| | Central government | | Local counties | | Local municipalities | |
	Real wage	*Nominal wage*	*Real wage*	*Nominal wage*	*Real wage*	*Nominal wage*
1973	36,828	41,988	n.a.	n.a.	32,124	36,624
1980	40,452	84,480	36,720	76,632	34,596	72,228
1990	39,744	177,552	37,356	166,908	34,176	152,748
2000	42,432	262,800	41,496	254,400	34,056	208,800

Source: Statistics Sweden.

Table 5.8   Nominal and real wage trend for industrial workers, 1970–90

	Nominal wages after taxes	*Real wages after taxes, (acc. to 1970 prices)*
1970	16,870	16,870
1980	46,300	19,170
1990	100,770	20,100

Source: SAF, *Facts about the Swedish Economy*, 1999, p. 24.

view, as Sweden had very high employment rates until the beginning of the 1990s.

However, all this changed very rapidly during the economic crisis that his Sweden in 1992–4, when the rates of labour force participation and employment fell by some 10 percentage points (see Table 5.9).[2]

Table 5.9   Employment rates, 1976, 1990 and 1998

	Men	Women	Total
1976	0.87	0.68	0.78
1990	0.85	0.81	0.83
1998	0.74	0.69	0.72

Source: Statistics Sweden.

Problems of the welfare state: trading income for leisure?

Thus we might say that the traditional Swedish welfare state came to an end with the crisis of the early 1990s. Countries close to Sweden in their attitudes to the welfare state, such as Denmark and the Netherlands, had already changed their policies in the early 1980s by reducing benefits and putting higher demands on their citizens to qualify for the various benefits – unemployment support, early retirement benefits and so on. Their labour market trends were also different. In Denmark, employment increased from 69.9 per cent to 71.2 per cent during the 1990s, and in the Netherlands it increased from 39.7 per cent to 55 per cent (Lidbeck, 1999).

Sweden, on the other hand, has not been able to make any real turnaround as far as high public expenditure and high tax rates are concerned, mainly for political reasons. At the time of writing, it still has the highest such levels among the OECD countries. From the 1980s, there is little doubt that its welfare policies started to induce negative attitudes to work.

Another issue that has become increasingly important at the beginning of the twenty-first century is the question of absence from work because of sickness. The costs of sickness 'insurance' have risen dramatically and consistently, and at the time of writing, in 2003, amount to SEK 120 billion, or 5.5 per cent of GDP. There has been a sharp increase in the cost of this form of 'welfare' over the years, and the cost of absence from work because of illness have now become a major policy issue and a major threat to the functioning and survival of the welfare state.

This issue is of central importance, as it casts a very interesting light on the functioning of the rules and regulations necessary for successful forms of the welfare state, and its less well-functioning forms and the role that changing social norms may play in the future of the welfare state.

Figure 5.6 shows that there is a clear correlation between absences on paid sick leave and the business cycles. In times of boom and increasing employment (1955–75 and 1985–91), there is an increase in paid sickness absence, and in times of falling employment, it falls. The latter phenomenon was especially striking during the years 1991–5, when the Swedish economy underwent its greatest crisis since the 1930s. In recent years, from 1995 to 2001, absenteeism has once more risen sharply.

The figure shows that absenteeism related to sickness was much lower in the 1950s than in the year 2000. There is a clear upward trend in sickness absenteeism as the welfare state matures. Why was absenteeism related to illness much lower in the 1950s and 1960s, than in the late 1990s? Why did the figure show a large peak during the full employment years of the late 1980s?

It is important to note that economic incentives play a significant role when it comes to the use of sickness insurance. The figures in Table 5.10 clearly illustrate this point. The incentive effects are very clear. The reforms making sickness insurance more generous (that is, those in 1963, 1967, 1974, 1987 and 1998) all led to an increase in the rate of absence from work, and increased use of sickness insurance. The reforms making the sickness insurance more restrictive (in 1991 and 1995), on the other hand, led to a fall in absenteeism. The reform in 1963 increased the average 'number of sickness days' by 2.62 days per person per year, while the less restrictive rules introduced in 1995 reduced absenteeism by 1.79 days.

There also seems to be a 'learning process,' so the effects in the long run are typically larger than those in the short run. Thus the more generous reforms introduced in 1998 led to an immediate increase in

Table 5.10   The effects on the average number of sickness days related to changes in sickness insurance

Reform in sickness insurance	Effects on days
1963	1.18
1967	2.62
1974	1.39
1987	0.98
1991	–0.03
1995	–1.72
1998	2.43

Source: Henrekson and Persson, 2004.

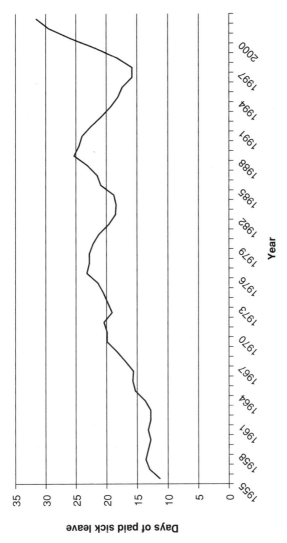

Figure 5.6 Average number of days of paid sick leave per person, per year
Source: Henrekson and Persson, 2004, plus updates received directly from the authors.

absenteeism of 2.43 days, while the long-run effect amounted to 4.12 days (Henrekson and Persson, forthcoming 2004).

The reasons for this trend are not completely clear. Some would argue that modern life, characterized as it is by stress and demanding work conditions, produces sickness. Within the medical profession, there seems to be no agreement about whether to grant people the right to stay away from work for assorted and vague medical reasons. Some doctors argue that being on sick leave does not cure people claiming to be sick, while others are more lenient.

It should also be observed that absence from work related to illness is about 30 per cent higher among women than among men, and also tends to be higher among people with low skills and involved in manual work, than among white-collar workers. The interrelationship between work environment and illness is a hotly debated issue. It does, however, seem undeniable that there is a negative correlation between unemployment and sick leave. When unemployment increases, absence related to illness decreases, and when unemployment falls, absence from work because of illness increases. This was witnessed once again during the boom years 1997 to 2000.

It is therefore important to realize that the work force is not a constant, but changes with changing conditions in the labour market. In times of recession, workers leave the labour force because of shrinking job opportunities. As a consequence, there is an increase in the number of people leaving the labour force and instead going on long-term sick-leave, into early retirement and so on (see Jonasson and Pettersson, 2002).

It is obvious that the existence of a welfare state itself changes the incentives of individuals and families, and it does so in rather complex ways. Returning to examine Figure 5.6 again, the sharp increase in unemployment can be said to have had a beneficial effect on work behaviour. During the height of the boom in late 1980s, roughly 250,000 people on average were absent from work because of illness every day. This figure then fell sharply and was halved during the years of high unemployment between 1992 and 1995. What are the reasons for this sharp decline in absence from work during the years of unemployment at the beginning of the 1990s? It can hardly be explained in medical terms.

Swedish society has traditionally been characterized by a strong work ethic. It seems that the growth of the welfare state, with its generous benefits for not working (for example, sickness and unemployment benefits) has changed these attitudes. In more recent years, the

Swedish state has become more of a 'soft' state. We have just referred to a behavioural change regarding sickness and work, where unemployment created a behavioural change that might be characterized as not being beneficial to society as a whole.

Some of the welfare reforms, however, seem to have created changes in the behaviour of the citizens that may be deemed undesirable. During the latter half of the 1980s, it may be argued that the rules for pay for sick leave were so generous as to make a worker indifferent as to whether to work or not. This behaviour changed with bad times, and accompanying changes in the remuneration when absent from work.

Still, even at the time of writing, it seems to be the case that some of the welfare reforms have turned out to function as subsidies to non-work, and to forms of behaviour that are not necessarily good for society as a whole, such as strong support to people who are long-term unemployed, generous support to people living in single-parenthood situations, parental leave from work and so on (see Lindbeck, 1995).

There also exist poverty traps for low-income groups, and disincentives to work for some of these. This is shown, for example, by the fact that over 40 per cent of the unemployed received a degree of compensation that was 90 per cent of their income or more. The average rate of compensation was 85 per cent.

There has been an intense debate in Sweden whether a so-called 'last parenthesis' – a final date after which unemployment insurance would no longer be available for the unemployed – should be introduced. So far, the social democratic government has not dared to introduce such legislation, primarily because of pressure from the trade unions. It is also well known, both from Swedish studies and the international scientific literature, that high rates of compensation in unemployment insurance (which in Sweden is over 90 per cent financed by taxes) lead to an increase in search periods, and thereby increases in the persistence of unemployment and decreases in the labour force participation rates we showed in Table 5.8 (see Harkman, 1997; Carling *et al.*, 1999; Holmlund, 2000).

The combined effects of high income taxes, generous welfare and day-care benefits often lead to very high marginal effects when moving from unemployment to employment; they can often be as high as 90 per cent (ESO, 1997). This reduces incentives to work and leads both to a high degree of unemployment and a 'discouraged worker effect', which implies that many of the people leaving the labour force during the depression of the early 1990s never came back. That helps to explain why the labour force at the beginning of the year 2000 is about 7–8 per cent smaller than it was ten years before.

Is there a U-turn or is Sweden becoming a dual economy?

As we have seen, the performance of the Swedish economy was quite poor from the early 1970s to the crisis years in 1992–4. The Swedish economy lost momentum and slid down from position number 4 to number 17 among the OECD countries. One important reason was that productivity growth fell to low numbers in the internationally competitive sectors, and that productivity fell in absolute numbers in the government sectors from 1965 to the early 1990s.

The 1990s, especially the latter half of the decade, showed remarkable changes, both on the productivity side and in terms of macro policies and employment patterns. The changes in the welfare-state side of the economy have, however, been small or non-existent, while the weaknesses of the Swedish economy at its welfare-state level have become even more visible and pronounced. It is both legitimate and necessary to ask the question: is the Swedish economy becoming a dual economy? Is it a fact that it consists of a small but highly effective export sector combined with an inefficient government sector? Is it furthermore the case that the levels of labour force participation are decreasing, and that large doses of absenteeism are combined with high taxes and low remuneration for active work?

To look for an answer to these questions, it is opportune to start with an analysis of the foreign trade or international side of the economy.

We have divided the export sector into two basic parts, one consisting of what we call the Heckscher–Ohlin sectors, and the other we call technology-driven sectors. Together, these two sectors comprise 80 per cent of Sweden's total exports; the exact definitions of the sectors are given in Table 5.11.

During the era of devaluation, from 1975 to 1990, the export share of GDP was more-or-less stagnant at around 30 per cent, which must be viewed as a disappointing result, as GDP growth was also low. This once more demonstrates that the devaluation policies were not successful, as the value of the Swedish krona deteriorated by around 40 per cent against a basket of trade-weighted currencies.

The Swedish export share of GDP remained stable at around 30 per cent from 1975 to 1990. There were several reasons for this rather disappointing performance. One was that inflation was high; another that, as we have seen, on the real side, productivity growth was low in the trad-

Table 5.11 Percentage shares of total exports

	Heckscher–Ohlin industries[2]	Technology- and R&D-intensive industries[3]	Other industries
1971[1]	67.7	9.5	22.8
1980	63.1	10.1	26.8
1985	60.7	11.5	27.8
1990	61.8	13.4	24.8
1995	59.5	19.1	21.4
2000	49.8	29.3	20.9
2002	53.9	22.0	24.1

Notes: 1 For 1971, data is based on SITC rev. 2, while SITC rev. 3 is used for the other periods; 2 Heckscher–Ohlin industries: wood, pulp, paper, metals, manufacturers of metals, motor vehicles and equipment (SITC rev. 3: 24, 25, 63, 64, 67–74, 78, 79); 3 Technology and R&D-intensive industries: telecoms, radio, electrical domestic appliances, other electronic apparatuses and components, medical and pharmaceutical products (SITC rev. 3: 54, 76, 77, 87, 88).
Source: Statistics Sweden.

able sector and negative in the public sectors. Another factor was that wages, even though only growing very slowly in real terms, tended to be too high in the public sectors, thereby making the traded sectors internationally less competitive (see Leamer and Lundborg, 1997).

With the 1990s, a change occurred, exports started to grow rapidly, and Swedish economic growth became export-led. There were several reasons for this change, purely economical and institutional.

We have divided Swedish exports into 'Heckscher–Ohlin type' industries on the one hand and 'technology-driven' sectors on the other for the following reasons. The first sectors basically comprise wood products and paper and pulp, manufacturing products and motor vehicles. The comparative advantage of these sectors rests on factor endowments (forests and mining deposits) and their technologies are rather old or at least well developed and tested (car and truck production). The comparative advantage of these industries rests on a combination of factor endowments, arrived technologies, capital and traditional labour skills. The share of exports of these 'H & O-industries' still comprises 50 per cent of Swedish exports, but their share is falling.

The 'technology-driven' export sectors consist of the ICT sector (information and communication technology industries) and the pharmaceutical industry. These two sectors have shown a very rapid growth since the 1980s, as demonstrated in Figure 5.7, and their share of total exports has grown from 10 per cent to over 30 per cent (see Table 5.11). This is a remarkable development and shows some of the 'new'

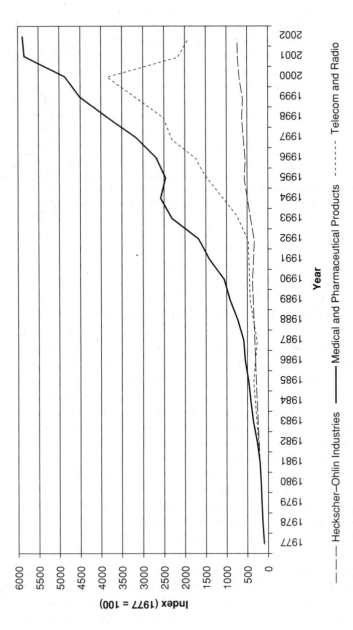

Figure 5.7 Export growth per sector
Source: Statistics Sweden.

internationally exposed parts of the Swedish economy to be very competitive. This is demonstrated by the ITC and pharmaceutical parts of the Swedish economy. We should observe that the ITC-sector is completely dominated by Ericsson, and that the pharmaceutical industry is largely concentrated in some major international firms such as Astra-Zeneca and Pharmacia Corporation.

The upturn in labour productivity in the competitive sector that occurred during the 1990s depended largely on productivity growth in the ITC sector (see Edquist and Henrekson, 2001; Lind, 2002).

As is demonstrated by Figure 5.8, Swedish export performance has been strong since 1992. Two important factors that have influenced this performance are that Sweden changed to a floating exchange rate regime in 1992, and in connection with this move, the Swedish krona was depreciated by 20 per cent, which had a strong, positive influence on exports as inflation also fell sharply, despite the depreciation of the currency.

Another positive factor for the Swedish economy was that Sweden joined the European Union in 1995. Swedish exports to EU countries have since increased from an already high level and comprised 60 per cent of total Swedish exports in 2001.

Concluding remarks

We have analysed the major crisis that occurred in the Swedish economy in 1991–4. As we have shown, GDP fell by some 5 per cent, the rate of employment fell by 11 percentage points (by around 500,000 people in absolute numbers), and the rate of 'non-employment' increased by 11 per cent between 1991 and 1995. These crisis years certainly sent a shock through the Swedish economy. Until 1990, Sweden had the highest employment rate of all OECD countries, even though the growth record had been poor since the early 1970s.

Then unemployment, or 'non-employment' as we prefer to put it, became an important feature of the Swedish economy. The increasing strain on the Swedish welfare state that had developed during the 1970s and 1980s now took its toll and the employment situation became more in line with other OECD countries. Sweden was no longer the country with no unemployment, but just an ordinary OECD country from this point of view, with rather large groups of the population not included in the regular labour market, while at the same time having the largest share of publicly-employed people and the highest rate of government expenditure within the OECD.

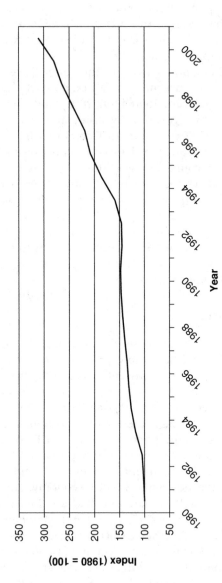

Figure 5.8 Real export growth
Source: Statistics Sweden.

With hindsight, however, the crisis of the early 1990s could also be viewed as a blessing in disguise. One very important factor was that inflation was pushed out of the Swedish economy. This is well demonstrated by comparing Swedish inflation with that in Germany. Since 1992, inflation in Sweden has been around 2 per cent or even less per year. When the crisis hit Sweden in 1992–4, it was impossible to increase prices as sales fell, and with a large rise in unemployment, wage increases were no longer possible.

Around the same time, the Swedish central bank was given its independence in line with Germany and several other European and Western countries. This autonomy has been respected by the government and the inflation rate has been maintained at around 2 per cent or lower since the Bank of Sweden became independent.

Another at least potentially important factor is that a ceiling on government expenditure has been introduced by Parliament, thereby giving more discipline to fiscal policies. How well this new attitude to fiscal policies will work still remains to be seen.

The Swedish growth rate did pick up in the latter half of the 1990s, and was 2.5 per annum from 1995 to 2001, (but only 1.7 per cent for the 1990s as a whole). The recovery of the Swedish economy was primarily due to exports.

The Swedish economy has thus rather become more of a dual economy in the 1990s, and the problems of the welfare state remain unresolved. Another important aspect is that the earlier employment pattern that persisted from 1975 to 1995 and consisted of a steady expansion of employment in the public sector accompanied by a decrease in the private sector has now started to change. If we look at the crisis years from 1990 to 1995, employment fell in both sectors, by 284,000 people in the public sector and 249,000 in the private sector; thus overall employment in these years decreased by over 10 per cent of the total labour force. From 1995 to 2001, employment in the public sector fell by another 70,000 people, while it increased by some 360,000 people in the private sector. The Swedish economy has shown a good deal of resilience in its private sector, in recovering from the crisis of the early 1990s. The internationally competitive parts of the economy have also performed fairly well.

When we consider the public sector and the welfare state arrangements, there have been fewer changes. Here, most of the problems remain, as witnessed by the large increase in non-employment by some 15 per cent of the labour force, for example. The drift towards exchanging income for leisure – often subsidized by the state – has not decreased. On the contrary, it has increased, which is shown by the large figures for non-employment and sick leave that are two characteristics of the Swedish welfare state.

Notes

1   The failure of devaluation policies when it came to improving market shares has also been demonstrated by Jakobsson and Jagrén (1993).
2   We simply state the facts here, as the development in the labour market is analysed in detail in Chapter 8 of this volume, by Erik Jonasson and Lars Pettersson. For a more complete analysis of the Swedish labour market, we refer readers to that chapter.

References

Bentzel, R. (1991) 'Produktivitetens utveckling under 1970- och 1980-talen', in Expertrapport 3 Government Official Report, (SOU), no. 82, Stockholm.

Bureau of Labour Statistics, Foreign Labour Statistics, US Labour Department, http://stats.bls.gov

Carling, K., Holmlund, B. and Vejsiu, A. (1999) 'Do Benefit Cuts Boost Job Findings? Swedish Evidence from the 1990s', Working Paper No. 20, Department of Economics, Uppsala University.

Edquist, H. and Henrekson, M. (2001) 'Solowparadoxen och den nya ekonomin', Ekonomisk Debatt, vol. 29, no. 6, pp. 409–19.

ESO (1997) Lönar sig arbete, Department Series (Ds) no. 73, Ministry of Finance, Stockholm.

Feldt, K. O. (1991) Alla dessa dagar-: i regeringen 1982–1990, Stockholm: Norstedt.

Freeman, R. B., Topel, R. and Swedenborg, B. (1997) The Welfare State in Transition: Reforming the Swedish Model, Chicago: University of Chicago Press.

Harkman, A. (1997) 'Arbetslöshetsersättning och arbetslöshetstid – vilken effekt hade sänkningen från 90 till 80 procents ersättningsnivå?', in A. Harkman, F. Jansson, K. Källberg and L. Öhrn, Arbetslöshetsersättningen och arbetsmarknadens funktionssätt, Stockholm: AMS.

Henrekson, M. and Persson, M. (forthcoming 2004) 'The Effects on Sick Leave of Changes in the Sickness Insurance System', Journal of Labour Economics, vol. 22, no. 1

Henrekson, M., Lantto, K. and Persson, M. (1992) Bruk och missbruk av sjukförsäkringen, Stockholm: SNS.

Holmlund, B. (2000) 'Svensk arbetsmarknad', in B. Södersten (ed.), Marknad och politik, Stockholm: SNS.

Jakobsson, U. and Jagrén, L. (1993) 'Den underliggande konkurrenskraften', Appendix 15 in Government Official Report SOU (no. 16), Nya villkor för ekonomi och politik, ekonomikommissionens förslag, Ministry of Finance, Norstedt, Stockholm.

Jonasson, E. and Pettersson, L. (2002) Employment and Non-Employment. A Study of the Swedish Labour Market, Paper presented at the SNEE Conference on Economic Integration in Europe, Mölle, May.

Leamer, E. E., and Lundborg, P. (1997) 'A Heckscher–Ohlin View of Sweden Competing in the Global Marketplace', in R. B. Freeman, R. Topel and B. Swedenborg (eds), *The Welfare State in Transition. Reforming the Swedish Model*, Chicago, Ill.: NBER.

Lind, D. (2002) 'ITK-sektorns betydelse för den svenska tillverkningsindustrin – en kommentar till Edquist och Henrekson', *Ekonomisk Debatt*, vol. 30, no. 6, pp. 61–70.

Lidbeck, Å. (1999) *Hur gör man? Om sysselsättnings- och välfärdsreformer i fyra EU-länder*, Department Series (Ds) no. 37, Stockholm.

Lindbeck, A. (1995) 'Hazardous Welfare-State Dynamics', *American Economic Review*, vol. 85, no. 2, May, pp. 9–15.

Lindbeck, A. (1997a) *The Swedish Experiment*, Stockholm: SNS.

Lindbeck, A. (1997b) 'Incentives and Social Norms in Household Behavior', *American Economic Review*, vol. 87, no. 2 May, pp. 370–7.

Lindbeck, A. (1998) *Det svenska experimentet*, Stockholm: SNS.

Lindbeck, A. (1999) 'Svensk ekonomisk tillväxt i ett internationellt perspektiv', in L. Calmfors and M. Persson (eds), *Tillväxt och ekonomisk politik*, Lund: Studentlitteratur.

MacKenzie L. W. (1987) 'General Equilibrium' in J. Eatwell, M. Milgate and P. Newman (eds), *The New Palgrave Dictionary of Economics*, Vol. 2, Hong Kong: Macmillan.

Murray, R. (1997) 'Public Sector Productivity in Sweden', *Papers on Public Sector Budgeting and Management in Sweden*, Vol. 3, Stockholm: Swedish Ministry of Finance.

OECD (1997) *OECD Historical Statistics, 1960–95*, Paris: OECD Publications.

OECD (1999) *OECD Economic Outlook*, vol. 66, Paris: OECD Publications.

OECD (2001) *OECD Revenue Statistics, 1965–2001*, Paris: OECD Publications.

OECD Statistics Portal; Price Statistics, http://www.oecd.org/topicstats portal.

Pempel, T. J. (1990) *Uncommon Democracies. The One-Party Dominant Regimes*, New York: Cornell University Press.

Pettersson, L. and Södersten, B. (1999) 'EMU and the Adjustment Mechanism', Paper presented at SNEE Conference on Economic Integration in Europe, May, Mölle.

SAF (1999) *Facts about the Swedish Economy 1999*, Stockholm: Svenska arbetsgivareföreningen, SAF (The Swedish Employers' Confederation).

SCB (2001) *Statistical Yearbook of Sweden*, vol. 87, Stockholm: SCB.

Schön, L. (2000) *Tillväxt och omvandling i svensk ekonomi*. in B. Södersten, (ed), *Marknad och politik*, Stockholm: SNS.

Södersten, B. (1992) 'One Hundred Years of Swedish Economic Development', in M. Blomström, and P. Meller (eds), *Diverging Paths: Comparing a Century of Scandinavian and Latin American Economic Development*, Washington, DC: Inter-American Development Bank. *Statistics Sweden*, http://seb.se.

6
What to Make of the Dutch and Danish 'Miracles'?

Christoffer Green-Pedersen

What has happened and what is happening to welfare states in advanced industrial countries is one of the big research questions within many branches of the social sciences. The reasons for the interest are evident. First, welfare states – of different kinds – are among the core features of the political economies of all advanced industrial countries, and significant changes in their construction will have considerable societal consequences. Second, for a number of reasons, these welfare states have come under pressure since the 1980s. Poor economic performance, changing family patterns, ageing populations and globalization are among the factors argued to force welfare states to reforms.

Among these factors, globalization is much discussed. Politicians and political commentators often use globalization as an argument for the need for changes to welfare states, and numerous scholars have looked at the effects of globalization on welfare states (for example Garrett, 1998b; Rieger and Leibfried, 1998; Mosley, 2000; Schwartz, 2001b; Kite, 2002; Swank, 2002). Not surprisingly, the findings of this research do not lead to simple conclusions about the effects of globalization on welfare states. However, looking at the literature within political science and comparative political economy,[1] there is at least agreement to dismiss popular arguments about the impossibility of extensive welfare states in a global economy. However beyond that, agreement is limited. There are many different accounts of what globalization is, how important it is as a challenge to welfare states, and through what mechanisms globalization affects them.

This chapter discusses the welfare state experiences of Denmark and the Netherlands since the 1980s in light of the globalization literature. The two countries are among the most open of the advanced industrial countries. Compared to many of the other advanced industrial countries, in particular many of the larger countries such as Germany and France, Denmark and the Netherlands have also been successes in the 1990s in terms of macroeconomic outcomes. Significant decreases in unemployment, low inflation, high growth and budget surpluses are some of the achievements that have caused scholars to discuss a Dutch and a Danish miracle (Visser and Hemerijck, 1997; Schwartz, 2001a; Delsen, 2003).

Both countries have implemented welfare state reforms. However, in most respects, they are still very generous welfare states, and their success in the 1990s is thus an argument against popular ideas about the incompatibility of generous welfare states and positive macroeconomic outcomes. However, the 'lessons' from the Dutch and Danish success stories for the debate about globalization and the welfare state go beyond that. As will be argued below, while the effects of globalization on the welfare state in general are often somewhat unclear, the internationalization of financial markets has obviously affected welfare states, including the Danish and Dutch ones. Through their macroeconomic policies, governments need to show financial markets that they can keep the economy on track by delivering low inflation, balanced budgets and so on. Otherwise they risk higher interest rates with negative effects on the economy.

Denmark and the Netherlands are success stories in exactly the sense that they have managed to secure the confidence of international financial markets to the extent that, no matter the party composition of the government, a macroeconomic policy focused on low inflation, balanced budgets and so on will be pursued. The question analysed in this chapter is thus how the broad political agreement that is across-political-blocs agreement around macroeconomic policy, which lies behind the confidence of international markets, came about. In this connection, the chapter argues that it is crucial to look at the position of social democratic parties. The reason is that the need to satisfy the demands of international capital is much more troublesome for social democratic parties than for right-wing ones. Therefore, they are key actors with regard to the establishment of across-political-blocs agreement around macroeconomic policy.

The chapter is organized as follows. It starts with a short review of the the welfare state literature on globalization. This review is meant to establish basic arguments about the effect of globalization on the welfare state. It thus constitutes the starting point for the perspective of this chapter, which is laid out in the following section.

Subsequently, there will be an analysis of the two countries, and the chapter ends with some further deliberations on globalization and welfare states.

Globalization and the welfare state

As mentioned above, questions about globalization and the welfare state have been much researched in recent years. A short introduction to the debate is offered below, looking first at the different definitions of globalization found in the literature, and then by discussing how the literature conceptualizes the impact of globalization on the welfare state.

Empirically, globalization means at least three things in the literature (Garrett, 1998a). First, globalization is often taken to imply increased openness of the economy measured as trade (export and import) relative to GDP (Garrett, 1998b; Rieger and Leibfried, 1998). Linking the openness of the economy to the development of the welfare state is, however, hardly new. A classical study on the development of the modern welfare state by Cameron (1978) linked its development with the openness of the economy, but argued that the more open the economy, the more extensive the welfare state would be. The reason was that the exposure to the volatility of international markets would create increased insecurity among workers, favouring trade unions and social democratic parties arguing for more extensive welfare states. Further, as argued by Huber and Stephens (1998), countries with the most extensive welfare states (Scandinavian countries and the Netherlands) have always been among the most open economies in the world.

This compensation argument about the relationship between the welfare state and an open economy has also been put forward in the recent globalization debate by, for example, Rodrik (1998) and Adsera and Boix (2002). The argument linking increased trade to an expansion of the welfare state has been criticized by others (for example, Iversen and Cusack, 2000; Andersen, 2003), but whether or not there is in fact a positive link between trade openness and the size of the welfare state is less important for this chapter. What is clear is that there is little evidence for the negative link that higher openness leads to smaller welfare states. Further, as argued by Swank (2002, pp. 15–28) and Weiss (2003), the increase in international trade since 1960 has been much less dramatic than conventional wisdom has it. Thus, if welfare states were being dismantled, it is difficult to see it as a consequence of

significantly increased levels of trade. Altogether, defining globalization as increased levels of international trade does not seem to be a
promising way to look for the pressures of globalization on the welfare
state.

The second way of defining globalization is to define it as increased
mobility of production that could lead to downward pressure on taxation and social expenditure. As argued by Andersen (2003), there is
little evidence that the workforce, apart from a few specialized groups,
is becoming internationally mobile, but that does not imply that jobs
are not internationally mobile. Production has become internationally
mobile as companies have become willing to move production to the
most favourable locations. Since, for example, employer contributions
to welfare programmes, corporate tax levels and wages are likely to be
decisive elements in the location of companies' production, the
funding of the welfare state could come under strong pressure from
increased mobility of production. However, theoretically as well as
empirically, this second understanding of globalization is also problematic. Theoretically, there are a lot of factors other than simply wage
and tax levels involved in a decision of production location. The educational levels of the workforce, the availability of workers with the
necessary skills, cultural and language factors, proximity to markets
and so on are also crucial factors in determining where to locate production. Of course, for some types of production that do not require a
high level of skills, wages and wage-related costs, such as social contributions, are likely to be decisive, but for many types of production this
is not the case.

Empirically, it has also been difficult to find evidence for the type of
'race to the bottom' logic that international competition to attract
companies on the basis of just wages and taxation would imply. Swank
(2002) found little evidence for a decrease in taxation of business, and
Hobson (2003) shows that while levels of corporate taxation have
decreased, a number of tax credits for business have disappeared,
leaving business taxation at the same level. Altogether, also with regard
to this second understanding of globalization, there is evidence that
this is not the right place to look for the impact of globalization on the
welfare state.

A third way of defining globalization is to look at the effects of international capital markets. This definition of globalization is used in, for
example, the studies of Swank (2002) and Mosley (2000). As argued by
Swank (2002, pp. 15–20), the reason why the effects of international
capital markets is an attractive way to define globalization is that

international capital markets have been almost completely deregulated (Quinn, 1997), capital flows have grown enormously, and interest rates have been converging. Further, as argued by Huber and Stephens (1998), while the most advanced welfare states such as the Scandinavian ones had built their models of welfare capitalism around trade openness, they were also built around restrictions on capital mobility, which allowed governments to keep interests at low level (thus stimulating investments), and to use depreciations of the currencies to secure competitiveness. While rising trade openness was nothing new to the most advanced welfare states, the internationalization of capital markets was a challenge to their models of welfare capitalism. In other words, while there is reason to be sceptical towards the arguments connecting globalization defined as increased trade openness and production mobility to welfare state reforms, the emergence of truly international financial markets seems to be the best argued challenge to welfare states (Weiss, 2003).

One of the most detailed studies of the impact of international financial markets on welfare states is the work by Mosley (2000, 2003). Her work investigates how international financial markets evaluate countries when investing money in their capital markets. If investing in a country is considered to be risky, interest rates in that country have to be higher than the international level in order to attract capital. Governments thus have two options with regard to international capital markets: one is to adjust policies to the demands of international markets; and the other is to accept the risk premium in terms of higher interest which, *ceteris paribus*, is negative for the economy. However, with regard to international financial markets' evaluation of governments, Mosley's (2000, 2003) findings are that international financial markets in fact give governments room for manoeuvre in the sense that they do not punish countries for having extensive welfare states leading to high tax levels as long as governments are able to combine this with especially low inflation and balanced budgets. The situation in which this leaves governments is both simple and difficult. Through their macroeconomic policies they need to secure the trust of financial markets that they will be able to keep the economy on track by delivering low inflation, balanced budgets and so on. Otherwise, they will have to raise interest rates to prevent capital outflows. However, if they are able to win the trust of international markets, having an extensive welfare state is not an issue.

The second question is how the literature has conceptualized the connection between globalization and the welfare state. In many popular debates, globalization is argued to affect welfare states directly and force them to change. The political economy debate has distanced itself from such discussions by arguing (Kite, 2002) that the effects of globalization are filtered though national political institutions (Weiss, 2003). For instance, a study by Garrett (1998b) argues that, if combined with encompassing trade unions, social democratic welfare states can still perform well in a globalized economy. Globalization is a threat to welfare states if it is not combined with encompassing trade unions able to control wage demands. Swank (2002) argues that globalization puts downward pressure on welfare states in countries that have majoritarian electoral institutions, pluralist interest representation, decentralization of policy-making authority, and liberal welfare programme structures. Whereas in countries characterized by inclusive electoral institutions, social corporatist interest representation, centralized political authority, and universal and social-insurance-based welfare programmes, globalization will not lead to downward pressure on the welfare state.

The perspective of this chapter

The following discussion of the Dutch and Danish miracles in the 1990s follows the globalization debate in two ways. The main effects of globalization on the welfare state are indirect and come from the internationalization of financial markets. International financial markets affect welfare states because they punish governments for not balancing budgets, keeping inflation down, and so on. Achieving these goals can imply welfare state retrenchments to secure a balanced budget, for example. In this way, the pressure from international financial markets joins forces with other challenges, such as an ageing population, to create what Pierson (1998) describes as 'permanent austerity' for the welfare state. Austerity is not something related to economic downturns. Governments have to focus constantly on keeping down the costs of the welfare state.

The arguments of Swank (2002) and Garrett (1998b) identify broad groups of nations, based on certain institutional traits, which are more or less vulnerable to the negative effects of globalization on their welfare state. The weakness of such analyses is that the variation within the groups of countries with the same types of institution is often considerable. For example, the Netherlands has been more successful in terms of macroeconomic outcomes in the 1990s than has Germany, and Denmark more than Sweden, even though these pairs of countries would in most cases be classified in the same categories.

Further, if one wants to identify the room for manoeuvre provided by globalization, looking at success stories such as Denmark and the Netherlands seems to be more appropriate than looking at the average performance of a group of countries, especially if variance within in the group is great. If some countries have been able to meet the challenges of globalization, it should be possible for other countries to do so as well. Focusing on the failure of some countries can easily lead to the identification of constraints that are not really there. Instead, the question should focus on why some countries seem to have been more successful than others. Following this line of argument, it seems that while studies by, for example, Swank (2002) and Garrett (1998b) focus on political institutions, party politics has received too little attention when considering that party political developments provide the key to understanding the Danish and Dutch successes.

Party politics is important because it is decisive for the predictability and stability of macroeconomic policy, which again is crucial for the macroeconomic outcomes that international financial markets are concerned about. If a change of government leads to radical changes in overall macroeconomic policy, international financial markets may respond by taking their money out of the country concerned, thus forcing increased interest rates to defend the currency. On the other hand, if there is agreement across all important parties about a macroeconomic policy focused on balancing budgets and keeping inflation down, international financial markets will be indifferent to changes of government and other political events. The question, of course, is what it takes to establish broad political agreement across the political blocs, around the kind of macroeconomic policy that international financial markets prefer. Here, the position of social democratic parties is crucial.

Keynesianism is one of the keys to the success of social democratic parties in many countries in the post-war period. Keynesianism was attractive to social democratic parties because it allowed a combination of welfare state expansion and an effective macroeconomic policy. What was just was also efficient (Green-Pedersen and van Kersbergen, 2002). In an era of permanent austerity, however, the situation of social democratic parties is more difficult. Balancing budgets may necessitate cutbacks in the welfare state, or at least make a further expansion extremely difficult. This does not imply that social democratic parties are forced to dismantle the welfare states they constructed, but it does suggest more limited space for the welfare states. The social democratic parties have to operate within the constraints of a macroeconomic policy focused on balancing budgets and keeping inflation down.

For right-wing parties this is not really a challenge to their political platforms. The welfare state has never been part of the core of political right-wing projects, which have always focused more on macroeconomic balances. Therefore the strategies of social democratic parties are crucial: they have to make the largest political changes in order to secure across-political-blocs agreement. They hold the key to the establishment of the broad political agreement that means a political institutionalization of the kind of macroeconomic policy preferred by international capital markets (Green-Pedersen and van Kersbergen, 2002; Kitschelt, 1999). However, acceptance of such a macroeconomic policy within social democratic parties can easily lead to internal conflict, as exemplified by the conflict between the more spending-orientated minister of finance, Oscar La Fontaine, and the more austere prime minister, Helmut Schröder, in Germany in the spring of 1999. Thus one important factor in determining whether a stable macroeconomic policy meeting the demands of financial markets can be pursued is whether internal agreement in social democratic parties can be achieved about such a policy.

In some countries, christian democratic parties have, to some extent, had the same welfare orientation as social democratic parties. In those countries, christian democratic support for a new macroeconomic & policy is necessary, but is at the same time not likely to come about without internal turbulence in these parties. It poses a threat to the 'social capitalism' project that has been part of the political success of christian democratic parties, in parallel with the role of Keynesianism for social democracy (van Kersbergen, 1999).

The following analysis of Denmark and the Netherlands is aimed at showing that, in both countries, social democratic parties, and in the Netherlands the christian democratic party, have long ago accepted this new context for the welfare state. Consequently, the basic macroeconomic policy has long been a non-political issue with across-the-political-blocs agreement. Balancing budgets and keeping inflation down are central goals of macroeconomic policy, no matter which government governs. This is one of the elements behind the Danish and Dutch miracles.

From disasters to miracles: macroeconomic policies in Denmark and the Netherlands, 1973–2000

Denmark and the Netherlands are considered to be among the success stories of the advanced industrial countries. However, as can be seen from Tables 6.1 and 6.2, in the early 1980s this was certainly not their situation. Both countries witnessed a constant deterioration of their economies during the 1970s, resulting from incoherent responses to the first and second oil crises. In both countries, attempts to fight inflation through wage restraint failed, and so did attempts to control budget deficits. After the second oil crisis, both countries thus found themselves in severe economic crisis (see Tables 6.1 and 6.2). The fumbling policies had political explanations (Green-Pedersen, 2003).

In Denmark, the causes were the polarization of the party systems following the entrance into Parliament of new radical left-wing (and in particular, right-wing) parties, and a leftist turn of the Danish social democrats. The latter party was very much focused on establishing economic democracy through central wage earners' funds, an idea supported by no other party (Green-Pederson, 2003). Apart from the general leftist turn, the reasons for the social democratic focus on eco-

Table 6.1 Macroeconomic indicators for Denmark, 1982–2001

	Growth of real GDP	Current account balance (percentage of GDP)	Inflation (change in consumer prices)	Standardized unemployment	General government financial balances (percentage of GDP)
1982	3	–3.9	10.1	8.4	–9.1
1990	1	0.9	2.6	7.7	–1.6
2001	1	2.5	2.4	4.3	3

Source: OECD, *Economic Outlook*, various years.

Table 6.2 Macroeconomic indicators for the Netherlands, 1982–2001

	Growth of real GDP	Current account balance (percentage of GDP)	Inflation (change in consumer prices)	Standardized unemployment	General government financial balances (percentage of GDP)
1982	–1.2	3.4	5.9	8.1	–7.1
1990	4.1	3.1	2.5	6.2	–5.3
2001	1.3	0.6	5.1	2.5	0.1

Source: OECD, *Economic Outlook*, various years.

nomic democracy was that it was a demand from Danish trade unions in return for wage restraints. However, as it was impossible for the social democrat party to gain parliamentary support for its version of economic democracy, the relationship between the social democrats and the trade unions was more than tense during the period (Nannestad, 1991).

In the Dutch case, the fumbling policies were also the result of turbulence in the party system. The Dutch party system had been dominated by three christian democratic parties, but in the late 1960s they lost their majority in the Dutch second chamber. For the christian democratic parties, this was the beginning of a merging process that was completed in the late 1970s when the CDA (Christen Democratisch Appèl) was established. In this period, the Dutch christian democrats were divided internally over macroeconomic policy, most obviously in a strong fight over welfare cutbacks between a CDA minister of social affairs and a CDA minister of finance in the christian democratic/liberal government in power from 1977 to 1981 (Toirkens, 1988, pp. 53–85). At the same time, the Dutch social democrats had turned left, as had many of its sister parties in Europe (Green-Pedersen and van Kersbergen, 2002).

The fumbling and incoherent responses to the two oil crises from both Dutch and Danish governments can also be found in their exchange-rate policies, especially the Danish one. In the later part of the 1970s, Denmark had participated in the monetary co-operation known as the 'snake', and then the European Monetary System (EMS) trying in this way to peg the Danish krone to, in reality, the German mark. However, inflation rates above German level and a tense relationship between the social democratic governments and the trade unions meant that financial markets had no confidence that the exchange rate could be kept (Nannestad and Green-Pedersen, forthcoming). As expected from the perspective of financial markets, the Danish currency was devalued several times in the late 1970s, resulting in a significant risk premium in terms of higher interest rates (Iversen and Thygesen, 1998). As can be seen from Figure 6.1, Danish interest rates were more than double the German levels. In 1982, they reached 21.9 in Denmark compared to 8.9 in Germany. This level of interest rates, of course, was highly damaging for the economy.

Dutch governments had also struggled with the country's exchange-rate policies during the late 1970s, and participated in both the snake and the EMS (Jones, 1998). Fumbling policies and lack of wage restraint was also part of the Dutch problems. Still, compared to

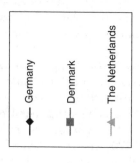

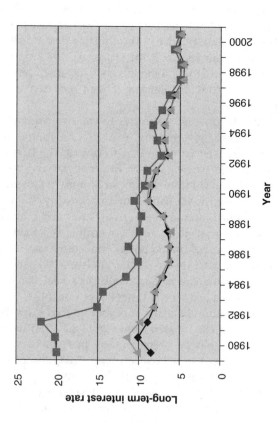

Figure 6.1 Long-term interest rates in Denmark, Germany and the Netherlands, 1980–2001
Source: OECD, *Economic Outlook,* various years.

Denmark, inflation rates were close to German ones, and Dutch governments had not used depreciation as an element in its economic policy. As can be seen from Figure 6.1, the risk premium paid by the Dutch was therefore much smaller than the Danish one – 1–2 per cent in the early 1980s.

In both Denmark and the Netherlands, the deterioration of their economies was, of course, set in motion by the challenge from the two oil crises. Still, the reasons why both countries handled the challenge badly and ended up in severe economic difficulty can be found in the position of the social democratic parties in both countries, and in the Netherlands also in the situation of the christian democrats. The social democratic parties in both countries were on a left-wing course at a time when financial markets expected economic policies to be focusing on balanced budgets and low inflation, a macroeconomic policy potentially conflicting with the social democratic welfare-state project. Political agreement across the blocs on a new macroeconomic policy was thus impossible to establish. In both cases, but especially in the Danish case, financial markets punished the countries through a risk premium on interest rates. Winning the confidence of the international financial markets was thus one of the important tasks for the new centre-right governments that came into power in both countries in the autumn of 1982.

In Denmark, the new government launched an economic policy abolishing the automatic indexation mechanism of wages and social benefits, cutting public expenditure, taxing the yield of private pensions and, not least, pegging the Danish currency firmly to the German mark. Of course, the confidence of financial markets was not established overnight. However, unlike the years before, the decision to peg the Danish krone was supported by a new economic policy, including strong measures to fight inflation, especially the abolition of the indexation mechanism. Further, the Danish government decided not to follow the large 'strategic devaluation' made by the Swedish government later in 1982. These two elements gave the new exchange-rate policy credibility but, as can be seen from Figure 6.1, Danish long-term interest rates remained considerably above German levels in the 1980s.

The continuing risk premium paid by Denmark during the 1980s reflects the fact that the new economic policy continued to be a matter of political controversy. Agreement across the political blocs around a new macroeconomic policy continued to be very limited because of the strategies of the social democrats. They quickly accepted the pegging of the Danish krone to the German mark, but opposed the policies aimed at ensuring credibility. To have them passed in Parliament, the government had to attract support of the entire bloc of non-socialist parties, a troublesome process because to the unpredictability of, in particular, the right-wing Progress Party (Green-Pedersen, 2001). During the early years, the centre-right government was able to follow its political aims despite the difficult political situation, but in the mid-1980s, 'fumbling' policies such as huge wage increases in 1987, and reversal of earlier welfare cutbacks, returned (Nannestad and Green-Pedersen, forthcoming). The reason was partly because of constant attacks from the social democrats. These gave the government an 'anti-social' image, which they tried to counter through improvements to the welfare state. Another reason is that the government found it increasingly difficult to bring together the non-socialist majority in the Danish Parliament behind its policies (Green-Pedersen, 2001).

Whereas, the Danish economy had witnessed a remarkable recovery in the mid-1980s, it moved into recession again after 1987, with low growth and rising unemployment. However, from the perspective of financial markets, the Danish economy was in good shape at the end of the 1980s: inflation was low, public budgets were under control, and risk premiums continued to decrease. Behind this was an emerging political agreement between the government and the social democratic opposition on more elements of macroeconomic policy than just a fixed exchange rate. The focus on low inflation and control of public budgets was no longer a controversial issue. Instead, disagreements centred around supply-side reforms of the welfare state, the labour market, and the tax system. However, such issues attracted much less interest from financial markets.

The emerging across-blocs consensus on the major elements of macroeconomic policy reflects pressure on the social democrats. By 1987, the trade unions had accepted the necessity of wage restraints, and they put pressure on the social democrats for a strategy of increasing compromise towards the government. The party itself was also realising that the small centre parties controlling the parliamentary majority saw acceptance of the macroeconomic policy as a demand for potential support for the social democrats. However, with regard to supply-side reforms of the welfare state and the labour market implying welfare state retrenchments, the social democrats were not willing to compromise as long as the party was in opposition. Attacking the government for attempts to dismantle the welfare state was an important element of social democratic strategy to regain power (Green-Pedersen and van Kersbergen, 2002).

In 1993, more than ten years of centre-right government in Denmark ended. The centre-right had had the restoration of the Danish economy as its primary goal, but from a general perspective, the results had been mixed. The current account had been turned from deficit to surplus, the public deficit controlled, inflation brought down, but the cost of this was high unemployment. Politically, the macroeconomic policy focused on low inflation, control of government deficits was accepted by the social democrats, but supply-side reforms were refused. Still, financial markets were largely satisfied, and in 1993, the difference in long-term interest rates between Denmark and Germany was less than 1 per cent. The satisfaction of financial markets can also be seen from the fact that during the turbulence of international financial markets in the autumn of 1992, which forced, among others, Sweden and the UK to float their currencies, the Danish currency was never under serious attack.

The confidence of financial markets was also hardly a problem for the social democratic-led governments that ruled Denmark from 1993 to 2001. One of their first deeds was to introduce an expansive tax reform aiming at kickstarting the Danish economy. This caused no reaction from financial markets. When Denmark voted against joining the EMU (economic and monetary union) in 2000, there was also no reaction from financial markets. At that time, all parties in Parliament supported a fixed exchange rate with the UR currency and more or less also the policies necessary to secure the credibility of this. The social democratic-led governments instead focused on the supply-side-orientated reforms that had been discussed but never implemented under the centre-right governments. These were now passed, and provided an important background to the Danish 'miracle' that emerged in the 1990s (Green-Pedersen, 2001).

At the time of writing, political disagreement around macroeconomic policy is marginal. Even the radical left and right-wing parties support the basic elements of macroeconomic policy, but some political disagreement still exists around the priorities of the budget and about supply-side measures. However, with regard to the elements of macroeconomic policy, such as the focus on low inflation and balanced budgets that financial markets are concerned about, political agreement across the blocs is very strong. This was the case after the 2001 election, where a right-wing government replaced the social democratic-led government.

To meet the demands of financial markets in terms of credibility, the task for the centre-right government taking office in the Netherlands in 1982 was much less wide-ranging than that faced by its Danish counterpart. The policies launched by the Dutch government were nevertheless quite similar, and included the abolition of the indexation of welfare benefits, and cutbacks in public expenditure (Green-Pedersen, 2001). With regard to exchange rate policies, the determination of the Dutch government was, however, less clear than that of its Danish counterpart. At the beginning of 1983, the Dutch minister of finance decided not to follow a revaluation of the German mark. The punishment came promptly from financial markets. The long-term interest rate differential between the Netherlands and Germany doubled (Jones, 1998, p. 154). From then on, Dutch governments remained as committed to the pegging of the Dutch guilder to the German mark as the Danish governments were to the pegging of the Danish krone to the German mark.

Politically, the new macroeconomic policy was possible because the internal disagreements within the CDA, which had paralysed the christian democratic/liberal government from 1977 to 1981, had come to an end. The government taking office in 1982 was the first Dutch government during the economic crisis that had not been plagued by strong internal disagreements. Therefore the government, with a no-nonsense policy motto could withstand public outcries over welfare retrenchments (Green-Pedersen, 2002, pp. 96–104). Unlike its predecessors, it was also able to coerce its social partners into an agreement about wage restraints (Van Wijnbergen, 2002).

With the definite CDA support for the new macroeconomic policy, across-political-bloc agreement around the new macroeconomic policy was thus on its way in the Netherlands. However, in the beginning, the Dutch social democrats launched an opposition to the macroeconomic policy of the christian democratic/liberal government. Still, as the next election approached in 1986, the Dutch social democrats reduced their criticism of the government. The reason was clear: for the Dutch social democrats, their only hope of returning to power was if the christian democrats chose them as their next coalition partner. This would only be possible by their acceptance of the new macroeconomic policy, an acceptance which made it possible for the Dutch social democrats to return to government in 1989 (Green-Pedersen, 2003). In other words, from around the mid-1980s, a macroeconomic policy meeting the demands of international financial markets finally ceased to be a matter of political controversy in the Netherlands. Therefore, when international financial markets attacked the pegging of several European currencies to the German mark in the autumn of 1992, the

Dutch guilder was not a target. The Dutch case is thus a very clear example of how a macroeconomic policy accommodating the wishes of international financial markets becomes a non-political issue. It was ultimately the result of the pivotal position of the CDA that forced the Dutch social democrats into accepting this policy (Green-Pedersen and van Kersbergen, 2002).

Just as in Denmark, political attention in the Netherlands in the late 1980s changed towards supply-side reforms of the welfare state and the labour market. On this point, Dutch governments were also able to move faster than the Danish government because of the position of the Dutch social democrats. These reforms added the final policy elements of the Dutch 'miracle' of the 1990s (Green-Pedersen, 2003). During the late 1990s, of course, the Dutch exchange rate lost its last elements of political controversy as it became clear that the Netherlands would join the UR, leading to a complete convergence of Dutch and German long-term interest rates.

In both Denmark and the Netherlands, winning the confidence of international financial markets was the first step in the mix of policies that led to the success of the two economies in the 1990 (Green-Pedersen, 2003). This was a process that took place largely in the 1980s. In both countries, winning the confidence of the financial markets meant securing political support across the political blocs for a macroeconomic policy focused on keeping inflation low and public budgets under control. Such an agreement ensures that, for example, a change of government has no implications for the basic elements of macroeconomic policy. In the Dutch case, winning the confidence of international financial markets was fairly fast, partly because that confidence was much higher than in Denmark to begin with, and partly because the Dutch social democrats were only opposed to this kind of macroeconomic policy for a short time after it was introduced. For the centre-right government in Denmark, the task was much greater because of the depreciations dwing the preceding social democratic governments and much more opposition from the Danish social democrats, who did not accept the new macroeconomic policy until towards the end of the 1980s.

Conclusions

Denmark and the Netherlands are examples proving that generous welfare states can thrive in a global world economy. For these two countries, the main challenge from globalization has been to meet the demands of international financial markets for a macroeconomic policy delivering low inflation and only limited budget deficits. Meeting these demands was in both countries the first step towards economic success which were later followed by reforms of the welfare state and the labour market, which financial markets were much less concerned about.

As argued by Garrett (1998a), this 'pressure' from financial markets was partly voluntary, as the countries could have opted for floating exchange rates, which would provide more room for a national monetary policy. However, from the perspective of governments, the pressure from international financial markets is also attractive, since it puts pressure in particular on the labour market because international competitiveness can only be secured through wage moderation and other labour market policies.[2] In other words, exposing oneself to the demands of international financial markets may be the lesser of two evils from a government perspective.

Pressure from international financial markets has political as well as economic implications. The crucial question is whether a political agreement ranging across the political blocs can be secured behind the type of macroeconomic policy that international financial markets demand. The answer to this question depends to a large extent on whether social democratic (and in the countries where they are important political actors, christian democratic) parties are willing to support the new macroeconomic policy. This is evident in the Danish and Dutch cases. In the Netherlands, broad political agreement had already secured been in the mid-1980s when first the christian democratic party and then the social democrats accepted the new macroeconomic policy, which has not been a political issue since that time. The confidence of international financial markets was thus quickly secured. In Denmark, however, securing the confidence of international financial markets was a more troublesome undertaking, for two reasons. Because of the depreciations of the Danish krone in the 1970s and early 1980s, confidence there was to begin with much more limited. Second, whereas the Dutch social democrats had no choice but to accept the new macroeconomic policy of the CDA if they wanted to get back into power, the Danish social democrats for a long time in the 1980s sought to win parliamentary control with other left-wing parties (Green-Pedersen and van Kersbergen, 2002). It was not until the late 1980s that the new macroeconomic policy was at least partly accepted by the social democrats, and elements such as welfare-state retrenchments were not supported by the party until it was back in government in 1993.

With the focus on party politics for the ability of different countries to respond to pressure from international financial markets, this chapter differs from most of the literature on globalization and the welfare state. As exemplified in the work of Garrett (1998b), the approach of the literature has been to look at how domestic institutions make countries able to respond more-or-less successfully to globalization. However, as pointed out by Kite (2002), the ability of such institutional arguments to predict the success stories of the 1990s is often limited. Countries with similar institutional set-ups vary considerably with regard to their performance in the 1990s. The different institutional set-ups provide governments with enough room to respond both effectively and ineffectively to pressures from international markets. The lesson from the Dutch and Danish cases is that party politics is decisive for the responses (Green-Pedersen, 2003).

It should also be stressed that the social democratic adaptation to the demands of international financial markets was not an automatic reaction forced along by the pressure on the national economies. In both countries, it was a political struggle where the outcome was not decided in advance, and in the German SPD for example, adherence to the type of macroeconomic policy pursued in Denmark and the Netherlands is still controversial.

Another much debated question with regard to globalization and the welfare state is the consequences for social democracy. On the one hand, Garrett (1998b) argues that globalization has only very limited consequences for the possibility of traditional social democratic policies, whereas authors such as Kurzer (1993) see the possibilities of traditional social democratic policies as being much more limited. The lessons from the Danish and Dutch cases as presented here fall somewhere in between these two extremes. One the one hand, winning the confidence of international financial markets and internal pressures for supply-side reforms forced social democratic parties in both Denmark and the Netherlands into a considerable move away from the policy stances they had had in the 1970s. However, this does mean that they have become neo-liberalists in disguise. The policies of social democratic governments in Denmark and the Netherlands in the 1990s still incorporate clear elements of social democracy, such as, for example, a strong focus on active labour market policies and redistribution (Green-Pedersen *et al.*, 2001). Further, it should be remembered that many social democratic parties, including the Dutch and Danish ones, made significant moves towards the left during the 1970s. Compared to the position of social democratic parties in the 1950s and 1960s, the course of the social democratic parties in the 1990s is less innovative (Green-Pedersen *et al.*, 2001).

Notes

1   Generally speaking, economists probably tend to see globalization as a more serious threat to the welfare state than do political economists and political scientists.
2   With the introduction of the UR in the Netherlands from 2000, the question of the exchange is, of course, settled once and for all, and the Netherlands can only secure its competitiveness with its European trading partners through the labour market. For further discussion of the consequences of the EMU.

References

Adsera, Alicia and Boix, Charles (2002) 'Trade, Democracy, and the Size of the Public Sector: The Political Underpinnings of Openness', *International Organization*, vol. 56, no. 2, pp. 229–62.

Andersen, Torben M. (2003) 'European Integration and the Welfare State', *Journal of Population Economics*, vol. 16, no. 1, pp. 1–19.

Cameron, David (1978) 'The Expansion of the Public Economy: A Comparative Analysis', *American Political Science Review*, vol. 72, no. 4, pp. 1243–61.

Delsen, Lei (2003) *Exit Poldermodel*, New York: Präger.

Garrett, Geoffrey (1998a) 'Global Markets and National Politics: Collision Course or Virtuos Circle?', *International Organization*, vol. 52, no. 4, pp. 787–824.

Garrett, Geoffrey (1998b) *Partisan Politics in the Global Economy*, Cambridge University Press.

Green-Pedersen, Christoffer (2002) *The Politics of Justification. Party Competition and Welfare-State Retrenchment in Denmark and the Netherlands from 1982 to 1998*, Amsterdam: Amsterdam University Press.

Green-Pedersen, Christoffer (2003) 'Small States, Big Success, Party Politics and Governing the Economy in Denmark and the Netherlands 1973–2000', *Socio-Economic Review*, vol. 1, no. 3, pp. 411–37.

Green-Pedersen, Christoffer and van Kersbergen, Kees (2002) 'The Politics of the "Third Way": The Transformation of Social Democracy in Denmark and the Netherlands', *Party Politics*, vol. 8, no. 5, pp. 507–24.

Green-Pedersen, Christoffer, van Kersbergen, Kees and Hemerijck, Anton (2001) 'Neoliberalism, the "Third Way" or What? Recent Social Democratic Welfare Policies in Denmark and the Netherlands', *Journal of European Public Policy*, vol. 8, no. 2, pp. 307–25.

Hobson, John M. (2003) 'Disappearing Taxes or "Race to the Middle"? Fiscal Policy in the OECD', in Linda Weiss (ed.), *States in the Global Economy*, Cambridge University Press, pp. 37–57.

Huber, Evelyne and Stephens, John D. (1998) 'Internationalization and the Social Democratic Model', *Comparative Political Studies*, vol. 31, no. 3, pp. 353–97.

Iversen, Torben and Thygesen, Niels (1998) 'Denmark: From External to Internal Adjustment', in Erik Jones, Jeffrey Frieden and Francisco Torres (eds), *Joining Europe's Monetary Club*, New York: St Martin's Press, pp. 61–81.

Iversen, Torben and Cusack, Thomas R. (2000) 'The Causes of Welfare State Expansion: Deindustrialization or Globalization?', *World Politics*, vol. 52, no. 3, pp. 313–49.

Jones, Erik (1998) 'The Netherlands: Top of the Class', in Erik Jones, Jeffry Frieden, and Francisco Torres, (eds), *Joining Europe's Monetary Club*, New York: St. Martin's Press, pp. 149–70.

Kite, Cynthia (2002) 'The Globalized, Generous Welfare State: Possibility or Oxymoron?', *European Journal of Political Research*, vol. 41, no. 3, pp. 307–43.

Kitschelt, Herbert (1999) 'European Social Democracy between Political Economy and Electoral Competition', in Herbert Kitschelt, Peter Lange, Gary Marks and John Stephens (eds), *Continuity and Change in Contemporary Capitalism*, Cambridge University Press, pp. 317–45.

Kurzer, Paulette (1993) *Business and Banking: Political Change and Economic Integration in Western Europe*, Ithaca, NY: Cornell University Press.

Mosley, Layna (2000) 'Room to Move: International Financial Markets and National Welfare States', *International Organization*, vol. 54, no. 4, pp. 737–73.

Mosley, Layna (2003) *Global Capital and National Governments*, Cambridge University Press.

Nannestad, Peter (1991) *Danish Design or British Disease?*, Aarhus: Aarhus University Press.

Nannestad, Peter and Green-Pedersen, Christoffer (forthcoming) 'Keep the Bumblebee Flying: Economic Policy in the Welfare State of Denmark, 1973–1999' in Erik Albæk, Leslie Elliason, Asbjørn Sonne Nørgaard and Herman Schwartz (eds), *Managing the Danish Welfare State under Pressure: Towards a Theory of the Dilemmas of the Welfare State*, Aarhus: Aarhus University Press.

OECD (various years) *Economic Outlook*, Paris: OECD.

Pierson, Paul (1998) 'Irresistible Forces, Immovable Objects: Post-industrial Welfare States Confront Permanent Austerity', *Journal of European Public Policy*, vol. 5, no. 4, pp. 539–60.

Quinn, Dennis P. (1997) 'The Correlates of Change in International Financial Regulation', *American Political Science Review*, vol. 91, no. 3, pp. 531–51.

Rieger, Elmar and Leibfried, Stephan (1998) 'Welfare State Limits to Globalization', *Politics and Society*, vol. 26, no. 3, pp. 363–90.

Rodrik, Danny (1998) 'Why Do More Open Economies Have Bigger Welfare States?', *Journal of Political Economy*, vol. 106, no. 5, pp. 997–1032.

Schwartz, Herman (2001a) 'The Danish "Miracle": Luck, Pluck or Stuck?', *Comparative Political Studies*, vol. 34, no. 2, pp. 131–55.

Schwartz, Herman (2001b) 'Round Up the Usual Suspects! Globalization, Domestics Politics and Welfare State Change', in Paul Pierson (ed.), *The New Politics of the Welfare State*, Oxford University Press, pp. 17–44.

Swank, Duane (1998) 'Funding the Welfare State: Globalization and the Taxation of Business in Advanced Market Economies', *Political Studies*, vol. 46, no. 4, pp. 671–92.

Swank, Duane (2002) *Diminished Democracy? Global Capital, Political Institutions, and Policy Change in Developed Welfare States*, Cambridge University Press.

Toirkens, Jose (1988) *Schijn en werkelijkheid van het bezuinigingsbeleid 1975–1986*, Deventer: Kluwer.

van Kersbergen, Kees (1999) 'Contemporary Christian Democracy and the Demise of the Politics of Mediation', in Herbert Kitschelt, Peter Lange, Gary

Maarks and John D. Stephens (eds), *Continuity and Change in Contemporary Capitalism*, Cambridge University Press, pp. 346–70.

van Wijnbergen, Christa (2002) *Imposing Consensus: State Steering of Welfare and Labour Market Reforms in Continental Europe*, Ph.D. dissertation, North Western University, Evanston, Ill.

Visser, Jelle and Hemerijck, Anton (1997) *A Dutch Miracle. Job Growth, Welfare Reform and Corporatism in the Netherlands*, Amsterdam: Amsterdam University Press.

Weiss, Linda (2003) 'Introduction: Bringing Domestic Institutions Back In', in Linda Weiss (ed.), *States in the Global Economy*, Cambridge University Press, pp. 1–36.

7

An Essay on Welfare State Dynamics

Assar Lindbeck

It is useful to discuss welfare-state arrangements and their consequences in the context of *dynamic processes*, with the development in
one period having a critical influence on subsequent developments.
For example, the expansion of welfare-state arrangements during the
twentieth century may be seen as the result of dynamic interaction
between market behaviour and political behaviour over time, often
with considerable time lags. Such interaction may also result in
either virtuous or vicious spirals. Moreover, welfare-state dynamics
may involve induced (endogenous) changes in social norms and
political preferences, which also tend to occur only after considerable time lags. After a discussion of these topics, I make some final
comments on the dynamics of reforms and retreats of welfare-state
arrangements.

Clearly, theory and speculation are far ahead of systematic empirical
research in the field of welfare-state dynamics. This chapter may be
seen partly as a call for more empirical research in the field.

The expansion of welfare-state arrangements

Generally speaking, welfare-state arrangements are, of course, meant to
enhance income security and provide social ('human') services for broad
population groups, as well as to mitigate poverty. In some countries,
welfare-state arrangements, and the taxes to finance them, have also
been designed to compress the overall distribution of disposable income.
Against this background, it is easy to understand that welfare-state
spending was boosted by the emergence of a general franchise in
Western countries in the early twentieth century, since this strengthened the political voice of low- and middle-income groups.

But why did it then take about half a century to build up elaborate welfare-state arrangements? One explanation may be that organizing and mobilizing new voters in the political process takes considerable time. Another reason is that there was only a gradual increase in interest among voters for formal systems of income protection and personal services outside the family. Naturally, I refer to the industrialization process, which over time increased the demand for formal arrangements of income protection in the case of unemployment, sickness and retirement, and so on. Moreover, because of the urbanization process, which separated family members geographically, families gradually became less able to provide income protection and human services to their members.

Thus expanded welfare-state spending may be seen as a combined effect of discrete shifts of political (electoral) powers, a gradual mobilization of new voters, and a rising interest among the population in new institutional arrangements for income security and social services. It is also likely that the demand for income protection and social services tends to rise more than does income (an income elasticity greater than one). An additional explanation of the observed gradualism may be the uncertainty about the economic and social consequences of new welfare-state arrangements, and their financing. In this sense, gradualism also reflects an experimental process, with information feedback from previous policy experiments.

Gradualism is, however, also a result of capacity limitations in political decision-making, which means that decisions must necessarily be recursive (sequential) rather than simultaneous. Indeed, such 'incrementalism' has been much discussed in the political science literature; see, for example, Wildavsky (1984). This recursivity of political decision-making interacts with the well-known fact that benefits are usually more selective – that is, more group-specific – than taxes, which means that the per capita gain for beneficiaries is greater than the per capita income loss for taxpayers. Metaphorically speaking, in January of a given year, Group A is offered (or asks for) a special benefit at the expense of the general taxpayer, in February Group B, in March Group C, and so on. A specific interest group may also push for new benefits for itself in response either to previously increased benefits to others, or in anticipation of such benefits in the future (Lindbeck, 1985). A recursive political process of this type may keep aggregate government spending gradually rising (as a share of GNP) for a long period of time.

It is sometimes also argued that welfare-state spending is influenced systematically by constitutional rules and other institutional arrangements. Indeed, there is empirical evidence that proportional (compared to majority) voting, strong unions and social democratic or christian democratic political dominance tend to boost such spending (Pierson, 2001; Persson and Tabellini, 2002). There is also evidence that majority voting tends to result in a *structure* of spending that favours special interest groups, compared to political regimes with proportional voting (Persson and Tabellini, 2002).

The structure of new welfare-state arrangements also seems to depend critically on the previously chosen structure – that is, on a country's previous choice of 'welfare regime' (in Esping-Andersen's (1990) terminology). In other words, the welfare regime exibits strong 'history dependence'. For instance, in several countries on the European continent, high minimum wages, rigid relative wages, high payroll taxes, generous and long-lasting unemployment benefits and strict job-security legislation, introduced in the 1960s and 1970s, have contributed to unemployment persistence, with a pronounced insider–outsider divide in the labour market, in particular for low-productivity workers (Lindbeck and Snower, 1988; Lindbeck, 1996). A common policy response in the late 1970s and early 1980s was to make unemployment benefits even more generous, further strengthen job-security legislation and (in particular) encourage early retirement. To counteract tendencies towards large budget deficits, governments often further raised payroll taxes which, in some cases, contributed to a new round of redundancies among low-productivity workers, and hence to more outsiders.

In the Nordic countries, expanded public-sector employment and so-called active labour market policies (such as public works and retraining programmes) have largely taken care of labour-market outsiders. Thus, while countries on the Continent have experienced 'welfare without work', in the Nordic countries the result has tended towards large public-sector employment.

In the Anglo-Saxon countries, without much ambition to push up the wage costs for low-skilled workers, and with low unemployment benefits and very little legislated job security, the 'continental' insider–outsider divide has largely been avoided. It has, however, been replaced by a large number of 'working poor' – a phenomenon accentuated by the inadequate education and training of individuals at the low end of the labour market (compared to the situation in many European countries). This, in turn, constitutes the background for recent policies in the USA and the UK to introduce and expand employment subsidies for low-wage workers (so-called 'in-work benefits'), rather than to subsidize non-work (as on the Continent), or increased public-sector employment (as in the Nordic countries). This is another example of history dependence of welfare regimes.

Interdependencies between family structure and welfare-state arrangements are another example of the dynamics related to the expansion of the welfare state. For example, the welfare regimes on the Continent have traditionally been designed to fit families with a single, male breadwinner, which means that such regimes are adjusted rather poorly to the contemporary reality of female participation in the labour market. The limited provision of childcare and old-age care outside the family in these countries is an important example. The resulting low number of females in the labour force, in turn, helps explain the limited political pressure for government arrangements in the fields of child care and old-age care – another example of the mutual interaction of market behaviour and political behaviour.

In contrast, in the Nordic countries, high subsidies for child care and old-age care may be seen both as a cause and an effect of the rapid increase in female labour-force participation. High average tax rates for most individuals have further boosted female labour force participation, although usually on a part-time basis. It has simply become difficult for a single income earner to finance a family with small children (reflecting a positive income effect, or perhaps rather a liquidity effect, of household taxes on the labour supply of females). The labour supply of married women has been further stimulated by shifts to an individual rather than a family assessment of income taxes; this shift has mitigated the rise in the marginal tax rate for females in countries with progressive taxes. Moreover, subsidies for child care and old-age care outside the family is presumably an important explanation of why birth rates in the Nordic countries are not lower, and indeed are often somewhat higher, than in European countries, where female labour-force participation is smaller.

There may, however, also be serious problems with large subsidies for child care and old-age care, the most obvious one being that they contribute to high taxes, and hence, large tax distortions. In Norway and Sweden, it has also been hypothesized that not only single parents, but also families with two adult income earners (with children), in many cases run into serious time constraints. This is asserted to be the case for females, in particular, who still have the main responsibility for children and household work. The high marginal tax rates and the high relative wages for personal services make it difficult to afford such services in the market. For example, if both I and a potential supplier of personal services have a marginal tax rate of 50 per cent, I would have to earn four times as much before tax as the service supplier gets after tax. As a result, the 'legal' market for household services tends to break down. The ensuring scarcity of time among adult family members is sometimes assumed to be an important explanation for stress symptoms, and a reason for the exceptionally high level of sick leave in Norway and Sweden, in particular among females.[1] Some evidence for this assertion is that the (medically measured) stress level among females (in executive positions) with 'double work' seems to reach its daily peak *after* work, rather than during the working day (Frankenhaeuser *et al.*, 1991).

Families in the USA have been able to combine high female labour-force participation, often in the form of full-time work, with a considerably higher birth rate than most other developed countries (including the Nordic ones). One explanation may be that many high- and medium-income families in the USA save time by being able to buy personal services on the market, since relatively low average taxes implies high disposable income, and since low marginal tax rates and a dispersed wage distribution make such services inexpensive for families. This has presumably dampened the political pressure for generous government subsidies for child care and old-age care – although there are also many complaints in the USA about the scarcity of inexpensive services of these types.

Virtuous and vicious welfare-state dynamics

Certain types of dynamic interdependencies between welfare-state arrangements and private behaviour may be characterized as virtuous spirals. Such dynamics were highlighted in Gunnar Myrdal's (1944, app. 3) classical study of socioeconomic developments among the black population in the USA in the 1930s. Myrdal emphasized what he called processes of 'cumulative causation' among socioeconomic characteristics, in terms of 'employment, wages, housing, nutrition, clothing, health, education, stability in the family relations, manners, cleanliness, orderliness, trustworthiness, law observance, loyalty to society at large, absence of criminality, and so on'. In Myrdal's view, certain types of welfare-state policies may turn vicious social spirals into virtuous ones – in particular, if the policies operate simultaneously on several social phenomena.

At the time of writing, there is broad empirical support for the relevance of Myrdal's vision of virtuous spirals, in response to policies designed to improve the quality and quantity of human capital among low-income groups, in particular in developing countries. The most obvious examples might be improved elementary education, better nutrition and sanitation, and fewer incidents of infectious disease; see references in Lindbeck (2003). Indeed, there is evidence of such childhood improvements being transmitted to future generations. Since government spending to boost human capital in these fields also tends to expand the future tax base, via higher labour productivity, such spending may even be self-financing for the government viewed over a long perspective.

It is often also hypothesized that welfare-state arrangements may contribute to social and political stability, and that this tends to favour real investment and economic growth. Indeed, Alesina and Rodrik (1994) find empirical support for this hypothesis in cross-country regressions covering both poor and rich countries. In a somewhat similar fashion, Persson and Tabellini (1994) find empirical support for the hypothesis that a reduced dispersion of *factor* income ('gross income' before taxes and transfers) is favourable to economic growth for a large sample of both poor and rich countries.[2]

It is, however, widely (and realistically) believed among economists that the relationship between government spending, on the one hand, and economic efficiency and growth, on the other, is hump-shaped rather than monotone. In rich countries, where government spending has already reached high levels (as a share of GNP), there is therefore a possibility that a further rise in government spending would move the economy into the downward-sloping part of the 'hump'. Nevertheless, special interest groups may be able to push through such spending increases in the context of the recursive political process outlined above. Thus there may be an 'overshooting' of government spending in the sense that the majority of voters would have preferred lower aggregate spending – if it had been politically and administratively feasible to take all spending decisions simultaneously rather than sequentially (Lindbeck, 1985, 1994). The emergence of such an overshooting of welfare-state spending, then, assumes that the sequential nature of the political process makes the co-ordination of group demands impossible (a co-ordination failure), or that voters and/or politicians do not anticipate rationally the disincentive effects of welfare-state policies (cognitive limitations). The widely held view in the early 2000s that it is important to cut welfare-state spending indicates that such overshooting may have occurred.

Overshooting is more likely in countries with so-called 'universal' welfare-state arrangements covering the entire population than in countries with means-tested, so-called 'residual' welfare-state arrangements. The reason is that a greater number of population groups compete for benefits from the government in the former than in the latter type of society. Obvious examples of competing groups, then, are pensioners, unmarried parents, individuals with small children, public-sector employees, people living in owner-occupied houses, unemployed workers, individuals on long-term sick leave, and so on. Conflicts of interests among such socioeconomic groups of voters tend to arise as soon as the 'veil of ignorance' of the individual's socioeconomic position is lifted during the course of the life cycle. By contrast, 'overshooting' of welfare-state spending, as defined above, is not usually regarded as an issue in Anglo-Saxon countries, where welfare-state arrangements are more selective (hence less universal) than in other countries.

Formalized political theories emphasizing competition for benefits among socioeconomic groups are often based on probabilistic voting models (rather than on the median voter model). In the special case when politicians are only interested in power *per se*, the announced pre-election policies of different parties converge on a utilitarian optimum, or a mean value of utility, rather than on the policy preferred by the median voter (Lindbeck and Weibull, 1987). But if political parties are also motivated by policy preferences, such voting models instead predict that competing parties adopt different policy platforms in political equilibrium, and that the winning policy lies between a utilitarian optimum and the more popular party's preferred policy, and closer to the latter position (Lindbeck and Weibull, 1993).

It is hardly controversial to say that both the explicit and implicit tax wedges in different benefit systems distort economic incentive, although the magnitude of these distortions is controversial. I do not have much to add to the general discussion of *how* such distortions reduce economic efficiency, and in some cases also retard economic growth. My only point is that a realistic analysis of this issue requires that we take into account the effects on a great number of individual decisions: leisure, household production, barter, the intensity and quality of work, promotion, work in the 'shadow economy', tax avoidance, tax evasion, the willingness of workers to move between jobs, savings, the allocation of assets, and so on. The estimates of the 'deadweight costs' of tax distortions are most probbly heavily underestimated if the analysis is confined to only one, or a few, of these decisions.[3] It is also important to look at the implicit tax rates in various benefit programmes since, in reality, these programmes are not actuarially fair, in the sense that the capital value of expected benefits, in particular on the margin, is often much smaller than the expected capital value of contributions paid by the individual (directly or via the employer). For example, if the capital value of my additional contribution to a certain social insurance system, such as the pension system, is £10,000, while the capital value of my expected future benefit increase is £5,000, the implicit marginal tax rate is about 50 per cent. Naturally, it is also well known that social insurance is connected with 'moral hazard' problems, in the sense that some individuals adjust their behaviour to be able to draw on social insurance benefits, and that the authorities cannot observe or influence such behaviour adjustments.

It is particularly difficult for voters and politicians to anticipate realistically such aggregate disincentive effects of taxes and benefits if these effects only emerge after time lags. A trivial example is that it may take time for individuals to understand and react to changes in benefit and tax rules. Individual behaviour may also be constrained for a time by 'binding' institutional arrangements which adjust only after time lags, in response to changes in the economic incentives for individuals. For example, even if individuals might want to cut their working hours in response to more generous benefits for non-work and higher marginal tax rates on labour income (which makes the private costs of leisure lower than the social costs), such a cut may be difficult for them to make until labour market organizations or government legislation have (collectively) agreed to shorten working hours (Lindbeck, 1994).[4] As a consequence, the effects of tax distortions are delayed, and politicians and voters may therefore support higher welfare-state expenditure and taxes than if no such lags existed. Indeed, such time lags (of uncertain length) also make it difficult for researchers to identify the effects on individual behaviour of changes in taxes and welfare-state arrangements, even in retrospect.

Changes in social norms and political preferences

My main point about welfare-state dynamics is, however, that individual adjustments to changes in economic incentives are constrained by social norms for some time, and that some of the disincentive effects therefore materialize only after the norm adherence has weakened (Lindbeck, 1995). It is reasonable to assume that norms in favour of work, or against living off handouts from others, initially emerged in societies where it was difficult to survive without working. The norms may have emerged either via an evolutionary process, when successful individuals were imitated by others, or via actions of specific 'norm senders', including parents, employers and colleagues. Before the emergence of the modern welfare state, such work norms therefore were quite consistent with, and indeed complementary to, the prevailing economic incentives.

Then came the welfare state, with generous benefits and high taxes. As long as earlier established norms were adhered to, these constrained potentially negative disincentive effects on work of higher taxes and more generous benefits for non-work. But it is reasonable to assume that tensions built up gradually between the norms inherited from the past and the new (weaker) economic incentives to work. As a result, some 'entrepreneurial' individuals started to exploit the new, generous welfare state arrangement by changing their behaviour in ways that made them, as individuals, qualify for benefits they had not previously been eligible to receive – a classic example of moral hazard.

This constitutes another conceivable explanation why disincentive effects of higher taxes and more generous benefits are likely to be stronger in the long run than in the short run. We may then hypothesize that the strength of the work norm tends to fall with the number of individuals living on benefits, in the sense that the guilt or shame connected with breaking the norms is then reduced (Lindbeck *et al.*, 1999). This, in particular, is likely to take place when the norm is 'social' in the sense of being upheld by the approval or disapproval of others. We would also predict that parents' incentives to instil work norms in their children fall if the taxpayers take over increasingly the future responsibility for the economic security of their children, via the build-up of social insurance. Indeed, this prediction follows from a formal model of the family as a 'norm sender' for its children (Lindbeck and Nyberg, 2001). The enforcement of social work norms by the administrators of the social insurance system may also weaken over time when more individuals live on benefits – for example, as a result of unemployment-creating macroeconomic shocks.[5]

So far, there has not been much systematic empirical research about social norms in connection with welfare-state policies. There is, however, some general empirical documentation of the *existence* of social norms in favour of work, rather than living off government benefits.[6] Such norms are often believed to be particularly strong in the case of highly selective benefits such as social assistance ('welfare' in US terminology). For example, Moffit (1983) has documented such norms, reflected in 'welfare stigma'. The stigma of living off 'universal entitle-ments' – such as unemployment benefits, paid sick leave and subsidized early retirement – is likely to be smaller than in the case of selective benefits. There may, however, be norms against 'over-using' or 'misusing' universal benefits. In other words, there may be norms limiting moral hazard and cheating over benefits, respectively, also in the case of universal benefits.

Let us take *unemployment benefits* as an example. There is a strong case for generous unemployment benefits, since many individuals lose their jobs through no fault of their own. But the more generous the benefits, in particular the longer periods the benefits can be paid, the more people will be unemployed at a specific point in time. Traditional economic analysis in terms of economic incentives and moral hazard takes us a long way towards explaining this prediction. There is also empirical evidence on this issue; see Layard *et al.*, 1991. It is, however, likely that social norms towards work, and endogenous changes in these, also play a part. For example, Åberg *et al.* (2003) find that an individual with given characteristics is more likely to be unemployed, and less likely to exit from unemployment, if *aggregate* unemployment in the individual's own neighbourhood is high. (The study was of young people in 699 neighbourhoods in metropolitan Stockholm.) Moreover, on the basis of a study of attitudes in England, Clark (2003) concludes that unemployed workers suffer less psychologically from their predicament if many 'relevant others' are also unemployed. Both studies are consistent with the notion that the social norms against living off unemployment benefits weaken when there is an increase in the number of individuals living in that way. Hence the studies are consistent with the hypothesis of endogenous social norms concerning work, and the emergence of 'unemployment cultures'. Moreover, a sociological study for the Netherlands (Engbersen *et al.*, 1993) in the late 1980s indicates that a substantial fraction of young, healthy people living on benefits in that country regarded this way of life as a 'social right'. The authors interpret this as being consistent with the notion of 'benefit cultures' in some sections of the Dutch population, after a prolonged period of generous benefits and a large number of beneficiaries.

There is also a strong case for generous *sick pay*. But the more gen-erous the sick benefits, the weaker the requirements for doctors' certification, and the weaker the administrative controls, the greater number of individuals would be expected to be drawing sick pay at a given point in time. Sick-pay insurance is therefore also highly susceptible to disincentive effects and moral hazard. After all, to a considerable extent, the individual him/herself defines whether he/she is able to work or not. Several econometric studies conclude that a generous benefit rule, *ceteris paribus*, raises the incidence of sick leave (Drago and Wooden, 1992; Johansson and Palme, 2002; Persson, 2003). It has, however, been difficult to explain by economic incentives alone the huge rise in the number of sick-pay beneficiaries in recent years (basically a doubling) in some countries, such as the Netherlands, Norway and Sweden. It has also been difficult to fully explain this development by changes in the composition of the labour force, or a deterioration in the health of the population.[7] It is therefore tempting to assume that a weakening of the social norms against using the sick-pay system for other purposes than sickness plays a part. It is also difficult to explain the wide geographic variation in paid sick leave across regions and local communities within countries such as Sweden without reference to geographic variations in norms against moral hazard and benefit cheating. Since work norms are likely to weaken only gradually in response to a rise in the number of beneficiaries, we would expect a time lag between changes in economic incentives and the incidence of sick leave. Indeed, in a study of the relationship between the generosity of sick-pay benefits and sickness absentees in Sweden, Persson (2003) finds the effects to be stronger in the longrun than the short run.

Since the capacity to work rapidly falls with increasing age for some individuals, there is also a strong case for generous rules for *early retirement* on health grounds. But the more generous the rules, the more individuals will choose early retirement. Early retirement is therefore another field that is vulnerable to moral hazard. Empirical studies clearly indicate that generous conditions for early retirement tend to generate many early retirees (Gruber and Wise, 1999) – an obvious example of the consequences of economic incentives and moral hazard. For example, the effective retirement age in EU countries at the time of writing is below 60 (and as low as 57 in Italy). As a result, the average employment rate in the EU in the age group 55–64 is only about 38 per cent. Another illustration is that about 12 per cent of the labour force in the Netherlands lived on disability pensions in the 1980s, without any evidence that the health situation in the Netherlands could possibly explain this. Although traditional economic incentives and moral hazard go a long way towards explaining the high frequency of early retirement, it is also tempting to hypothesize that the social norms against applying for early retirement have been weakened by the rising number of individuals living on such benefits. Otherwise it would, once more, be difficult to explain the apparent geographical clustering of the taking of early retirement.

Moral hazard is also unavoidable in the case of economic support for *single parents* (in fact, usually single mothers). There is a strong social (humanitarian) case for government support to single parents, not least to mitigate the poverty of children in such households. But it is unavoidable that generous benefits encourage both divorce and birth outside marriage (or outside cohabitation) – another example of moral hazard. It is, however, also obvious that the social norms (stigmatization) against single motherhood were gradually weakened during the final decades of the twentieth century, although we do not know to what extent government support to single mothers has contributed to this development.

Outright *benefit cheating* is also unavoidable – for example, when individuals in receipt of unemployment benefits work in the black economy, and when others call in sick when, in fact, they have stayed off work to paint their home, repair their summerhouse, help sick relatives or simply enjoy an additional holiday. This type of behaviour is not more surprising than tax cheating, which surprises nobody. It is also well known that some individuals receiving support because of single parenthood do not, in fact, live alone. While the existence of benefit cheating may be explained largely by economic incentives, we would expect the *strength* of the effect to depend on social norms, including the norm of honesty. Indeed, an opinion poll in Sweden in 2002 indicated that a majority of Swedes thought that it was acceptable to stay at home claiming sickness even when not sick – for example, because of family problems or because the individual regards his/her job, or boss, as unpleasant (Modig and Boberg, 2002). Moreover, administrative controls (via sampling) by the Swedish Insurance Board in 2001 found that 10 per cent of individuals given paid leave to take care of sick children were in fact at their jobs, or their children were at day-care centres. Skogman Thoursie (2002) found that a considerable number of males in Sweden had called in sick when radio and television has international sporting events with important participation by Swedish athletes.[8]

These fragmented examples of moral hazard and endogenous work norms at least suggest that the issue is worth-more systematic empirical research. The examples also suggest that induced changes in social norms may be important not only in the case of 'selective' (or residual) welfare states (with means tests), but also for the so-called 'universal' welfare state – hence, when benefits are tied to citizenship or residence rather than to low income. Indeed, the distinction between these two types of welfare state is often strongly exaggerated in the literature. 'Deserving' beneficiaries must be separated from 'non-deserving' ones by discretionary administrative decisions, not only in the case of selective benefits but also in the case of universal ones. For example, the authorities must find out who among the claimants of 'universal' benefits for unemployment, sickness, disability, single parenthood and so on, really qualifies for such benefits according to the rules.

As a result, taking a long perspective, it is not self-evident that the administration costs are smaller in universal than in selective systems. They are probably smaller *per person*, but it may be necessary for the authorities to control many more individuals in a universal welfare state than in a selective one. One advantage of universal compared to means-tested benefits, though, is that the implicit marginal tax wedge will be smaller for low-income earners. But the marginal tax rates will instead be higher for the general taxpayer.[9]

So far, I have concentrated on changes in market behaviour. Voting behaviour may, however, also be influenced by existing welfare-state arrangements, since those living on benefits have a greater interest than others in supporting generous benefit rules and high taxes. When we consider the possibility that social norms change with the number of beneficiaries, a society may wind up in quite different political equilibrium positions, depending on the previous path of welfare-state spending. If benefits are only moderately generous and the norms against living on benefits are strong at a given point in time, the vast majority of voters are likely to support policies with only moderate benefit levels (and taxes). However, if for some reason the economy has found itself in a situation with a great number of transfer recipients – for example, after a huge negative macroeconomic shock – the adherence to work norms is likely to weaken after a time, and more voters will support generous benefits (and hence higher taxes).

Indeed, multiple equilibria of this type have been modelled formally in the literature. In a theoretical model by Lindbeck *et al.* (1999) with homogenous preferences, there is a critical wage rate that separates individuals choosing to live on benefits and individuals choosing to work. Assuming, for simplicity, that everyone can predict the consequences for the number of beneficiaries of policy changes, there turn out to be only two alternative political equilibria – a low-tax equilibrium, where most individuals work, and another high-tax equilibrium, where the majority of voters live on benefits. Alternatively, we may assume that individuals differ in their sensitivity to social norms. In this case, there will instead be a critical value for the intensity of guilt or shame, when breaking the existing social norms, that separates individuals.[10]

In principle, at some point in time a society may 'flip' from the first to the second type of economic–political equilibrium. One example is when a great negative macroeconomic shock has thrown a large fraction of the population into various safety nets. It may be difficult to get a political majority for less generous benefits after such events.[11] Another example is when voters and politicians turn out to have underestimated the long-term disincentive effects (including moral hazard) of taxes or benefits, and perhaps also the weakening of social norms when the number of beneficiaries increases. We do not yet know much about the empirical relevance of these hypotheses and inferences.

Naturally, aggregate political preferences may also change in other respects as a result of the previous path of government spending and taxes. For example, suppose that subsidies for child care and old-age care outside the family have induced a great number of females to move into the labour market. As a result, some of them may have come to appreciate their economic independence and the non-monetary benefits of work outside the household. After all, preferences are, to a large extent, a social phenomenon. There may naturally also be reverse causation: 'spontaneous' (unexplained) increases in preferences among females for economic independence and work outside the household may boost their political demand for subsidized child care and old-age care. Ideological developments, including feminism, may lie behind such spontaneous changes in preferences. In reality, mutual interaction between spontaneous changes in preferences and induced changes in preferences in response to new experiences is probably the most proper way of looking at the issue.

We may also speculate that the respect for the existing distribution of disposable income tends to recede gradually when people learn that this distribution is, to a large extent, politically determined – via taxes and welfare-state benefits – rather than market-determined by the distribution of skills and efforts of individuals (Lindbeck, 1994). As a result, political taboos against government intervention to redistribute income may gradually recede. The legitimacy of remaining income differentials is then likely to fall. As a result, political conflicts about the distribution of income may increase rather than reduce. Thus, I hypothesize (speculate) that conflicts about the distribution of income may be large, not only in societies with huge income differences (as predicted by the median voter model) but also in societies with a rather *even* distribution of disposable income, if the latter is a result of progressive taxes and transfers. In other words, I hypothesize that distributional conflicts do not necessarily fall monotonically with a reduction in the dispersion of the distribution of disposable income, when this reduction results from tax and welfare-state policies. For example, it is my impression that the huge, gradual squeeze of the distribution of disposable income in Sweden from the late 1950s to the mid-1980s was accompanied by larger rather than smaller political conflicts about the remaining income differentials. It should be possible to investigate whether this hypothesis is consistent with empirical data about redistributional conflict in the political arena.

It is also likely that social norms on *saving* are influenced by welfare-state policies. Before the emergence of the modern welfare state, individuals had probably learned from experience that it is proper to save for rainy days and old age. Subsequently, however, increasingly generous welfare-state arrangements made voluntary saving to deal with such contingencies less important. As in the case of work norms, it is therefore likely that the adherence to saving norms subsided only gradually when the government started to provide individual income security. This assertion is consistent with the experience that voluntary household savings only fell slowly in Sweden after the initiation of the new, quite generous government pension system in 1960 (the ATP-system).

We may also speculate that welfare-state arrangements have conse-quences for *entrepreneurship*, which certainly is an important element of economic dynamics. It is sometimes argued that entrepreneurship is stimulated by welfare-state arrangements, since failed entrepreneurs are said to be protected by unemployment benefits and social assistance. In other words, it is assumed that the risk of entrepreneurship is reduced by welfare state arrangements; see, for example, Sinn (1996). But do entrepreneurs really regard unemployment benefits and social assistance as being important alternatives ('fall back positions') to entrepreneurial success? Is it not more likely that they believe they can support themselves as employees if they fail as entrepreneurs? Moreover, in many countries, entrepreneurs are not even covered by the unemployment insurance system.

I would therefore hypothesize that features of the welfare state other than the safety nets are more important for entrepreneurship. For example, the Alesina–Perotti argument that social policies may contribute to social and political stability is relevant not only for investment in incumbent firms, but also for new entrepreneurship. On the other hand, the after-tax return for entrepreneurial activities may be so small in a high-tax society that entrepreneurship is seriously harmed.[12] We would also expect low household savings to have negative consequences for entrepreneurship, since investment in new and small firms often requires personal equity capital obtained outside the stock market.

This is not the whole story, however. Since entrepreneurs try, and sometimes also succeed in, building up personal wealth, they may be regarded as 'alien' figures in societies with advanced welfare states that emphasize income equality. The social acceptance of entrepreneurs may therefore unfold in highly egalitarian welfare states, and this is likely to harm entrepreneurship. This may occur both directly via the attitudes in society towards entrepreneurs, and indirectly via political decisions induced by these attitudes. Indeed, studies in Sweden during the 1970s and early 1980s revealed quite negative attitudes towards entrepreneurship and entrepreneurs among the population (Henrekson and Jakobsson, 2001). In 1978, only 30 per cent of the respondents in an opinion poll in Sweden believed that it was 'important to encourage entrepreneurship'. Moreover, only 37 per cent believed that business leaders (entrepreneurs) were 'capable of running firms most efficiently'; the majority believed that government officials or union leaders would be more capable of running them. These negative views were preceded and accompanied by legislation and taxation that made entrepreneurship less rewarding and more difficult administratively. (The situation has subsequently changed considerably.)

Reforms and retreat of the welfare state

Welfare-state dynamics is potentially important not only in order to understand the emergence of today's welfare-state arrangements, but also when analysing how such arrangements are subsequently reformed or cut down. Familiar situations in which this may happen are when existing welfare-state arrangements encounter financial difficulties; when serious disincentive effects emerge for the domestic economy; and when new socioeconomic developments make existing welfare-state arrangements less relevant than before.

An obvious situation where the welfare state runs into serious *financial difficulties* is when the domestic economy is exposed to unexpected shocks – for example, unfavourable demographic developments, slower productivity growth or unemployment-creating macroeconomic disturbances. The creation of generous welfare-state arrangements in the 1960s and 1970s was based on quite optimistic assumptions about the future growth of the general tax base. It is therefore easily understood that the subsequent slowdown of GDP growth created financial problems for several welfare-state arrangements, and that suggestions for reforms of and retreats from such arrangements have thus emerged. The most usual policy responses to restore financial viability seem to have been reduced replacement rates (that is, simply lower benefits and hence more co-insurance in the sense that the insured shares the risk with the insurance provider), more waiting days and shorter periods of time during which benefits can be obtained (including a later retirement age). Such retreats of the generosity of social insurance have taken place, for example, in the case of sick pay, unemployment benefits and pensions.

While the financial vulnerability of the welfare state to shocks is relatively easily to detect, *disincentive effects* are more difficult to observe and to measure. Indeed, the first instinct of many proponents of generous welfare-state arrangements is to deny that such problems exist, or, if acknowledged, to deny their importance. Some countries have, however, recently started to reform their welfare-state arrangements (and the financing of these) as a result of noticeable disincentive problems. The most obvious example is the fairly comprehensive tax reforms in several countries in the 1980s and 1990s, generally designed to broaden the tax base, reduce tax rates and mitigate the progressivity of the tax system. The most frequently suggested and implemented reforms of the benefits systems (including social insurance) have simply been higher contribution rates, benefit cuts and (in the case of the pension system) a later retirement age. Some countries have, however, also strengthened the link between the individual's lifetime contributions and his or her subsequent pension benefits – hence a shift to what may be called a 'quasi-actuarial' pension system (Lindbeck and Persson, 2003).

Socioeconomic developments that have made existing welfare-state arrangements less appropriate include increased labour force participation among married women, and the increased instability of the family, the latter reflected most dramatically in higher divorce rates. Naturally, such developments do not only constitute the background to the demand for a greater provision of organized child care and old-age care outside the family, but also for suggestions to tie welfare-state benefits to individuals rather than the family.

Better-educated individuals with higher incomes also generate political demand for more differentiated systems of income protection and social services, as well as for increased individual choice. This development may be regarded as a parallel to an increased demand for differentiated consumer goods resulting from similar forces. In the case of income insurance, recent shifts to contribution-based systems with individual accounts in some countries may be seen as a response to these new demands. Such developments are particularly noticeable in the pension system. In the case of social ('human') services, the new demands for individualization are probably easiest to satisfy if government subsidies of such services 'follow' the individual's own choice of service provider (that is, 'voucher systems' in the broad sense of the term). However, increased individualization of welfare-state arrangements are bound to encounter strong political resistance from groups having traditionally regarded the uniformity of welfare-state arrangements as an advantage, partly because such uniformity is seen as a reflection of egalitarian values.

When discussing retreats in welfare-state spending, certain asymmetries between the politics of expansion and retreat, respectively, are exposed. While the combination of selective benefits and general taxes, as argued above, tends to boost the expansion of government spending, the same combination is likely to make it difficult to cut existing benefits. Thus there may be some irreversibility because of special features of the political process. Moreover, every new type of benefit tends to create a new interest group of beneficiaries, which accentuates the irreversibility. Individuals are also likely to be more dissatisfied at losing benefits they already have than if they had not received such benefits in the first place. Indeed, this point may be regarded as a simple application of the Tversky–Kahneman prospect theory (1981), according to which the utility function is steeper to the left than to the right of the individual's initial position. Strong voter resistance to benefit cuts has also been recorded in numerous opinion polls and is, of course, highly noticeable in the political process itself. At the time of writing, Sweden is an extreme example, since about 60 per cent of the population gets practically *all* its income from the government – either as employees in public administration and service production, or as transfer recipients (Lindbeck, 1997).

Another complication of reforms and retreats in welfare-state spending is that such arrangements constitute a tightly interlocked network. It is difficult to remove one arrangement without causing complications to other arrangements. One illustration is that cuts in one type of benefit induce individuals to shift to other types. An illustration is that people in Sweden switched from sick leave to work injury leave in the late 1980s, when the replacement rate in the latter system was raised to 100 per cent of the previous income, compared to only 90 per cent in the case of sick leave. Similar shifts from unemployment benefits to sick leave benefits and early retirement have recently been noticed. Such shifts are particularly likely if social norms against 'over-using' or 'misusing' benefits have weakened.

The disincentive effects of generous benefits may, however, be mitigated by other elements of a benefit system. Disincentive effects may therefore be reduced if these elements are accentuated. An obvious example is a stiffening of requirements for doctors' certificates and administrative controls in both home and workplace in the sickness benefit system.

We would also expect that constitutional factors influence the political feasibility of reforms and retreats in welfare-state spending. Some political scientists (Bonoli, 2001; Huber and Stephens, 2001; Swank, 2001) argue that centralized political regimes, often with majority voting (such as the UK and New Zealand), have been able to make more dramatic reforms and retreats in welfare-state arrangements than more decentralized political regimes (often with proportional representation). Indeed, reforms and retreats in the UK and New Zealand, with majority parties, were made without an acute macroeconomic crisis, although both countries had experienced long periods of relative economic decline, which have often (realistically) been assumed to depend, at least to some extent, on government-created economic distortions. But the same authors also observe that some countries with quite fragmented political regimes have also been able to negotiate substantial reforms and retreats, such as Denmark and the Netherlands, and, to some extent, also Finland and Sweden. It might be argued, however, that the reforms and retreats in these countries were facilitated by *acute* economic crisis, partly as a result of severe negative macroeconomic shocks.

The internationalization of markets is often also regarded as a factor behind recent reforms and retreats in the traditional welfare state, which has basically been a 'national project'. Clearly, individual nations can no longer have much higher corporate and capital income tax rates than other counties. There has, indeed, recently been a race to a 'common level' of taxation in this field – in fact, in the neighbourhood of about 30 per cent. The consequences for the possibilities of financing the welfare state are, however, rather limited, since it is basically financed by the taxation of labour rather than capital. Although there is not (at least not yet) a 'race to the bottom' of taxation and social assistance in general, the internationalization process in the long run limits the ability of national governments to redistribute income among income classes.

We also expect increased mobility of poor people from poor to rich countries to induce the latter to continue, or even to sharpen, their strict immigration controls in order to limit the number of individuals expected to claim social benefits of various types. In principle, an internationalization of the markets for highly educated labour may also induce countries to reduce the progressivity of the tax system, although few strong tendencies have yet been observed in this direction. (Reductions in the maximum marginal tax rates in the 1980s and 1990s seem to have been induced mainly by domestic rather than international considerations.)

In a world with an increased geographical mobility of labour, we would also expect political demand for an expanded geographical 'transportability' of national welfare-state entitlements and the provision of services – within as well as across nations. In the case of social insurance, these demands are probably easiest to satisfy in the context of contribution-based systems with individual accounts, 'tied' to individuals regardless of where they live. In the case of social services, such as medical care or old-age care, a way to satisfy the demand for international transferability might be to request that the social insurance system in one country pays the bills for its citizens when they take advantage of services in other countries. This would simply be an international extension of the 'voucher method' of financing and allocating social services.

It is too early at present to say whether the continuing internationalization of the economic system will result in a more far-reaching co-ordination of welfare-state arrangements and their financing across nations. The alternative to formal co-ordination ('harmonization') is, of course, that individual countries adjust their systems independently to the ever more international character of markets for products, services, labour and capital – 'system competition' rather than centralized co-ordination. There will most probably be some combination of these two developments.

Notes

1 The average number of sick days in Sweden in 2002 was estimated to be about 30 per year. The figure for females was about 50 per cent higher than for men (according to statistics from previous years); see Persson (2003).
2 Persson and Tabellini (1994) hypothesize that a fall in the dispersion of the distribution of factor income ('gross income') makes voters (along the lines

of the median voter model) prefer less redistributive taxes. If this hypothesis makes sense, education policies reducing the dispersion of factor income would not only result in higher labour productivity among low-income groups, but also reduce the political demand for redistributive and distortionary taxes.

3 Martin Feldstein (1995) has tried to summarize the aggregate effects of several different market distortions in a single measure, namely income. He then produces much larger distortions than those in traditional empirical studies, where the effects of distortions in the labour market are often measured by hours of work.

4 Note that the economic distortion created by taxes is tied to the substitution effect and not to the income effect. There are, however, also two mutually counteracting income effects on labour supply: a positive income effect of higher average taxes, and a negative income effect caused by the rise in government spending.

5 Ljungqvist and Sargent (1998) have tried to explain unemployment persistence in Europe in the 1980s and 1990s resulting from an increasingly lax administration of the unemployment benefit system. This may be interpreted as a weakening of the enforcement of work norms by the administrators of the system.

6 Some of this literature is briefly summarised in Lindbeck and Nyberg (2001).

7 For example, about 8 per cent of the Swedish labour force did not go to work because of stated sickness on a given day in the year 2002 (Persson, 2003).

8 Among males, approximately 16 per cent more than normal reported sick when two international skiing competitions were reported on TV and radio (the World Championship and Olympic Games).

9 Means tests exist also in countries emphasizing universal welfare state arrangements. Examples are social assistance, income-dependent housing subsidies and income-dependent fees for services such as child care and old-age care.

10 Multiple political equilibria of the 'boot-strap' type, without social norms, have been analysed by Hassler *et al.* (2003). In this model, the multiplicity comes from the assumption that voters rationally expect investment in human capital today to influence voters' interest in redistribution policies in the future.

11 Formally, a process of the 'unwinding' of social norms is rather similar to certain types of ecological process. Initially, ecological disturbances may hardly be noticeable, but they may speed up after a time, possibly after a sudden 'ketchup effect' in connection with an exogenous disturbance – for example, in weather conditions.

12 For example, the marginal tax rates in Sweden for small firms approached 100 per cent in real terms in the 1970s and 1980s, if all taxes are considered (Du Rietz, 1994).

References

Åberg, Y., Hedström, P., and Kolm, A.-S. (2003) 'Social Interactions, Endogenous Processes, and Youth Unemployment', Manuscript, Department of Sociology, Stockholm University.

Alesina, A. and Rodrik, D. (1994) 'Distributive Politics and Economic Growth', *Quarterly Journal of Economics*, vol. 109, pp. 465–90.

Bonoli, G. (2001) 'Political Institutions, Veto Points, and the Process of Welfare State Adaption', in P. Pierson (ed.), *The New Politics of the Welfare State*, Oxford University Press, pp. 238–64.

Clark, A. E. (2003) 'Unemployment as a Social Norm: Psychological Evidence from Panel Data', *Journal of Labour Economics*, vol. 21, pp. 323–51.

Drago, R. and Wooden, M. (1992) 'The Determinants of Labour Absence: Economic Factors and Workgroup Norms across Countries', *Industrial and Labour Relations Review*, vol. 45, pp. 764–78.

Du Rietz, G. (1994) *Välfärdsstatens finansiering*, Socialstatsprojektet 1994. 1, Stockholm: City University Press.

Engbersen, G., Schuyt, K., Timmer, J. and Van Warden, F. (1993) *Cultures of Unemployment: A Comparative Look at Long-Term Unemployment and Urban Poverty*, Boulder, Col.: Westview Press.

Esping-Andersen, G. (1990) *The Three Worlds of Welfare Capitalism*, Cambridge: Polity Press.

Feldstein, M. (1995) 'The Effects of Marginal Tax Rates on Taxable Income: A Panel Study of the 1986 Tax Reform Act', *Journal of Political Economy*, vol. 103, pp. 551–72.

Frankenhaeuser, M., Lundberg, U. and Chesney, M. (eds) (1991) *Women, Work, and Health: Stress and Opportunities*, New York: Plenum.

Gruber, J. and Wise, D. A. (eds) (1999) *Social Security and Retirement around the World*, Chicago: University of Chicago Press.

Hassler, J., Rodríguez Mora, J. V., Storesletten K. and Zilibotti, F. (2003) 'The Survival of the Welfare State', *American Economic Review* vol. 93, pp. 87–112.

Henrekson, M. and Jakobsson, U. (2001) 'Where Schumpeter Was Nearly Right – the Swedish Model and Capitalism, Socialism and Democracy', *Journal of Evolutionary Economics*, vol. 11, pp. 331–58.

Huber, E. and Stephens, J. (2001) 'Welfare State and Production Regimes in the Era of Retrenchment', in P. Pierson (ed.), *The New Politics of the Welfare State*, Oxford University Press, pp. 107–45.

Johansson, P. and Palme, M. (2002) 'Assessing the Effect of Public Policy on Worker Absenteeism', *The Journal of Human Resources*, vol. 37, pp. 381–409.

Layard, R., Nickell, S. and Jackman, R. (1991) *Unemployment: Macroeconomic Performance and the Labour Market*, Oxford University Press.

Lindbeck, A. (1985) 'Redistribution Policy and the Expansion of the Public Sector', *Journal of Public Economics*, vol. 28, pp. 309–28.

Lindbeck, A. (1994) 'Overshooting, Reform and Retreat of the Welfare State', Tinbergen Lecture, *The Economist*, vol. 142.

Lindbeck, A. (1995) 'Welfare State Disincentives with Endogenous Habits and Norms', *Scandinavian Journal of Economics*, vol. 97, pp. 477–94.

Lindbeck, A. (1996) 'The West European Employment Problem', *Weltwirtschaftliches Archiv*, December, pp. 1–31.

Lindbeck, A. (1997) 'The Swedish Experiment', *Journal of Economic Literature* vol. 1273, p. 319.

Lindbeck, A. (2001) 'Changing Tides for the Welfare State – An Essay', Research Institute of Industrial Economics (IUI), Working Paper No. 550 and IIES Seminar Paper No. 694, Stockholm; forthcoming in *Festschrift for Richard Musgrave*, Berlin/Heidelberg: Springer-Verlag.

Lindbeck, A. (2002) 'From the Cradle to the Grave, A Prescription for Reform of European Welfare States over the Individual's Life Cycle', Publication in Skandia's Social Focus series, Stockholm.

Lindbeck, A. (2003) 'Social Model: Lessons for Developing Countries', in R. Pethig and M. Rauscher (eds), *Challenges to the World Economy*, Festschrift for Horst Siebert (Berlin/Heidelberg: Springer-Verlag, pp. 67–79.

Lindbeck, A. and Weibull, J. W. (1987) 'Balanced-Budget Redistribution as the Outcome of Political Competition', *Public Choice*, vol. 2, pp. 273–97.

Lindbeck, A. and Snower, D. S. (1988) *The Insider–Outsider Theory of Employment and Unemployment*, Cambridge, Mass.: MIT Press.

Lindbeck, A. and Weibull, J. W. (1993) 'A Model of Political Equilibrium in a Representative Democracy', *Journal of Public Economics*, vol. 5, pp. 195–209.

Lindbeck, A. and Nyberg, S. (2001) 'Raising Children to Work Hard: Altruism, Work Norms and Social Insurance', CESifo Working Paper No. 498, Munich.

Lindbeck, A. and Persson, M. (2003) 'The Gain from Pension Reform', Institute for International Economic Studies, Seminar Paper No. 712 and IUI Working Paper No. 580, Stockholm.

Lindbeck, A., Nyberg, S. and Weibull, J. W. (1999) 'Social Norms and Economic Incentives in the Welfare State', *Quarterly Journal of Economics*, vol. 114, pp. 1–35.

Ljungqvist, L. and Sargent, T. J. (1998) 'The European Unemployment Dilemma,' *The Journal of Political Economy*, vol. 106, pp. 514–50.

Meltzer, A. and Richard, S. (1981) 'A Rational Theory of the Size of Government', *Journal of Political Economy*, vol. 89, pp. 914–27.

Modig, A. and Boberg, K. (2002) *Är det OK att sjukskriva sig fast man inte är sjuk*, TEMO, T22785 (memo), Stockholm.

Moffit, R. (1983) 'An Economic Model of Welfare Stigma', *American Economic Review*, December, pp. 1023–35.

Myrdal, G. (1944) *An American Dilemma*, New York: Carnegie Foundation, app. 3.

Persson, M. (2003) 'Sjukskrivningarna och ersättningsnivån', in B. Swedenborg (ed.) *Varför är svenskarna så sjuka?*, Stockholm: SNS förlag.

Persson, T. and Tabellini, G. (1994) 'Is Inequality Harmful for Growth?', *American Economic Review*, vol. 84, pp. 600–21.

Persson, T. and Tabellini, G. (2002) *Economic Policy in Representative Democracies*, Manuscript, Institute for International Economic Studies, Stockholm.

Pierson, P. (ed.) (2001) *The New Politics of the Welfare State*, Oxford University Press.

Sinn, H.-W. (1996) 'Social Insurance, Incentives and Risk Taking', *International Tax and Public Finance*, vol. 3, January, pp. 296–80.

Skogman Thoursie, P. (2002) 'Reporting Sick: Are Sporting Events Contagious?', Mimeo, Department of Economics, Stockholm University, Sweden.

Swank, D. (2001) 'Political Institutions and Welfare State Restructuring. The Impact of Institutions on Social Policy Change in Developed Democracies', in P. Pierson (ed.), *The New Politics of the Welfare State* Oxford University Press, pp. 197–237.

Tversky, A. and Kahneman, D. (1981) 'The Framing of Decisions in the Psychology of Choice', *Science*, vol. 211, pp. 453–58.

Wildavsky, A. (1984) *The Politics of the Budgetary Process*, Boston, Mass.: Little, Brown.

8
Employment and Non-employment: A Study of the Swedish Labour Market

Erik Jonasson and Lars Pettersson

Introduction

The employment issue is one of the most important areas for economic research and policy. Political ambitions are determined by the employment rate, because of the link between employment and tax revenues. The problem of unemployment and non-employment is associated with negative effects for society. Behrenz and Delander (1998) analysed the economic effects of unemployment and labour market programmes in Sweden for the year 1995, when open unemployment plus labour market programmes amounted to 11 per cent of the labour force. The authors estimated the fiscal costs for the public sector, as well as the real resource costs (opportunity costs associated with, for example the potential loss in production output) for society as a whole, and the economic costs for the unemployed. According to their study, the sum of these effects might amount to SEK 165 billion (around 10 per cent of GDP in 1995).

Research shows that once unemployment has increased, it will probably remain at the higher level or decrease slightly, but will not return to its previous lower level. Layard *et al.* (1991) present an overview of a number of empirical studies of post-war unemployment in OECD countries and show that, in general, unemployment rates were higher in the 1980s compared to the 1960s. This observation is particularly strong for European countries. For a long time, Sweden had a record low unemployment. Unlike the rest of Western Europe, Sweden and a few other countries were able to avoid high unemployment until the 1990s.[1] However, there was a break in the first years of the 1990s, when the rate of open unemployment increased from around 2 per cent to

8 per cent. Even though this rate had declined by 2001 compared to the level in 1993–4, there still appears to have been a structural break in the early 1990s (findings also supported by, for example, Lindbeck, 1996). At that time, the ratio of people employed among the population of working age (20–64 years) decreased by around 10 per cent in Sweden. The ratio of people who were non-employed decreased in the latter half of the 1990s, but remains at a level where around 25 per cent of the working-age population do not have a regular job.

The purpose of this chapter is to explore and analyse the changes in the Swedish labour market over recent decades, focusing on the percentage of the population aged 20–64 that is not employed (non-employed). The substantial changes in the 1990s are analysed by decomposing the percentage of people who are not employed into different categories.

Labour market policy and non-employment

When the labour market situation was deteriorating in Sweden in the early 1990s, substantial policy efforts were implemented. Different types of active labour market policy tools were used to deal with the increasing unemployment – for example, labour market training, job broking and various forms of job creation. Scholars differ in their views on the effectiveness of different forms of active labour market policy programmes. Martin and Grubb (2001) present an overview of experiences from active labour market policy programmes in OECD countries, primarily using OECD data from the 1980s and 1990s. Martin and Grubb also surveyed the evaluation literature in the field. Their general conclusion is that active labour market programmes appear to have little success in terms of 'increasing future employment and earnings prospects', which is a problem in particular for disadvantaged youngsters. The same kind of negative view of the unemployment problem with regard to youngsters' response to labour market programmes is also found for the US labour market (Heckman *et al.*, 1999). At the same time, job-search assistance, wage subsidies in the private sector and labour market training programmes seem to work for some 'target' groups, in so far that the post-programme employment prospects for the participants are improved.

Concerning evaluations of the labour market policy strategies in Sweden, IFAU (the Institute for Labour Market Policy Evaluation) has carried out a number of studies, at both micro and the macro levels. According to Ackum Agell and Lundin (2001), different conclusions can be drawn from the experiences of labour market policy with respect to the formation of present-day policy. One interesting result from this research is that it cannot be claimed that the probability of becoming employed is considerably higher for individuals participating in active labour market programmes compared to those who do not.

Calmfors *et al.* (2001), in particular, question the volume of active labour market programmes in Sweden from the beginning of the 1990s. The authors' conclusion is that the Swedish practice in this field has shortcomings when it comes to dealing with unemployment problems. An interesting issue related to the increase in the volume of active labour market programmes in the 1990s is how to interpret labour market data. As an example, there was a significant decrease in open unemployment between 1993 and 2000. This is not the whole picture, however. The unemployment and the employed do not constitute the entire working-age population. In fact, the working-age population (aged 20–64) can be divided into several groups, and in order to get a total picture of the changes in the labour market, the total population must be analysed. To get a total overview of the changes in the labour market, it is important to analyse all the different forms of occupation, both regular employment and various forms of non-employment. In this chapter, we consider the whole working-age population. The argument for applying this method is that unemployment does not constitute a perfect measure of problems concerning changes in the non-working groups in the population.

There is an extensive literature in the field of labour economics focusing on the unemployment problem (in particular, the poor employment performance in the labour market in Western Europe from the 1970s onwards). One theoretical approach aimed at explaining why unemployment occurs and becomes persistent relates to the way prices and wages are determined in the economy. Economic models in this field combine both short-run and long-run interactions in the labour market to explain how unemployment and inflation are determined.[2]

Typical questions of interest are why excess supply (unemployment) occurs, and why the labour market does not clear, as well as why wages do not fall when there is an excess supply of workers. In the literature, the answers to these questions are usually that (i) firms are not free when setting the wages (usually because of wage bargaining); and/or (ii) firms choose to pay high wages because it is in their interest to do so. The latter relates to the theory of efficiency wages, stating that firms will choose freely to pay high wages in order to motivate effort and keep their employees (Layard *et al.*, 1991).[3]

Concerning wage bargaining and wage formation, the performance in the labour market is, for example, explained by union behaviour. A central issue for the European economies is the role of central wage negotiations found in many countries – in Sweden for example. A particular way of stressing the importance of the wage-setting procedure in central wage negotiations is the insider–outsider theory – initiated by, for example, Blanchard and Summers (1986) and Lindbeck and Snower (1988). In the light of this theory, it can be explained how long-term unemployment may increase in relation to different phases of the business cycle. According to the insider–outsider theory, there is a risk that there might be an increase in the number of outsiders in the economy in times of depression and, hence the number of long-term unemployed. This is explained by the difficulties faced by outsiders trying to enter a labour market governed by the behaviour of insiders defending their positions. The way wages are settled can be assumed to generate difficulties for outsiders. If wages are set with respect to marginal productivity conditions among insiders, outsiders will face problems in entering the labour market if their marginal productivity is at a lower level than the insiders'. This situation can deteriorate if the human capital for outsiders decreases over time. This means that people becoming unemployed in times of recession are likely to face difficulties in competing for jobs when the economy is booming, because of this insider–outsider relationship.

There are a number of empirical studies analysing the presence of unemployment in the labour market. One kind of analysis focuses on the equilibrium level of unemployment at the so-called NAIRU (non-accelerating inflation rate of unemployment) level. Examples of these, focusing on the Swedish labour market, are Forslund (1995), Assarsson and Jansson (1996), and Lindblad (1997). These studies have taken into account both open unemployment and people on labour market programmes. A general conclusion from these studies is that the equilibrium level of unemployment increased in Sweden during the 1990s.

In an international study covering Germany, the UK, Canada and the USA, Jaeger and Parkinson (1994) found evidence of the persistence effects in unemployment being greater in Europe than in the USA. Layard *et al.* (1991) present the results of a study of the European labour markets in the 1970s and 1980s. Their results shows that, while unemployment in the USA decreased in the years following the second oil crisis (in the early 1980s), it increased in the EC countries. However, the EFTA countries managed to avoid high unemployment at that time.

One problem often recognized in empirical studies is that the labour force is treated as a constant. In other words, the cyclical changes in labour force participation are often ignored or paid little attention. Naturally, many scholars are aware of this problem, and keep it in mind when carrying out their analyses. The focus of our study is on non-employment in Sweden since the 1970s. In this respect, we divided the part of the working-age population without a 'regular job' into different categories (based on data from the *Labour Force Surveys*, Statistics Sweden). Thus we also incorporate various 'intermediate' types of unemployment, and instead of using the traditional unemployment rate, we use a definition of *not-employed*, defined as:

$$NE = U + LMP + WH + ST + DW + OTH \qquad (8.1)$$

where we define non-employment (NE) as the sum of open unemployment (U), people involved in labour market policy programmes (LMP), people working in their own homes (WH), full-time students (ST), people too disabled to work (DW), and other people of working age not participating in the labour force (OTH).[4] Adding the sub-population that is employed (E) to the non-employed (NE) gives the total population of working age. Thus, $E + NE = 1$, when E and NE are reported as shares of the total population.

Figure 8.1 shows *non-employment* (NE) as a share of the total population of working age (20–64 years). NE decreased until the early 1990s, there was then a significant shift in the trend, and since the mid-1990s non-employment has been at a significantly higher level.[5] In the mid-1990s, the rate of non-employment was at a similar level to the early 1970s.

When comparing European countries, we find that the Swedish labour market was in a peak position with respect to high employment in 1990. Table 8.1 presents a comparison of the open unemployment rate and non-employment in a number of European countries. The data in this table includes people aged 15–64 (not the same definition as that used in the analysis in the other sections of this study), and shows the situation for the years 1990 and 2000.

In 1990, open unemployment in Sweden was 1.8 per cent. At the same time, non-employment was also at a very low level – 17.2 per cent. The average rate of unemployment (unweighted) for countries in the European Union was at the same level (8.3 per cent) in both 1990

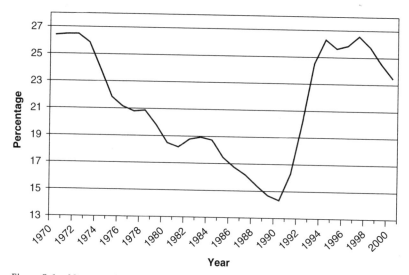

Figure 8.1 Non-employment as a share of the working age population (20–64) in Sweden
Source: Statistic Sweden, *Labour Force Survey* (1970–2001).

Table 8.1 Open unemployment and non-employment in European countries, people aged 15–64 years, 1990 and 2000, percentages

Country	Open unemployment, 1990	Open unemployment, 2000	Non-employment, 1990	Non-employment, 2000
Belgium	7.3	6.6	48.6	41.4
Denmark	8.5	4.5	26.1	24.5
Finland	3.2	9.9	26.6	35.6
France	9.2	10.1	43.2	42.1
Germany	6.2	8.1	37.8	35.9
Ireland	13.2	4.4	53.0	37.0
Italy	9.9	11.0	50.1	51.1
Luxembourg	1.6	2.4	41.5	38.2
Netherlands	7.7	2.7	41.5	27.8
Norway	5.3	3.5	28.2	22.8
Portugal	4.8	4.1	36.0	33.1
Spain	16.1	14.1	55.2	48.8
Sweden	1.8	5.9	17.2	27.0
UK	6.8	5.6	29.0	29.0
OECD Europe	8.1	8.9	41.3	41.7
European Union	8.3	8.4	40.9	38.9

Source: OECD *Employment Outlook*, 2001.

and 2000. The rate of non-employment (unweighted) decreased by 2 per cent points (from 40.9 per cent to 38.9 per cent). This means that, on average, a larger proportion of the population in the EU countries aged 15–64 was working in the year 2000 than in 1990. A number of countries (for example, Belgium, the Republic of Ireland, the Netherlands, Luxembourg and Norway) decreased their rate of non-employment substantially during the 1990s. Naturally, some of these changes might depend on demographical changes, catch-up effects in female employment and so on. Sweden, and Finland, show sharp increases in the rate of unemployment and non-employment, making these two countries special cases.[6]

There are several possible explanations why Sweden and Finland performed differently compared to other European countries. First, it could be argued that there is a so-called 'catch-up effect', meaning that Sweden and Finland were at a higher level in the first place, and that the other countries have narrowed the gap. This explanation could be valid for Sweden to some degree, but Finland was at the same level as Norway, Denmark and the UK. The 'catch-up' explanation to similar phenomena regarding growth patterns has also been questioned in other studies, since, for example, countries with a comparatively high purchasing power have remained at the top for a long time (for example, the USA). Second, according to other scholars, it is possible that the poor Swedish performance resulted from policy failures (see, for example, Chapter 5 by Bo Södersten in this volume).

The labour market and labour force participation in Sweden

In Sweden, a far-reaching intervention policy with an active public sector has been used for a long period of time. It was implemented from the Second World War onwards (during the 1950s and 1960s), and is known as the 'Swedish model'. The basic targets for economic and social policy have been (i) economic security; and (ii) egalitarianism (Lindbeck, 1997). The policy has been guided by Keynesian-type ideas, and consequently, economic security includes full employment. The 'golden years' for this particular policy are usually considered to be the period from the beginning of the 1950s to the middle of the 1970s, when both inflation and unemployment in Sweden were kept at comparatively low levels (Södersten, 1981). At the same time, Sweden also had strong economic growth.

In the middle of the 1970s (at the time of the first oil crises), the Swedish economy started to perform less well than before. The currency was devalued several times in the late 1970s and early 1980s. In the mid-1980s, there was an improvement in the trade balance as well as a recovery in the economic performance. However, the problems continued and in the early 1990s a severe crisis hit the economy. The banking and real estate sectors played a central role in the crisis and the currency was converted from a fixed-exchange-rate regime to a floating one. In the first years of the 1990s, when the fixed exchange rate was defended, the economy was suffering from a high interest-rate level. Such a significant shock naturally did affect the economy, resulting in a decrease in demand, and thus the very strong recession of the first half of the 1990s was triggered.

The recession in the early 1990s had to be handled differently from previous ones. The government debt had to be reduced and various reforms adopted in order to adjust the markets towards international competition criteria. The stated intention to fulfil the criteria of the European Monetary Union (EMU) and the global trend of deregulating markets are often mentioned as two important factors behind the changes that were implemented. Deeper questions were also asked about the viability of the welfare arrangements in Sweden (for example, the pension system) (Björklund *et al.*, 1998). As a consequence of the deep recession and the structural problems in the economy at that time, there was a sharp increase in the unemployment rate.[7]

Table 8.2 shows the Swedish population of working age (20–64), divided into those inside and outside the labour market in the period 1970–2000. Our measure of employment in this case does not include people involved in labour market programmes. The motivation for excluding this group from the regular measure of employment is because employment is related to a labour market policy tool. The earlier increase in the employment rate, defined as employment as a share of the working-age population, is to a substantial degree explained by women entering the labour market during the period 1970–90.[8] In the latter half of the 1990s, the employment rate fell to a lower rate compared to the situation in the 1980s. But, the employment rate is still, at the time of writing, at a comparatively high level from an international perspective; the OECD average is less than 70 per cent (OECD, 2001).

In Equation (8.1), non-employment was defined as the sum of six non-working groups in the working-age population. The time series,

Table 8.2 The working-age population in Sweden, 1970–2000

	Working age population, aged 20–64	Labour force[a]	Employment[b]	Unemployment[c]	Outside labour force
1970	4,715,000	3,540,000 (75.4%)	3,494,000 (74.1%)	46,000 (1.3%)	1,160,000
1980	4,767,000	3,975,000 (83.9%)	3,909,000 (82.0%)	66,000 (1.7%)	769,000
1990	4,941,000	4,322,000 (87.7%)	4,258,000 (86.2%)	64,000 (1.5%)	610,000
1995	5,116,000	4,147,000 (82.2%)	3,830,000 (74.9%)	317,000 (7.5%)	913,000
2000	5,200,000	4,196,000 (81.4%)	4,005,000 (77.0%)	191,000 (4.5%)	965,000

Notes: a) Labour force participation rate, as a share of the working age population, is given in brackets; b) Employment rate, as a share of the working age population, is given in brackets; c) Unemployment rate, as a share of the labour force, is given in brackets.
Source: Statistics Sweden, *Labour Force Surveys* (1970–2001).

showing the magnitude of these groups, are plotted in Figures 8.2a–8.2f below. As can be seen from the figures, open unemployment and the number of people engaged in labour market policy programmes increased dramatically at the beginning of the 1990s. Even if the unemployment rate has fallen during the latter part of the 1990s, the number of people employed was still 250,000 lower in 2000 than in 1990. This means that the decrease in unemployment does not cover the whole picture, including every aspect of dynamic changes in the labour force.

If we compare values over two periods, 1976–90 and 1991–2000, we find that non-employment, *NE*, has a mean that is 350,000 higher in the 1990s than in 1976–90. The explanation is to be found both inside and outside the labour market: on average, 180,000 more people were unemployed, while the number of people outside the labour market (of working age) was 170,000 higher during the 1990s. Looking at the five sub-groups of people outside the labour market, there has been a steady fall in the number of people working in their own homes, whereas the number of people involved in labour market programmes (LMPs), students, people too disabled to work, and those in the category of 'others' have all increased. Because of changes in statistical methods and definitions, the *Labour Force Surveys* do not allow meaningful comparisons of the different groups outside the labour market

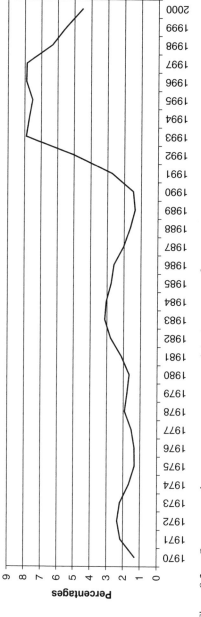

Figure 8.2a　Open unemployment as a percentage of the labour force[9]

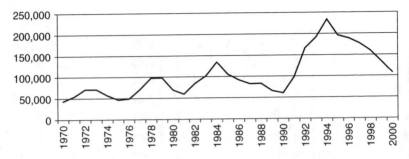

Figure 8.2b Number of people involved in labour market policy programmes [10]

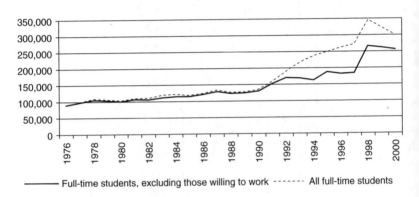

——— Full-time students, excluding those willing to work ------ All full-time students

Figure 8.2c Students[11]

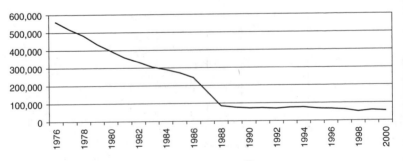

Figure 8.2d People working in their own homes[12]

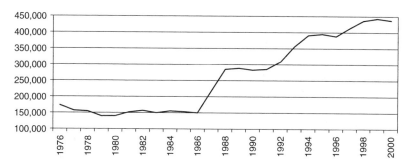

Figure 8.2e People too disabled to work[13]

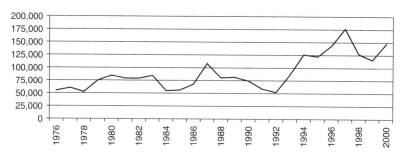

Figure 8.2f Other people outside the labour market[14]

Figure 8.2 Non-employment
Figure 8.2a shows open unemployment, while Figures 8.2b–f provide a subdivision of the people outside the labour market.

over time (at least, not before the 1990s). However, among the 440,000 'too disabled to work', there is a group of approximately 100,000 people who have chosen early retirement for non-health-related reasons. This group has been fairly stable during the 1990s. The remaining members of this group of people, those *reported to be long-term side or early retired for health-related reasons*, increased from about 130,000 at the end of the 1980s to 320,000 at the end of the 1990s. Among the people outside the labour market (most likely to be found in the non-categorized group 'others'), 80,000 are considered to be *discouraged workers* (that is, people who are willing to work but have not been able to get a job. In the 1970s and 1980s, this group ranged between 20,000 and 30,000 people; in the mid-1990s, it amounted to 140,000. The majority of this group are likely to be engaged in labour market policy programmes.

The changes in the labour market

Empirical analysis shows that there was a structural break in the Swedish labour market in the early 1990s. According to Perron's test for structural change, this break is significant if we study both open unemployment and non-employment (see the Appendix to this chapter on page 000). Unemployment and, as we measure it, non-employment, increase at this time. As mentioned earlier, this phenomenon has been noticed by several other scholars. It is also acknowledged that Sweden followed a similar trend to other European countries during the 1970s and 1980s.

One particular aspect of interest in our study is that the two measurements, non-employment and unemployment, are not significantly cointegrated (see the Appendix). This means that they do not generate the same picture of the development of the economy and the labour market. Open unemployment is not significantly cointegrated with either non-employment or the size of the population outside the labour force. Our judgement is that the measurement 'open unemployment' is not always the most appropriate, at least not in itself. Other measures, such as non-employment, could be used as a complement to open unemployment.

There are several possible explanations for the performance of the Swedish labour market and the increase in non-employment. One obvious first explanation is that there has been an increase in higher education. The university programmes have expanded, and there are more students in the system. Second, the fluctuations in the business cycle can explain changes in employment. The problem with persistent unemployment in Western Europe is well known. A notable amount of research has been carried out in this area. Calmfors and Holmlund (2000) provide the results of a survey in which they point out how both micro- and macroeconomic explanations are used to explain performance in the labour market.

Third, demographic changes can also contribute explanations related to the problem. One possible explanation for the performance of Sweden during the 1990s is the increased number of immigrants. A large number of immigrants entered the economy at a time of recession, when demand for labour was weak, and they have had difficulty in becoming integrated through the labour market. The stream of immigrants to Sweden has changed since the 1970s. Rolf Ohlsson (1995) compares the level of vacancies in the manufacturing industry with the stream of immigrants to Sweden, and points out that there has been a link between the demand for labour and immigration. In particular, immigrants before 1975 could be considered as labour-force migration. After 1975, immigration cannot be characterized as labour force migration in the same way, although the stream of immigrants appears to follow business cycles trends (at least until the end of the 1980s). The increase in non-employment can be related to immigration, since employment is lower among immigrants than in the rest of the population, as shown by for example, Ohlsson (1995) and Rooth (1999). There are also differences in the employment rate between immigrants with respect to their nationality (also shown by Rooth, 1999, and Ekberg and Ohlsson, 2000).

Demographic changes in the age distribution can also contribute towards explaning labour market performance. If the average age of the working-age population increases, it is possible that more people will be found outside the labour market. In the Swedish case, we should not expect this 'ageing effect' to have a large impact. In a study by Johansson and Palme (2002), it was shown that older people in the work force in Sweden have a high employment rate compared to other countries.

Institutional factors constitute a fourth explanation for the labour-market performance. It is well documented in economic research that rules within the welfare system determining the benefits from unemployment, sickness and so on can explain behaviour among employees. Björklund *et al.* (1996) show how benefits from unemployment insurance affect the probability of proceeding from unemployment to employment. The probability increases when the benefits are close to expiring. Henrekson and Persson (forthcoming, 2004) also show that sick leave is very much influenced by the benefits of related sickness insurance. When the benefits become more generous, sick leave tends to increase by a time-lagged effect.

A fifth possible explanation behind the increase in non-employment is the change in social norms with respect to employment that has been in focus recently in a number of publications. Lindbeck (1996) argues that social norms in favour of non-employment might be established in an economy if the subsidies and welfare benefits are extensive. A change in the social norms may occur in a recession, when more people become dependent on public assistance. As time goes by, it is likely that more people will adopt a new way of living, without working, which was previously acceptable as 'good behaviour'. In this way, new social norms may emerge where 'good behaviour' is not attached to self-support through working income.

Summary and concluding remarks

We have analysed the labour market from the non-employment perspective. This means that our focus has been on the part of the population of working age (aged 20–64) who do not have a 'regular' employment. By 'regular', we mean ordinary jobs offered on the labour market – that is, we exclude labour market programmes and so on. However, it is not straightforward to acknowledge this by only considering the data series for open unemployment. There are problems to be addressed in analyses of open unemployment; for example, the connection between unemployment and the labour force participation rate. In this study, we include the whole population of working age.

According to our own analysis and previous research, Sweden started to experience more serious labour market problems in the 1990s. These problems are very similar to those in many other European countries. Our study, as well as other studies, show that there was a structural shift in the employment rate and non-employment in Sweden in the early 1990s. The employment rate showed an increasing trend during the 1970s and 1980s, mainly as a result of women entering the labour market during this period. Between the years 1990 and 1994 there was a sharp drop in the employment rate, which has remained at a substantially lower level since the mid-1990s compared to the 1980s. Sweden and Finland are the only countries among those included in our study that show a considerable increase in non-employment during the 1990s.

When scrutinizing the non-employed groups of the working-age population, we find interesting changes. First, we can state that the volume of labour market programmes was much more extensive during the 1990s compared to the 1970s and 1980s. At the time of the recession, this kind of policy tool was favoured by politicians (Calmfors *et al.*, 2001). However, their efficiency can be questioned in the light of evaluations that have lately been made concerning labour market policies (see, for example, the findings presented in Ackum Agell and Lundin, 2001).

Second, the number of students has doubled during the 1990s. The explanation is that (i) educational programmes have been extended with respect to their number of years in education; (ii) there are more educational positions offered in the higher education system; and (iii) more people are occupied in different types of labour market training schemes as a part of the labour market policy programmes. Third, an increasing number of people have been considered to be too disabled to work.

Within this category of individuals, there are, for example, those who are reported as long-term sick or early retired for health-related reasons. These two categories of individuals are the ones explaining the sharp increase in the total number of people too disabled to work.

There are also other explanations as to why the group of non-employed has increased. In recent years, different scholars argue that a change in social norms and preferences in favour of the non-employment position has taken place in many countries. Lindbeck (1996) argues that such social norms in favour of work may be weakened in countries with generous benefit systems when an economic shock occurs. As more people will be living on different welfare benefits, this may become a way of living that people accept and adopt instead of striving to become employed. This means that the change in non-employment should be analysed with respect to the benefits systems in the welfare state.

Our final conclusion is that the kind of study our analysis represents is very well motivated, and it is worth acknowledging the differences between the non-employment approach and studies of unemployment. There are future options for more research in this area – for example, making international comparative studies of this kind. Evidently, there are also policy implications that can be pointed at from this particular perspective. Our claim is that policy should be based on the situation for the whole population, not just on those who are employed or unemployed.

Appendix: Perron test for unit roots and structural change

In Figure A 8.1 the seasonally adjusted *unemployment rate* and *rate of non-employment* are found, 1976Q1–2002Q1. These are derived according to the following principle:

$$y_t = a_0 + D_1 + D_2 + D_3 + y\_adj_t \tag{A8.1}$$

where y_adj is the residual in regression (A 8.1) and D_i is the dummy variable for quarter i. Perron's test for structural change and unit roots has been run as:

$$ne_t = a_0 + a_1 ne_{t-1} + a_2 t + a_3 D_L + \sum_{i=1}^{4} \beta_i \Delta ne_{t-i} + \varepsilon_t, \tag{A8.2}$$

where ne is the seasonally adjusted non-employment, D_L is the structural dummy (1 for $t > 1992{:}4$, 0 otherwise) and i is the number of lags for Δne (See Table A8.1).

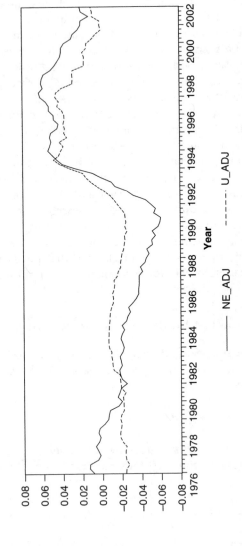

Figure A 8.1 Non-employment (NE_ADJ) and unemployment (U_ADJ), standardized and seasonally adjusted

It is important to remember that the *t*-statistics should be compared with Perron's critical values (which are somewhat higher than ordinary critical values for the *t* distribution). The AR(1) process does not seem to deviate significantly from 1, which indicates the presence of a unit root process. The trend and the intercept parameters both have low significance, whereas the structural dummy appears to be significant.

The results are similar for the unemployment rate (see Table A8.2). The conclusion from the two tests is that both variables follow a unit root process and have a structural break around year 1993.

Table A8.1   Perron´s test for structural break for non-employment in Sweden

Variables	Coefficient	Std. error	t-statistic	Prob.
C	–0.116908	0.122236	–0.956413	0.3415
TREND	0.001201	0.000953	1.260985	0.2106
DL	*0.014523*	*0.005099*	*2.848034*	*0.0055*
DNE_ADJ(-1)	–0.018488	0.123145	–0.150128	0.8810
DNE_ADJ(-2)	0.192181	0.161522	1.189809	0.2373
DNE_ADJ(-3)	0.256657	0.156137	1.643799	0.1038
DNE_ADJ(-4)	0.335691	0.122200	2.747073	0.0073
AR(1)	*0.978505*	*0.019034*	*51.40841*	*0.0000*
R-squared	0.987199	Mean dependent var.		0.000285
Adjusted R-squared	0.986180	S.D. dependent var.		0.040845
S.E. of regression	0.004802	Akaike info criterion		–7.760047
Sum squared resid.	0.002029	Schwarz criterion		–7.546351
Log likelihood	380.4823	F-statistic		969.4640
Durbin–Watson stat	1.565677	Prob(F-statistic)		0.000000

Table A8.2   Perron´s test for structural break for open unemployment in Sweden

Variables	Coefficient	Std. error	t-statistic	Prob.
C	0.192224	0.984355	0.195280	0.8456
TREND	–0.001099	0.004009	–0.274269	0.7845
DL	*0.013253*	*0.003067*	*4.320704*	*0.0000*
DU_ADJ(-1)	0.371373	0.102311	3.629860	0.0005
DU_ADJ(-2)	0.325696	0.103372	3.150705	0.0022
DU_ADJ(-3)	–0.016516	0.102809	–0.160653	0.8727
DU_ADJ(-4)	0.378196	0.103514	3.653581	0.0004
AR(1)	*0.990638*	*0.023837*	*41.55837*	*0.0000*

The cointegration test shown in Table A8.3 suggests there is no cointegration between non-employment and unemployment. If we consider the population outside the labour market (*OUT*) — that is, separating unemployment from non-employment, the Perron test indicates that this variable follows a unit root process (see Table A8.4). However, the level dummy variable is not significant, suggesting that the number of people outside the labour market did not suffer from any structural shift around 1993. Hence the structural shift in non-employment must be caused by the changes in unemployment.

Finally, a cointegration test between *OUT* and *U* gives the result shown in Table A8.5 and indicates that we have no cointegration between the two variables.

Table A8.3 LR test for cointegration between non-employment and open unemployment in Sweden

Sample: 1976:1 2002:1
Included observations: 100
Test assumption: No deterministic trend in the data
Series: NE_ADJ U_ADJ
Lags interval: 1 to 4

Eigenvalue	Likelihood ratio	5 per cent critical value	1 per cent critical value	Hypothesized no. of CE(s)
0.085327	11.96676	12.53	16.31	None
0.030019	3.047872	3.84	6.51	At most 1

Notes: *(**) denotes rejection of the hypothesis at 5%(1%) significance level.
L.R. rejects any cointegration at 5% significance level.

Table A8.4 Perron's test for structural break for population outside the labour market in Sweden

Variables	Coefficient	Std. error	t-statistic	Prob.
C	−0.077757	0.052675	−1.476167	0.1434
@TREND	0.000851	0.000502	1.694948	0.0935
DL93	0.005276	0.004049	1.302933	0.1959
DOUT_ADJ(-1)	−0.129265	0.106840	−1.209897	0.2295
DOUT_ADJ(-2)	−0.249083	0.128695	−1.935453	0.0560
DOUT_ADJ(-3)	−0.403674	0.122584	−3.293034	0.0014
DOUT_ADJ(-4)	0.080376	0.109760	0.732286	0.4659
AR(1)	0.963974	0.019321	49.89281	0.0000

Table A8.5 LR test for cointegration between open unemployment and the population outside the labour market in Sweden

Sample: 1976:1 2002:1
Included observations: 100
Test assumption: No deterministic trend in the data
Series: OUT_ADJ U_ADJ
Lags interval: 1 to 4

Eigenvalue	Likelihood ratio	5 per cent critical value	1 per cent critical value	Hypothesized no. of CE(s)
0.087048	12.09635	12.53	16.31	None
0.029450	2.989194	3.84	6.51	At most 1

Notes: *(**) denotes rejection of the hypothesis at 5%(1%) significance level.
L.R. rejects any cointegration at 5% significance level.

Notes

1 Other countries in Western Europe that also had comparatively low figures of open unemployment were the other EFTA-countries (Austria, Finland, Norway, Sweden and Switzerland).
2 An overview of labour market theory is, for example, presented in Layard *et al.* (1991). The phenomenon of unemployment and persistence in unemployment can, according to Layard *et al.*, be stressed using the NAIRU concept and the Phillips curve relation. This approach is slightly different from that used in 'new classical macroeconomics' (Lucas, 1972). However, both approaches make use of an equilibrium level of unemployment. Another way of studying the occurrence of unemployment would be to use the concept of real business cycles, which is not dealt with in this chapter.
3 For a further overview of efficiency wage theories, see Katz (1986) and Weiss (1990).
4 Closer definitions of these groups can be seen in Figures 8.2a–8.2f. All variables in equation (8.1) show non-stationarity at the 5 per cent level (according to an augmented Dickey–Fuller test), which means that there are no stable equilibrium levels for any of the variables.
5 In the Appendix, a Perron test has been used, analysing the presence of a structural break, which yields significant results at the 5 per cent level.
6 Italy is the only country in Table 8.1, besides Sweden and Finland, that shows an increase in non-employment (minor) between 1990 and 2000.
7 The sharp increase in unemployment in the 1990s was very much a Nordic phenomenon. The Nordic countries reached a level that other EC-countries had been at from the early 1980s onwards (Elmeskov, 1994).
8 Note that the employment rate differs from the labour force participation rate, which is defined as the labour force (employed + unemployed) as a share of the total population of working age.
9 Standard definition used. *Source*: Statistics Sweden, *Labour Force Survey* (1970–2001).

10   Some of the labour market policy programmes (LMPs), such as 'Relief Work' and 'Trainee Replacement Scheme' are considered to be employment in the Labour Force Surveys. In this study, all LMPs apart from programmes for disabled people are considered as non-employment. *Source*: The National Labour Market Board.

11   Refers to full-time students. The majority of the 'students willing to work' are involved in LMPs such as the Work Experience Scheme, Employment Training and Work Experience for Youngsters. *Source*: Statistics Sweden *Labour Force Survey* (1970–2001).

12   Unpaid assistants in firms owned by a member of the same household are considered to be employed. *Source*: Statistics Sweden, *Labour Force Survey* (1970–2001).

13   The variable includes early retirement, people reported long-term sick, and a smaller number of people being/working abroad. The break in the time series in 1987 is caused by a change in statistical methods in the Labour Force Surveys. From 1987, early retirement has been reported separately. Including this group among people too disabled to work, a one-time upward-shift of around 100,000 is created at the expense of downward-shifts in the time series, covering people working at home, even though other groups were also affected. From 1998, the number of people working/being abroad is reported separately in the *Labour Force Surveys* and amounts to about 50,000. *Source*: Statistics Sweden *Labour Force Survey* (1970–2001).

14   This group covers those people reported as being outside the labour market but who do not fit into the above groups. *Source*: Statistics Sweden *Labour Force Survey* (1970–2001).

References

Ackum Agell, S. and Lundin, M. (2001) *Erfarenheter av svensk arbetsmarknadspolitik*, Institute for Labour Market Policy Evaluation (IFAU), no. 1.

Assarsson, B. and Jansson, P. (1996) 'Unemployment Persistence: The Case of Sweden', Working Paper No. 140, FIEF, Trade Union Institute for Economic Research, Stockholm.

Behrenz, L. and Delander, L. (1998) *The Total Fiscal Costs of Unemployment: An Estimation for Sweden*, Working Paper: European Commission.

Björklund, A., Edebalk, P-G., Ohlsson, R. and Söderström, L. (1998) *Välfärdspolitik i kristid – håller arbetslinjen?*, Stockholm: SNS Förlag.

Björklund, A., Edin, P.-A., Holmlund, B. and Wadensjö, E. (1996), *Arbetsmarknaden*, Stockholm: SNS Förlag.

Blanchard, O. and Summers, L. (1986) 'Hysteresis and the European Unemployment Problem', in S. Fischer (ed.), *NBER Macroeconomic Annual 1986*, Cambridge, Mass.: MIT Press.

Calmfors, L. and Holmlund, B. (2000) 'Unemployment and Economic Growth: A Partial Survey', *Swedish Economic Policy Review*, no. 7, pp. 107–53.

Calmfors, L., Forslund, A. and Hemström, M. (2001) Does Active Labour Market Policy Work? Lessons from Swedish Experiences', Paper presented at the conference, 'What Are the Effects of Active Labour Market Policy?', Stockholm, 8 October.

Ekberg, J. and Ohlson, M. (2000) 'Flyktingars arbetsmarknad är inte alltid nattsvart', *Ekonomisk Debatt*, vol. 28, pp. 431–40.

Elmeskov, J. (1994) 'Nordic Unemployment in a European Perspective', *Swedish Economic Policy Review*, vol. 1, pp. 27–70.

Elmeskov, J. and Pichelmann, K. (1993) 'Interpreting Unemployment: The Role of Labour Force Participation', *OECD Economic Studies*, no. 21, Winter.

European Commission (2000) *The EU Economy – 2000 Review*, European Economy.

Forslund, A. (1995) 'Unemployment – Is Sweden Still Different?', *Swedish Economic Policy Review*, vol. 2, pp. 15–58.

Heckman, J. J., Lalonde, R. J. and Smith, J. A. (1999) 'The Economics and Econometrics of Active Labour Market Programs', in O. Ashenfelter and D. Card, (eds), *Handbook of Labour Economics, Vol. 3*, Dordrecht: North-Holland.

Henrekson, M. and Persson, M. (forthcoming, 2004) 'The Effects on Sick Leave of Changes in the Sickness Insurance System', *Journal of Labor Economics*, vol. 22, no 1.

Holmlund, B. (2003) 'The Rise and Fall of Swedish Unemployment', Working Paper 2003:13, Department of Economics, Uppsala University.

Jaeger, A. and Parkinson, M. (1990) 'Testing for Hysteresis in Unemployment: An Unobserved Components Approach', *Empirical Economics*, vol. 15, no. 2, pp. 185–98.

Jaeger, A. and Parkinson, M. (1994) 'Some Evidence on Hysteresis in Unemployment Rates', *European Economic Review*, no. 38, pp. 329–42.

Johansson, P. and Palme, M. (2002) 'Assessing the Effect of a Compulsory Sickness Insurance on Worker Absenteeism', *Journal of Human Resources*, vol. 37, pp. 381–409.

Katz, L. (1986) 'Efficiency Wage Theories: A Partial Evaluation', in S. Fischer, (ed.), *NBER Macroeconomic Annual 1986*, Cambridge, Mass.: MIT Press.

Layard, R., Nickell, S. and Jackman, R. (1991) *Macroeconomic Performance and the Labour Market*, Oxford University Press.

Lindbeck, A. (1996) 'Employment Problems', *Welwirtschaftliches Archiv*, vol. 132, pp. 609–37.

Lindbeck, A. (1997) *The Swedish Experiment*, Stockholm: SNS Förlag.

Lindbeck, A. and Snower, D. J. (1988) *The Insider–Outsider Theory of Employment and Unemployment*, Cambridge, Mass.: MIT Press.

Lindblad, H. (1997) 'Persistence in Swedish Unemployment Rates', Working Paper 1997:3, Department of Economics, University of Stockholm.

Lucas, R. E. (1972) 'Expectations and the Neutrality of Money', *Journal of Economic Theory*, vol. 4, no. 2, pp. 103–24.

Martin, J. P. and Grubb, D. (2001) 'What Works and for Whom: A Review of OECD Countries' Experiences with Active Labour Market Policies', Paper presented at the conference, 'What Are the Effects of Active Labour Market Policy', Stockholm, 8 October.

OECD (2001) *Employment Outlook*, June.

Ohlsson, R. (1995) *Svensk invandrings-och flyktingpolitik efter 1945*, Stockholm: SNS Förlag.

Rooth, D.-O. (1999) 'Refugee Immigrants in Sweden. Educational Investments and Labour Integration', Doctoral dissertation, Lund Economic Studies No. 84, Lund University.

Södersten, B. (1981) *One Hundred Years of Swedish Economic Development*, Department of Economics at the University of Lund, Reprint Series No. 151.

Södersten, B. (2002) 'The Welfare State as a General Equilibrium System', Paper presented at the Symposium, 'Globalisation and the Welfare State', Jönköping, June.

Statistics Sweden (1970–2001) *Labour Force Survey, annually*, Stockholm: Statistics Sweden.

Weiss, A. (1990) *Efficiency Wages: Models of Unemployment, Layoffs, and Wage Dispersion*, Princeton, NJ: Princeton University Press.

9
Immigrants in the Welfare State*

Jan Ekberg

Introduction

Since the Second World War, the number of immigrants in Sweden has
increased rapidly. In 1940, the proportion of foreign-born people
among the total population of the country amounted to only 1 per
cent. The proportion had increased to nearly 7 per cent by 1970, and
to about 11 per cent at the beginning of the twenty-first century –
about 1 million individuals. About 50 per cent of the foreign-born
individuals living in Sweden at the time of writing have acquired
Swedish citizenship. Moreover, there is a growing group of so-called
second-generation immigrants – that is, children born in Sweden with
at least one parent born abroad. This group amounts to about 800,000
individuals at present. Thus the total number of first- and second-
generation immigrants totals about 1.8 million individuals, some
20 per cent of the total population of Sweden.

The immigration pattern has changed. Until the mid-1970s, immigration to Sweden consisted primarily of labour-force immigration,
mainly from Europe. This was the first wave of immigration. A relatively large number of these immigrants went to the manufacturing
sector as blue-collar workers. This immigration varied with the labour-
market situation in Sweden: it increased with greater demands for
labour in the Swedish economy, and dropped when the demands
decreased. According to the 1970 census, about 60 per cent of foreign-
born people living in Sweden were born in other Nordic countries, and
more than 90 per cent were born in Europe, but after 1975, the character of immigration changed. The proportion of refugees and 'tied
movers' (relatives of already-admitted immigrants) increased and the
proportion of labour-force immigrants decreased. Many of those new

immigrants were born outside Europe, and the relationship between demand for labour in Sweden and immigration weakened. This was the second wave of immigration. The economic motivation for migration can be assumed to be weaker among refugees and tied movers than among labour immigrants. At the same time, a great many of the former labour-force immigrants returned to their home countries. Thus the composition of the immigrant population living in Sweden has changed. In 2000, the proportions of foreign-born people in the population were almost 30 per cent born in the other Nordic countries, about 35 per cent born in the rest of Europe, and almost 40 per cent born outside Europe.

The overall immigration pattern has been similar in most other immigrant countries in Europe. Up to the mid-1970s, most of the immigrants were labour-force immigrants. Since then, the proportion of refugees and relatives has increased, many of them being born outside Europe. However, in one respect, Sweden differs from many other European countries. As mentioned above, the proportion of the population born abroad is currently 11 per cent in Sweden. This is a large figure, compared to 5–6 per cent in Denmark and in Norway, 2 per cent in Finland, 8 per cent in France, 10 per cent in Netherlands and 9 per cent in Belgium and Germany, see OECD (2001). But there are some countries where the figure is higher than in Sweden – In Switzerland, for example, 18 per cent of the population was born abroad.

Immigration may affect the income conditions of the native population in many ways. There may be effects on the markets. Immigration may have impacts on relative factor prices and on employment opportunities for natives. Some native groups may lose while other native groups may benefit. However, studies from many countries show that these effects are probably fairly negligible (see, for example, Borjas, 1994 and Ekberg, 1999). Besides, the situation may also be affected by the publicly-financed redistribution of incomes. The direction of this distribution depends on whether the immigrants make more use or less of the public sector than they contribute to the system in taxes. If the immigrants contribute more/less in taxes than they receive from the public sector, there will be positive/negative income effects for the native population. Positive income effects for the native population means that disposable incomes increase, while negative income effects mean a decrease in their disposable incomes.

The immigrant labour market situation is a major determinant for how the public sector redistributes income between immigrants and the native population. There have been great changes over time, and since the late 1970s the immigrant labour market situation in Sweden has deteriorated. As a consequence, their use of the public welfare system has increased and their contribution to the tax system decreased. In political debate and among the public, there is a fear that this will reduce the disposable incomes of the native population. Poor labour market integration among immigrants, and therefore negative effects on the public budget, may lead to tensions between natives and immigrants, which might have implications for the political system.

Below, we shall describe and analyse the changed employment situation among immigrants during the post-war period. What are the reasons for these developments? For example, are there faults in the integration policy? How is the situation in Sweden compared to that in other countries? What are the effects on immigrant use of the public welfare system in Sweden and, consequently, the effects on the native population's disposable incomes?

Immigrants in the labour market

There have been great changes in the employment situation for immigrants during the post-war period. Many studies, such as those by Wadensjö, 1973; Ohlsson, 1975; Ekberg, 1983; Scott, 1999; Bevelander, 2000; and Hammarstedt, 2001, show that the employment situation for immigrants in Sweden was good up to the mid-1970s, with both native population and immigrants enjoying full employment. During long periods, employment levels among immigrants even exceeded those of the native population. This was especially the case for immigrant women. Moreover, a large number of employed immigrant women worked full-time, while most of the employed Swedish-born women worked part-time, therefore the annual work income per capita was high among immigrants. The occupational mobility among these early immigrants was also about the same as that among the native population, see (Ekberg, 1990, 1996).

At the end of the 1970s, the labour market integration of new immigrants began to deteriorate, and since then the trend has been maintained. A great number of the refugees that arrived during the 1980s have never entered the labour market. Not only was the rate of unemployment for immigrants high, but their participation in the labour force also was low, and many immigrants have now probably given up the idea of searching for work in the labour market. This has occurred despite the boom in the Swedish economy in the 1980s, despite the high level of education and skills among these new immigrants, and despite the goal for the Swedish immigration policy to integrate immigrants (also refugees) to about the same extent as the native population in the labour market. This goal has not been achieved.

In the 1960s the immigrants' educational level (number of years in school) was lower than for the native population (see Wadensjö, 1973). Since then, the educational level has increased among immigrants. At the time of writing, there are only small differences between broad groups of foreign-born (born in Europe or born outside Europe) and the native Swedish population. Most immigrants have a good educational level, which should make it easy for them to enter the Swedish labour market. However, there are large differences between smaller immigrant groups. Table 9.1 shows the proportions in the age 16–64 with only pre-secondary school education, with secondary school education and more than secondary school education (academic education). There is a tendency that the educational level for immigrants born outside Europe is more uneven than for natives and for immgrants from Europe. Among immigrant men born outside Europe there are a both larger part with only pre-secondary education and with academic education. There is also a tendency that women from outside Europe have somewhat shorter education than men from the same region.

Table 9.1   Educational level, ages 16–64, 2002, percentages

	Pre-secondary school	Secondary school	Academic level[*]
Men			
Native Swedes	24.8	48.5	26.6
Foreign-born	26.3	46.0	27.7
Of which			
Born in Europe	25.4	49.4	25.3
Born outside Europe	27.8	41.1	31.1
Women			
Native Swedes	20.7	48.1	31.2
Foreign-born	28.4	43.1	28.5
Of which			
Born in Europe	26.2	43.6	30.3
Born outside Europe	32.3	42.3	25.4

Note: * A very short academic education also included.
Sources: *Statistics Sweden: Labour Force Survey 2002.*

Although many immigrants are well-educated, the labour market situation has deteriorated for them. We do not know all the reasons for this development. The reasons may be discrimination, changes in the Swedish economy with increased demand for 'Sweden-specific' knowledge (for example, the Swedish language) to succeed on the labour market, or mistakes in the Swedish integration policy. During the 1980s and up to 1991, there was still full employment among the native population. During the recession, from 1992 onwards, the immigrant labour market situation, relative to that of the native population, deteriorated even further. However, it seems as if the situation stabilized in the mid-1990s. At the end of the 1990s, there was also a small improvement in the immigrant labour market situation. A summary of the development is given in Table 9.2. Changes in work income per capita among immigrants follow the changes in their employment rate.

There are large differences in employment situation between immigrants born in Europe and those born outside Europe. In Table 9.3

Table 9.2   Index for employment rate at ages 16–64 years, foreign born, standardized for age (index for native-born 100*)

Year	Index for employment rate			Index for work income per capita at the age 16–64**
	Men	*Women*	*Both sexes*	
1950	–***	–***	120	–***
1960	100	110	105	–***
1967	–***	–***	110	122
1978	95	101	98	99
1987	90	88	89	–***
1991	84	83	83	75
1994	77	74	75	62
1999	78	75	76	64
2001	82	77	79	–***
2002	81	77	79	–***

Notes: * The index can be interpreted as follows: in 1960, the index was 105. This means that the employment rate among foreign born was 5 per cent higher than the employment rate among natives. In 1994, the employment rate among foreign-born was 25 per cent lower than that among natives. For the years 1950, 1960 and 1967, the figures refer to foreign citizens. Most of the foreign-born living in Sweden in these years had foreign citizenship.
** Even including individuals at the age 16–64 with zero work income. There is not enough information to standardize for age and for work income.
*** No information available.
Sources: Ekberg (1983); processed data from 1950 and 1960 Swedish census, and from 1987, 1991, 1994, 1999, 2001 and 2002. *Labour Force Surveys*. Data from the Swedish Income Register in 1991, 1994 and 1999.

we have calculated the index for the period 1991–2002. The index was low during the whole period and especially for immigrants born outside Europe. During the depression in the beginning of the 1990s the employment situation deteriorated even further, and rapidly for those born outside Europe. In the late 1990s, the Swedish economy recovered and there was some improvement in the employment situation among these immigrants compared to native workers. However, since the start of the twenty-first century there have been no further improvements, and there is still a situation with a very low employment rate and very high unemployment, especially for immigrants born outside Europe.

It is to be noted that the tendency has been the same in many other immigrant countries. However, there are large differences between countries concerning the immigrant labour market. Investigations for the OECD countries show that the Netherlands, Sweden and Denmark have particularly high unemployment rates among immigrants (see OECD, 1999, 2001). In countries such as the USA, Australia and Canada, the unemployment rate among immigrants is about the same as for the native population. A summary is given in Table 9.4.

Explanations

There are probably many reasons for the worsening labour market position among immigrants. In Swedish research, the following main explanations have been put forward:

1   The risk for discrimination on the labour market increased when the immigration pattern changed from immigration from Europe to immigration from countries outside Europe.

Table 9.3   Index for employment rate at ages 16–64 years, foreign-born, in different regions, standardized for age (index for native-born 100)

| Year | Index for employment rate* | | | | | |
| | Born in Europe | | | Born outside Europe | | |
	Men	Women	Both sexes	Men	Women	Both sexes
1991	90	90	90	72	64	68
1994	87	86	86	62	49	55
1999	83	83	83	71	61	66
2001	86	85	86	74	68	70
2002	87	84	85	74	66	70

Notes: * The interpretation of the index is the same as in Table 9.2.
Sources: Statistics Sweden. Labour Force Surveys. 1991, 1994, 1999, 2001 and 2002.

Table 9.4 Unemployment rate among foreigners compared to natives, average 1999–2000*

Netherlands	2.8
Sweden	2.4
Belgium	2.3
Denmark	2.3
France	1.9
Germany	1.7
USA	1.2
Australia	1.1
Canada	1.0

Notes: * Interpretation is as follows: the figure for the Netherlands is 2.8, which means that the unemployment rate among foreigners is 2.8 times higher than among natives. For the USA, Australia and Canada, the unemployment rate among immigrants is about the same as for natives.

The figures show so-called open unemployment. In countries with high open unemployment rates among immigrants, the total unemployment rate among them compared to natives may be even higher. In such countries, immigrants are probably heavily over-represented in many labour market policy programmes. These individuals are not registered as open unemployed. We know from Sweden that immigrants are over-represented in such programmes.

Sources: OECD (2001).

2 Structural changes in the Swedish economy make it difficult for immigrants to enter the labour market. Changes from an industrialized to a post-industrial economy place greater demands on skills and know-how that are specific for the immigrant country, which in turn reduces immigrant opportunities on the labour market. This development has run in parallel with the increasingly distant ethnic and cultural background of these immigrants, which may have contributed to their human capital being poorly adapted to the Swedish labour market.

3 Mistakes in the Swedish integration policy of immigrants.

There may also be other explanations. Recently arrived immigrants are new on the labour market, and many of them are searching for employment. There are implications from the insider–outsider theory, which may also shed light on the immigrant labour market situation. Individuals who have a job – the insiders – often have a special position compared to those without a job – the outsiders. The reason for this is that a firm has turnover costs when replacing an insider, such as costs of hiring, firing and training. Because of the turnover costs, firms are not willing to replace insiders by outsiders as long as the wage differences between outsiders and insiders are negligible. Besides, there is a central wage formation system in Sweden, which probably reduces the possibilities for outsiders to underbid insiders' wages. A presentation of the insider-outsider theory is given in Lindbeck and Snower (2001).

The existence of turnover costs may be a special disadvantage to immigrants. We know that many immigrants plan to return to their home country. If an employer takes into account the risk that an immigrant may return to his or her country of origin in the near future, then there is a risk that, if this immigrant is engaged, the employer will have a new turnover cost in the near future.

Integration policy

Let us concentrate next on the Swedish integration policy for immigrants. There has been an intensive public debate about this policy (see, for example, Ekberg *et al.*, 2002; Delander and Behrenz, 2002; and Lundh *et al.*, 2002a). There was a parliamentary election in Sweden in September 2002, and the issue of the labour market integration of refugees was one of the largest issues in the political debate before the election.

Let us look at some components in the integration policy. The first is institutional changes in the policy. The second is a strategy to relocate refugees to different regions in Sweden. The third is labour market policy programmes for immigrants; such programmes are parts of the integration policy.

Responsibility for receiving refugees transferred from the Swedish Labour Market Policy Board (AMS) to the Swedish Immigration Board in the mid-1980s. With AMS in charge, the main focus was on employment. The Immigration Board, however, had a different philosophy once they took over. In practice, a greater emphasis was placed on the social integration of refugees in Sweden, and refugees must attend a specific training programme in Sweden before they were allowed enter the labour market. The time between the arrival in Sweden and the possibility of entering the labour market was increased. Rooth (1999) showed that early contact with the labour market is not only important for refugees in the short term, but also in their long-term efforts to succeed on the labour market. The Rooth's study stresses the importance of rapid contact with the labour market rather than participating in Swedish training programmes. In many respects, the most effective way to acquire 'Sweden-specific' knowledge is probably to participate in the labour market.

Some countries (for example, Denmark and the Netherlands) have used special settlement policies for refugees. The aim is to spread the refugees over the country. This method has also been used in Sweden. A new strategy of demographic relocation of refugees in Sweden was introduced in the mid-1980s, the so-called 'Whole Sweden' strategy. The strategy was in place from the middle of the 1980s to the beginning of the 1990s, but was in practice applied to some degree for some time after this period. The aim of this strategy was to relocate newly arrived refugees over the entire country. By avoiding demographic concentrations, immigrants were expected to have a better opportunity of learning the Swedish language, which in turn should improve their chances of gaining employment. However, this was not the case in reality. Refugees were often allocated to different municipalities based on the availability of accommodation rather than on opportunities to find employment. This can be seen as having a negative influence on the refugees' opportunities to gain employment. Studies carried out in the 1990 indicate this to be the case. In regions with no jobs, there was plenty of accommodation to choose from, because Swedish-born people had moved out from these regions. Edin *et al.*, 2000 found that earnings and employment levels among refugees had worsened as a result of this strategy.

A longitudinal study undertaken at Växjö University of Bosnians who had arrived in Sweden in 1993 and 1994, revealed that the level of integration in the labour market varied immensely depending on where they were located. The group of refugees arriving from Bosnia in 1993 and 1994 was very large (about 48,000 individuals) and were distributed among about 250 of the total 289 municipalities in Sweden.

Of course, it is not possible here for us to describe the labour market integration of Bosnians in all these municipalities. However, we shall give some examples to show the extremely irregular regional employment labour market situation for the group. One example is the so-called small business district consisting of the municipalities of Gnosjö, Gislaved, Vaggeryd and Värnamo in the west part of the county of Småland. There are almost 100,000 inhabitants in these four municipalities. The economy in the area is, to a great extent, based on small-scale industry. The rate of unemployment in the area is usually low. Another area is Malmö municipality, with about 250,000 inhabitants. The economy in Malmö has undergone structural changes since the 1980s, resulting in high unemployment. Both of these areas received many Bosnians. Let us look at the situation in 1997 and 1999; by 1999, the Bosnian group has lived in Sweden for 5–6 years.

The employment rate in the age group 20–59 for the years 1997 and 1999 is shown in Table 9.5. Already by 1997, the employment rate for Bosnian men in the small-business district exceeded 75 per cent. This was about the same level, on average, as for native-born men in Sweden. Bosnian women in this area also achieved a good labour market position. However, the situation in Malmö was very gloomy. The employment rate for Bosnian men was less than 15 per cent, and for women the situation was even worse. For Bosnian men, on average, in Sweden, the employment rate was about 30 per cent. Between 1997 and 1999, the labour market situation for Bosnians gradually improved, but the regional differences remained and, in Malmö, the situation had not improved. In the small-business district, the employment rate for Bosnians, at the time of writing, has reached levels that are probably closer to the theoretical maximum. More than 90 per cent of men and more than 80 per cent of women were employed on the labour market, a much greater percentage than for native-born Swedes.

In the 1980s and 1990s, the Malmö–Landskrona region in the western part of the county of Skåne had a very depressed labour

Table 9.5   Employment rate, Bosnians in Sweden, ages 20–59, in 1997 and 1999, percentages

	1997			1999		
Bosnians in	*Men*	*Women*	*Both sexes*	*Men*	*Women*	*Both sexes*
Small business areas (municipalities in Gnosjö, Gislaved, Vaggeryd and Värnamo)	76.8	51.5	64.7	90.3	80.2	85.7
Stockholm	34.9	20.9	28.3	61.6	53.6	57.8
Gothenburg	19.7	12.8	16.4	44.7	34.5	39.8
Malmoe	14.4	8.6	11.4	36.7	28.0	32.4
Bosnians in Sweden	30.1	17.2	23.8	58.5	45.6	52.2
All foreign-born in Sweden	59.4	53.7	56.2	64.9	58.2	61.4
Natives in Sweden	77.6	74.2	75.8	80.4	77.0	78.6

Sources: *Statistics Sweden*; Employment Register; 1997 and 1999 Working up from the Swedish Population Register and Employment Register; 1997 and 1999, Ekberg and Ohlson (2000).

market. Many among the native population moved out of the region because of difficulties in finding employment. This led to an increase in the number of vacant homes, and refugees were allocated to this area to fill them. This was, for example, the case with refugees from the Middle East in the 1980s and from Bosnia in the 1990s. Of course, many of these individuals found it difficult to enter the labour market, and many have remained unemployed, which has consequently led to heavy use of the public welfare system. This situation probably causes tension between native-born Swedes and immigrants. It is noticeable that, in the municipal elections in 2002, the extreme-right parties in the Malmö–Landskrona region were successful in exploiting this issue.

Regional differences in the general demand for labour are, of course, important in explaining the regional differences in the labour market integration of Bosnians. This is not, however, the full picture. There are a number of other explanations to take into consideration. The labour market situation in the Stockholm area has, for example, been good. However, Bosnians in Stockholm have had much greater difficulties in gaining employment compared to their counterparts in the small-business district. Another significant factor could be the structure of the economy in the region. The small-business district distinguished itself through small-scale industrial production, while the Stockholm region had high knowledge-intensive production. It can be assumed that 'Sweden-specific' knowledge is a more important requirement for those trying to find work in the Stockholm region compared to the small-business district. An econometric study carried out by Ekberg and Olsson, (2000) shows that the labour-market demand structure of the local economy plays a part, but this does not give the whole picture. There are obviously other circumstances that are of significance in promoting the labour market integration of Bosnians and other immigrants in the small-business district. Effective labour market procedures also play a part – that is, the market's ability to match job searchers quickly to suitable vacancies. Investigations of corporate culture, social networks and distribution of information in the small-business district suggest short decision procedures that often take place in informal networks (see Johannisson and Gustavsson, 1984). These networks also offer a direct link to public authorities such as employment offices and the commercial sector. Job-seeking procedures in the labour market can often mean using personal contacts, which may result in the formation of closer relationships between job-seekers and employers. If the employer already knows about the job-seeker, he or she can quickly access the job-seeker's qualifications, while the job-seeker can quickly make a decision on the suitability of the position in question. If the jobs-seeker does not fill the vacancy this time, he or she can still turn to his/her personal network for assistance in finding employment. Companies within the network are usually well aware of each other's needs for different forms of labour. The network and the close collaboration between the public and commercial sectors is likely to improve the way that refugees are received locally, and their introduction into the labour market.

It is likely that a different form of allocation of refugees, together with a system to transfer knowledge from successful regions regarding ways of organizing the reception and introduction of refugees to achieve rapid contact with the labour market, would have integrated refugees on more successfully with the Swedish labour market in the 1980s and 1990s.

There are, at the time of writing, very irregular levels of regional labour market integration of immigrants in Sweden. In this respect, large changes have occurred over time. These regional labour market irregularities seem to have arisen since the late 1980s. Ekberg (1983) concludes that there were only minor discrepancies in the levels of employment among immigrants living in different regions in Sweden up to the end of the 1970s. Immigrants arriving in the 1950s, 1960s and 1970s moved to regions in Sweden that offered employment; see, for example, Wadensjö (1973) and Ekberg (1995).

How labour-market policies are formulated is also of importance when it comes to the integration of immigrants into the labour market. Labour-market policies have a number of objectives, a significant one being to prevent segregation and the permanent marginalization of individuals from the labour market. According to the Swedish governmental proposition, 1995/1996, no. 222, priority is given to those groups that experience high levels of unemployment, especially immigrant groups, by implementing a series of active labour-market policies. It is surprising to find that only a few evaluations of labour-market programmes for immigrants have been carried out, considering the difficulties experienced by these individuals in gaining employment. One such evaluation was carried out by Ekberg and Rooth (2001) on behalf of the Parliamentary auditors. It showed that the immigrant groups who were most in need of support were included only to some extent by the programmes undertaken. As an example, immigrants from the Middle East, who experienced great difficulty in finding work, were rarely included in the active labour market programmes provided. However, Bosnian immigrants were, to a large extent, given access to these programmes. There are, quite clearly, major differences in the ways that different immigrant groups have been dealt with in relation to various active labour-market policies, despite similar high levels of unemployment in each group.

Immigrants in the welfare system

One effect of the deterioration of the employment situation for immigrants is that they are now using the social welfare system to a much greater extent than before. This process started as far back as the 1980s. With the help of linking and matching the income register to the population register, it has been possible to provide data for the year 1999 relating to immigrant dependence on social welfare allowances, housing allowances, unemployment benefits, and pensions before the age of 65. How much social welfare allowance, housing allowance and unemployment benefit is required by a population group depends on the prevailing labour market situation for the group. From the information in Tables 9.2 and 9.3, we may expect that immigrants, at the time of writing, are heavily over-represented as dependants on the welfare system. This is specially so in regard to social welfare allowances. Immigrants who have never entered the labour market are not in a position to receive unemployment benefit. Instead, they are dependent on social welfare allowances. This implies that immigrants are over-represented in the social welfare allowances group than in the unemployment benefit group. There are also many studies in Sweden showing a rapid transition to early-retirement pension (pension before the age of 65) among immigrants during the 1980s. There are many possible reasons for this development. One reason is, in all probability, the large number of immigrants who are employed in high-risk jobs, with negative health effects. Another explanation may be the worsening labour market situation among immigrants: it was possible, in the 1980s, to receive an early retirement pension if an individual found it difficult to find a job.

Table 9.6 shows the situation in 1999. The immigrants are greatly over-represented in many areas of the welfare system. This is especially the case with regard to social welfare allowances. The amount of social welfare allowances per capita in the age group 16–64 is about nine times higher for immigrants than for native-born Swedes. The amount of housing allowances for immigrants is more than three times higher for immigrants compared to native Swedes. The amount of unemployment allowances is about the same as for natives, although the unemployment rate is much higher for immigrants. The reason for this is that many unemployed immigrants have never had a job, and are therefore not qualified to receive unemployment benefit. Instead, they are entitled to social welfare allowances. The total budget for social welfare allowances, housing allowances and unemployment benefits per capita, in the age group 16–64, is more than the double for immigrants compared to native-born Swedes.

How the public sector redistributes incomes between immigrants and the native population is often a matter for political debate and among the public itself. In this respect, the situation has changed a great deal over time. We showed in Table 9.1 that up to the mid-1970s, immigrant employment rates were the same as, or, at certain times, even higher than those for the native population. The immigrant population also has a favourable age composition (a lower fraction of people in older groups old age people compared to the native population). The public sector usually redistributes incomes from individuals in the labour market to old-age individuals and heavy public expenditure is directed towards the older age group of people. This expenditure is mainly financed by taxes paid by employed individuals. Redistribution also occurs from employed to unemployed individuals. It can be expected that in a situation where immigrants are well integrated into the labour market and also offer a favourable age structure, they contribute more to the public sector, through taxation, compared to what

Table 9.6   Index of allowances, benefits and pensions, ages 16–64, foreign born*, 1999

1 Social welfare allowances	980
2 Housing allowances	320
3 Unemployment benefits	100
Sum of 1–3	210
4 Pensions before the age of 65 (early retirement pensions, survivors' pensions, partial pensions)	112

Notes: * For 1, 2 and 3, the index indicates the amount per capita, in the age group 16–64, for foreign-born compared with natives. All individuals in the age group 16–64 are included, that is, even those not receiving allowances. The index for social welfare allowances is standardized for family composition. For housing allowances and unemployment benefits, there is not enough information to standardize for age or for family composition. However, a sensitivity analysis shows that these circumstances only have small effects. The overall picture is the same. For 4, the index shows the participation in pensions before the age of 65 (mainly early retirement pensions). This index is standardized for age.
Sources: *Statistics Sweden*: Income Register 1999.

they receive from this sector, and the revenue gained is allocated to those who are native-born. This happened in the 1950s, 1960s and 1970s, and gave rise to a positive income effect for natives; (see Wadensjö (1973) and Ekberg (1983). The situation changed when the the immigrants' employment situation deteriorated. At the end of the 1980s, the yearly positive income effect had disappeared (see Gustafsson, 1990), but at the time of writing there is a negative income for natives-born Sweden – that is, immigrants contribute less to the tax system compared to what they receive from the public sector. At present, the yearly negative income effect is 1–2 per cent of GNP, that is, approximately SEK 30 billion; see Ekberg (1999). This negative income effect would disappear if the immigrant employment rate was increased by 15 percentage points. Thus we can say that the present cost of poor labour market integration of immigrants is at least SEK 30 billion per year.

The great importance of labour market integration among immigrants for the way that the public sector redistributes incomes between immigrants and the native population has also been found in studies of Denmark (see Wadensjö, 2000). Because of the poor employment situation among immigrants in Denmark, they make more use of the public sector than they contribute to the system in taxes, which implies a negative effect on the native Danish population's disposable income. Issues around immigration and the integration of immigrants into Danish society have had great implications for the political system in Denmark in recent years.

Conclusions and comments

For a long time during the post-war period there was full employment for both immigrants and the native population in Sweden. Up to the mid-1970s, immigrants were well-established on the labour market. This was the case not only for labour-force immigrants, but also for refugees who arrived in Sweden at the end of the war (around the mid-1940s), at the end of 1950s, and at the end of the 1960s. At the end of the 1970s, however, the first signs of a worsening labour market situation among immigrants appeared, and it intensified up to the mid-1990s. Since then the situation has stabilized, with a very low employment level and a very high uemployment rate for immigrants. A great number of refugees arriving during the 1980s did not enter the labour market at all. This was despite the 1980s boom in the Swedish economy, despite the fact that 1980s immigrants were better-educated than former immigrants, and despite the governmental integration policy goal of integrating immigrants (also refugees) as well as the native population in the labour market. At the beginning of the 1990s, this tendency strengthened even more. To make an international comparison, immigrants in Sweden at the start of the twenty-first century experience a very high unemployment rate. Besides, immigrant labour market integration differs a lot between different immigrant groups, and between different demographic regions in Sweden.

There are probably many explanations for this development. Among others, there is a body of evidence that mistakes have been made in the Swedish integration policy. The situation also creates tension between native Swedes and immigrants, which has implications for the political system. In regions with extremely low labour-market integration among immigrants, extreme-right political parties were successful in the 2002 municipal elections.

A very important issue for the future is to what extent the labour market position for the immigrants is transferred to their children who were born in Sweden – that is to say, the so-called second-generation immigrants. In recent years, certain studies relating to this matter have been conducted in Sweden – see, for example, Ekberg, 1997; Österberg, 2000; and Vilhelmsson, 2002. These studies show that second-generation immigrants, born before 1970, have about the same employment rate and about the same work income as natives of the same age and with both parents born in Sweden. These second-generation immigrants are children of the first immigration wave – that is, those who immigrated in the 1950s and the 1960s and who where well integrated in the labour market. The pattern is about the same for *their* children also. However, the situation is probably more pessimistic for subsequent waves of immigrants. (From the above discussion we know that, in particular, non-European immigrants in these waves were not integrated into the labour market. Recent studies indicate that the same pattern exists for their children born in Sweden, see Ekberg and Rooth (2002) and Lundh *et al.*, 2002b). The studies also show that parent composition has a clear effect on the probability of being unemployed. Second-generation immigrants with one native-born Swedish parent have a lower probability of being unemployed than when both parents were born within the same ethnic group.

Second-generation immigrants with a non-European background and who are of working age are at present a relatively small group, because of a late start for immigration from these countries. However, there are large numbers of second-generation immigrants with a non-European background of younger ages. Over the next 10–20 years a large number of second-generation immigrants with a non-European backgrounds will try to enter the labour market in Sweden. The chances of success for this group will, to a large extent, depend on how well their parents were integrated into the labour market, and whether they themselves have succeeded in the Swedish school system. This is a real challenge facing the government's integration policy and the school system in Sweden.

Note

* I am grateful to Rolf Ohlsson and Bo Södersten for their useful suggestions.

References

Behrenz, L. and Delander, L. (2002) 'Moralisk algebra' (Moral Algebra), *SVD-Debatt. Brännpunkt* 4 September.

Bevelander, P. (2000) 'Immigrant Employment Integration and Employment Change in Sweden', Ph.D. thesis, *Lund Studies in Economic History*, XV.

Borjas, G. J. (1994) 'The Economics of Immigration', *Journal of Economic Literature*, vol. 32, pp. 1667–717.

Edin, P.-A., Fredriksson, P. and Åslund, O. (2000) 'Settlement Policies and The Economic Success of Immigrants', in O. Åslund, 'Health, Immigration and Settlement Policies', Ph.D. thesis. *Uppsala Economic Studies*, LIII.

Ekberg, J. (1983) 'Inkomsteffekter av invandring' (Income Effects Due to Immigration), Ph.D. thesis, summary in English, *Lund Economic Studies*, XXVII.

Ekberg, J. (1990) 'Immigrants – Their Economic and Social Mobility', in I. Persson (ed.), *Generating Equality in the Welfare State: The Swedish Experience*, Oslo: Norwegian University Press, p. 289.

Ekberg, J. (1995) 'Internal Migration Among Immigrants in Sweden', *Scandinavian Population Studies*, vol. 10, pp. 236–46.

Ekberg, J. (1996) 'Labour Market Careers Among Young Finnish Immigrants in Sweden', *International Migration Quarterly Review*, vol. 34, XXXIV pp. 371–84.

Ekberg, J. (1997) Hur är arbetsmarknaden för den andra generationens invandrare? (How is the labour market situation among the second generation immigrants?) *Arbetsmarknad och Arbetsliv* 3:5–16.

Ekberg, J. (1999) 'Immigration and the Public Sector: Income Effects for the Native Population in Sweden', *Journal of Population Economics*, vol. 12, pp. 411–30.

Ekberg, J. and Ohlson, M. (2000) 'Flyktingars arbetsmarknad är inte alltid nattsvart' (The Labour Market for Refugees is Not Always Bad), *Ekonomisk Debatt*, vol. 28, pp. 431–40.

Ekberg, J. and Rooth, D.-O. (2001) 'Är invandrare oprioriterade inom arbetsmarknadspolitiken?' (Are Immigrants Not Given Priority to labour Market Policy Programmes?), *Ekonomisk Debatt*, vol. 29, pp. 285–91.

Ekberg, J. and Rooth, D.-O. (2003) 'Unemployment and Earnings for Second Generation Immigrants – Ethnic Background and Parent Composition', *Journal of Population Economics* vol. 16 (under publication in no. 4).

Ekberg, J., Södersten, B., Hammarstedt, M. and Rooth, D.-O. (2002) 'Hårdare tag mot invandrare att vänta' (Difficulties for Immigrants Are Expected), *DN-debatt*, 22 April.

Governmental proposition (1995/1996:222) *Vissa åtgärder för att halvera arbetslösheten till år 2000 (Some measures in order to halve the unemployment up to the year 2000)*, Stockholm.

Gustafsson, B. (1990) 'Public Sector Transfers and Income Taxes Among Immigrants and Natives in Sweden', *International Migration Quarterly Review*, vol. 28, pp. 181–99.

Hammarstedt, M. (2001) 'Making a Living in a New Country', Ph.D. thesis, *Växjö Acta Wexionensia*, IX.

Johannisson, B. and Gustavsson, B.-Å. (1984) *Småföretagande på småort. Nätverkstrategier i informationssamhället* (Small Business in Local Area. Strategies for Networks in the Information Society), Rapport Högskolan i Växjö.

Lindbeck, A. and Snower, D.-J. (2001) 'Insiders versus outsiders,' *Journal of Economic Perspectives* vol. 15, 165–88.

Lundh, C., Bennich-Björkman, L., Ohlsson, R., Pedersen, P. and D.-O. Rooth (2002a) 'Risken för arbetslöshet fyrdubblad' (Four Times Higher Risk for Unemployment) *DN-debatt* pp. 11–28.

Lundh, C., Bennich-Björkman, L., Ohlsson, R., Pedersen, P. and Rooth D.-O. (2002b) *Arbete? Var god dröj! Invandrare i välfärdssamhället* (Employment! Please wait! Immigrants in the Welfare State), Stockholm: SNS, p. 72.

OECD (1999) *Trends in International Migration*, Paris: Sopemi, p. 47.

OECD (2001) *Trends in International Migration*, Paris: Sopemi, p. 61.

Ohlsson, R. (1975) *Invandrarna på arbetsmarknaden* (Immigrants on the Labour Market), Ph.D. thesis), *Lund Ekonomisk-historiska förening*, XVI.

Österberg, T. (2000) 'Economic Perspectives on Immigrants and Intergenerational Transmissions', Ph.D. thesis, *Gothenburg Economic Studies* CII.

Rooth, D.-O. (1999) 'Refugee Immigrants in Sweden. Educational Investments and Labour Market Integration', Ph.D. thesis, *Lund Economic Studies*, LXXXIV.

Scott, K. (1999) 'The Immigrant Experience: Changing Employment and Income Patterns in Sweden 1970–1993', Ph.D. thesis, *Lund Studies in Economic History*, IX.

Vilhelmsson, R. (2002) 'Wages and Unemployment of Immigrants and Natives in Sweden', Ph.D. thesis. *Dissertation Series*, CVL. Swedish Institute of Social Research. Stockholm.

Wadensjö, E. (1973) 'Immigration och samhällsekonomi' (Immigration and Economy), Ph.D. thesis, *Lund Economic Studies* VIII.

Wadensjö, E. (2000) 'Immigration, the Labour Market and Public Finances in Denmark', *Swedish Economic Policy Review*, vol. 7, pp. 59–84.

Specific source data

From *Statistics Sweden*: data from 1950, 1960 Swedish census, data from 1987, 1991, 1994, 1999 2001 and 2002 Labour Force Surveys, data from 1991, 1994 and 1999 Income Register, data from 1997 and 1999 Employment Register.

10
The Stability of the Globalized Welfare State

Cynthia Kite

Introduction

Arguments about the decline of the welfare state as a consequence of globalization are well-known. The increased power of producers and capital owners to influence government policy by threatening to disinvest and/or abandon states that ignore their demands is usually identified as the biggest challenge posed by openness. While acceding to these demands – lower taxes, fewer/weaker regulations, reduced spending, flexible labour markets – might have undesirable effects, these are seen as being less serious than the consequences of disinvestment and capital flight. Governments therefore comply, albeit often reluctantly. Welfare states become increasingly similar because mobile capital punishes those who deviate in the direction of generosity.

While this logic of downward convergence is compelling, this chapter argues that empirical analysis does not support it. Neither levels of government revenue and expenditure, nor how governments spend are converging. Variation in spending patterns continues to sustain distinct types of welfare state. Furthermore, non-convergence should continue, because states that do not reduce welfare effort significantly are not punished automatically by market actors. Given this, domestic politics in the form of institutions, political parties, voters and interest groups will continue to influence the size and shape of national welfare states. Retrenchment will not necessarily occur where openness is greatest, because the strength of political resistance is also important.[1] That is, retrenchment is as much a manifestation of political strength as economic necessity. Given the historically positive relationship between openness and government spending (Katzenstein, 1984; Rodrik, 1997), retrenchment might in fact be greater in states whose economies are least open. In any case, developments will be influenced by the interaction of openness and domestic politics.

The remainder of this chapter is organized as follows. The next section reviews arguments about globalization's negative consequences for the welfare state, and the relationship between domestic political factors and welfare-state development. I then present a model that identifies four different openness – resistance mixes in which retrenchment politics are played out. To test the model, the third section presents an empirical analysis of economic openness, domestic political institutions, welfare state effort and economic performance in eighteen OECD states.[2] The final section discusses the implications of the findings and avenues for further research.

Theorizing retrenchment – globalization confronts domestic politics

The welfare state came to maturity when national economies were not fully open (Scharpf, 2000; Mishra, 1999). Political factors determined its size and shape during an era in which capital owners, taxpayers and consumers had limited exit options. Government spending and tax policy could be adjusted to accommodate party ideology, political business cycles and citizens' demands for social services with little risk of pushing investment, income-reporting or consumption across national borders. Firms could pass higher production costs on to consumers. Interest rates and budget deficits could be adjusted to promote high levels of employment and economic growth. Wage-setting and exchange-rate policy could be used to manage the economy, promote welfare goals and respond to economic difficulty.

A central question that emerged in the wake of increasing economic openness was, what happens when business and capital see 'exit' as a viable option? What does increased openness mean for the future of welfare states? It is widely agreed that openness leads to greater competition and capital mobility, which creates downward pressure on welfare states – that is, it encourages spending cuts (Garrett and Mitchell, 2001). Some argue that increased competition is problematic because public spending reduces economy-wide efficiency because of its negative effects on investment, allocation of resources and human performance (Barr, 1998; Pfaller *et al.*, 1991). While this might be affordable in some situations, when economies are open states cannot afford the luxury of a public sector that is much bigger than those of others. Greater competition also makes producers more cost-sensitive because they are less able to pass increases on to consumers. It pressures firms to innovate and improve production processes and products in order to maintain market shares, and this requires healthy profitability. These developments make producers less supportive of anything perceived to raise costs, including regulations and welfare programmes. For example, firms might oppose minimum wage laws and generous support programmes for those outside the labour market. Producers may also push for lower tax rates, which affects the state's ability to raise revenues (McKenzie and Lee, 1991; Steinmo, 1994).

It is also argued that capital's increased mobility has changed the world because its range of investment options has increased dramatically. Anything that reduces investment returns relative to those available elsewhere encourages capital flight, while anything that increases it promotes investment and attracts capital inflows. This can tempt governments to engage in races to the bottom as regards tax burdens and regulatory standards (Kahler, 1998; Mishra, 1999). There is little empirical evidence of such races, but the expansion of capital's exit option is broadly understood to have increased its structural power to veto policies it opposes, including tax, labour and social policies, and environmental regulations.

Capital mobility also reduces monetary and fiscal policy autonomy (Simmons, 1999). An expansionary monetary policy leads to capital flight, while a deflationary policy encourages capital inflows. Either response undermines government efforts to speed up or slow down the economy. With regard to fiscal policy, borrowing can lead to currency appreciation, which harms the traded goods sector. Moreover, since governments borrow at interest rates set in global markets, borrowing might be prohibitively expensive. Even if rates are low, capital holders might charge a premium to governments who fail to conform to strict macroeconomic standards (Garrett, 1998).

Do these arguments mean the end of welfare states? Not necessarily, because, even if they are correct, this does not mean that retrenchment necessarily follows, or that the biggest spenders are likely to cut the most. This is because, however similar the pressures of globalization, they are played out in domestic political contexts that vary considerably, and this variation matters. While some argue that it does not, because governments are powerless to refuse the demands of global capital,[3] most observers recognize that the dynamics of domestic politics are decisive for how governments respond to the pressures created by openness. As one author puts it: 'The logic of globalization comes into conflict with the "logic" of the national community and democratic politics. Social policy emerges as a major issue of contention' (Mishra, 1999; p. 105). In short, the interaction of the retrenchment voices of international capital and the anti-retrenchment voices of national political actors determines the development of the welfare state.

A simple model reflecting this view is presented in Figure 10.1. The model combines economic openness and domestic resistance. Openness is either high or low, and resistance is strong or weak. There are four possible cases, each representing a different mix of openness and resistance. Looking first at cases in which domestic resistance is weak (open and closed retrenchers), here there is limited effective opposition to cuts in social spending, so cuts should not create significant political conflict. On the other hand, demands for retrenchment are expected to be greater in Case 1 – open retrenchers – than in Case 3. This is because greater openness in the latter suggests that pressure from international capital should be greater. Given weak opposition, however, it is possible that closed retrenchers will engage in ideologically-motivated retrenchment.

The greatest political conflict over retrenchment is to be expected in Case 2 – open resisters, where both demands for retrenchment and opposition to it are significant. Given domestic resistance, it is likely that open resisters will implement more modest retrenchment than open retrenchers. Least retrenchment and political conflict over it is

DOMESTIC SOURCES OF RESISTANCE

		STRONG	WEAK
ECONOMIC OPENNESS	HIGH	Case 2 **OPEN RESISTERS** Economic performance: poor	Case 1 **OPEN RETRENCHERS** Economic performance: good
	LOW	Case 4 **CLOSED RESISTERS** Economic performance: same or worse	Case 3 **CLOSED RETRENCHERS** Economic performance: good or better

Figure 10.1   Economic openness and domestic resistance

expected in Case 4 – closed resisters. This is because there is strong opposition to spending cuts and less demand for it because of lower levels of openness.

I now turn to an empirical analysis based on Figure 10.1. If the globalization literature is correct, then empirical analysis should show that states' welfare spending is becoming more similar, regardless of domestic resistance potential (that is, the columns in Figure 10.1 are irrelevant). If domestic resistance matters, then retrenchment should vary, with open retrenchers showing the greatest retrenchment and closed resisters the least.

Are states converging?

In this section, empirical analysis is used examine whether or not states are converging on measures of openness, spending and resistance potential. The analysis is based on data from eighteen OECD states for the period 1980–97. The choice of time periods follows Huber and Stephens (2001), who identify four phases of welfare state development since the 1960s. The first ends with the oil price shock of 1973; the second is a short period from 1973 to 1979; and the third stretches from 1980 to 1990. During these years, governments stopped treating the economic downturn as a temporary disturbance and adopted new policy responses to promote recovery. The golden age of welfare state development ended. The end of the Cold War, the spread of financial deregulation, and a renewed European commitment to financial and monetary unity suggest that the 1990s are distinct from the 1980s and should be treated as a separate phase. Since the focus here is on globalization and retrenchment, the analysis includes the latter two phases. I discuss how to measure openness, welfare effort and domestic resistance, and present data on each. The analysis confirms that there is considerable cross-national variation on most measures, although some convergence on others.

Economic openness is used here as an indicator of pressure from globalization. Other things being equal, states with more open economies ought to experience greater international pressure than their less-open counterparts. I use several variables to measure economic openness. The first is trade exposure measured as exports and imports as a percentage of GDP. Data is presented in Table 10.1. The average value for the period 1980–97 is 65 per cent of GDP. Belgium, with exports and imports equal to 140 per cent of GDP, ranks first. The USA ranks last. The data are also presented for the two periods of interest. The picture that emerges is one of stability. The average level of exports and imports as a percentage of GDP is similar in the 1980s and 1990s. Moreover, most states experience little change, remaining either above-average, average or below-average in both periods. A few states record large increases in trade exposure – notably Canada and Ireland.

Another way to measure economic openness is to examine financial openness. Quinn's measure of current and capital account restrictions (Quinn, 1997) is a widely accepted indicator of this dimension of openness. This 14-point scale is based on national legislation regulating cross-border financial transactions and adherence to international agreements limiting the government's authority to enact such restrictions. Higher values indicate greater openness. Quinn-scale scores are also listed in Table 10.1.[4] The average value over the whole period is 12, which is quite open. There is an unambiguous trend toward greater openness over the period, and states have become much more alike. By the mid-1990s, fifteen of eighteen states had scores of 13 or 14.

A third indicator of economic openness is cross-border financial flows. Data on foreign direct investment (FDI) and portfolio investment is presented in Table 10.2. The average value of FDI during 1980–97 was 2.7 per cent of GDP, while the figure for portfolio investment was 4.5 per cent. Both increased over the period. A comparison of the early 1980s and late 1990s (data not shown) reveals this development even more clearly, with average FDI increasing from 1.3 per cent of GDP in 1982 to about 4 per cent by 1996, and portfolio investment rising from just under 2 per cent to almost 7 per cent. There is considerable variation among the countries. In the 1990s, FDI is close to 8 per cent of GDP in Belgium and the Netherlands, but still less than 1 per cent of GDP in Austria, Italy and Japan. Cross-border portfolio investment is as low as 1.5 per cent of GDP in Ireland and New Zealand, over 9 per cent in the UK and over 30 per cent in Belgium.

Considering all three measures of openness, the data supports the view that globalization increased between 1980 and the late 1990s. While trade openness remains about the same, capital flows have increased, and regulations governing them have been liberalized almost everywhere. At the same time, variation across states remains. The Netherlands and Belgium are clear examples of very open economies, while Japan and Australia are less open.

Turning now to public spending, two variables are used to measure welfare effort – social spending and government spending as a percentage of GDP. Government spending includes all government cash transfers and government final consumption. As shown in Table 10.3,

Table 10.1 Trade exposure and Quinn scale

Country	Exports and imports as percentage of GDP			Country	Quinn scale, average value		
	1980–97	1980–90	1991–97		1980–97	1980	1994
Australia	36	34	39	Australia	10.5	8	12
Austria	78	80	78	Austria	12	12	13
Belgium	141	144	136	Belgium	11	10	14
Canada	58	52	66	Canada	13	12	14
Denmark	67	68	66	Denmark	12	10	14
Finland	59	57	61	Finland	11	11	12
France	45	46	45	France	11.5	11	14
Germany	52	55	48	Germany	14	14	14
Ireland	118	112	128	Ireland	11	11	14
Italy	46	46	46	Italy	11.5	11	14
Japan	22	24	18	Japan	10.5	11	11
Netherlands	104	107	100	Netherlands	14	13	14
New Zealand	58	58	58	New Zealand	11.5	8	13
Norway	75	78	72	Norway	10.5	9	14
Sweden	65	64	67	Sweden	11.5	11	13
Switzerland	72	74	69	Switzerland	13	13	13
UK	53	53	54	UK	14	14	14
USA	21	19	26	USA	12	13	14
Mean	65	65	65	**Mean**	12	11	13.5
Variance	941.85	947.36	940.64	Variance	2.7	3.47	.95

Source: OECD Historical Statistics, various years.   *Source:* Quinn, 1997.

Table 10.2 Cross-border financial flows

Country	1980–97	1980–90	1991–97
Foreign direct investment as % of GDP			
Australia	2.9	2.9	2.9
Austria	1.1	0.7	1.7
Belgium	5	3.3	7.6
Canada	2.5	2.2	2.9
Denmark	1.9	1	3.3
Finland	1.9	1.4	2.8
France	2.3	1.6	3.3
Germany	1.3	1.1	1.6
Ireland	1.8	0.8	3.4
Italy	0.9	0.7	0.9
Japan	0.7	0.8	0.5
Netherlands	6.1	5.3	7.5
New Zealand	4.5	4.7	4.1
Norway	2.1	1.6	3.0
Sweden	4.1	3.2	5.6
Switzerland	4.6	3.8	5.5
UK	4.6	4.5	4.8
USA	1.5	1.2	1.8
Mean	**2.7**	**2.2**	**3.5**
Variance	**0.05**	**0.043**	**0.064**

Country	1980–97	1980–90	1991–97
Portfolio investment as % of GDP			
Australia	3.5	2.7	4.3
Austria	4.3	3.2	5.6
Belgium	17.9	6.7	32
Canada	4.1	3.3	5.1
Denmark	3.2	1.7	5.1
Finland	3.7	2.5	5.4
France	2.5	1.9	3.5
Germany	3.5	2.4	4.7
Ireland	3.3	4.5	1.4
Italy	3	0.8	6.1
Japan	3.3	3.6	3
Netherlands	4.7	3.2	6.3
New Zealand	0.6	1.1	1.4
Norway	2.3	2.1	2.6
Sweden	2.1	9.4	3.9
Switzerland	8.9	8.4	8.6
UK	7.3	5.8	9.2
USA	2.3	1.2	3.6
Mean	**4.5**	**3.1**	**6.2**
Variance	**0.377**	**0.885**	**0.677**

Source: IMF Financial Statistics Yearbook.

during 1980–97 average government spending as a percentage of GDP was 35 per cent. Average spending was higher in the 1990s than the 1980s, with the biggest increase occurring in Finland. Social spending measures government and mandatory private spending on thirteen social needs.[5] Average social spending was 23 per cent of GDP during 1980–97. It was highest in Sweden, Demark and the Netherlands, and lowest in Japan, Australia and the USA. Average spending was several percentage points higher in the 1990s, and even here Finland records the biggest increase. Government expenditure as a percentage of GDP declined in the 1990s in Belgium, the Republic of Ireland and the Netherlands. However, the social spending data suggest that it is only in the Netherlands that these cuts affected total social spending in a negative way. As the measure of variance shows, states are less similar with regard to both government and social spending in the 1990s than they were in the 1980s. This is true despite the fact that, as shown above, states are more open today than they were in the 1980s.

The last variable examined here is domestic resistance potential. I have identified a number of domestic political factors linked to the likelihood of retrenchment. I use them to construct a resistance potential index that summarizes the political strength of anti-retrenchment forces at the national level. To find relevant domestic political factors I borrow from comparative politics literature about the development of the welfare state. This research seeks to explain national-level variation in social spending and welfare policies, including variation in retrenchment. As a complement to this literature, where appropriate – and particularly for operationalization – I also borrow from comparative politics literature on democratic institutions.

So what domestic level factors influence the development of the welfare state? Broadly speaking, they can be grouped into two categories – ideologies/values and institutions.[6] Ideological factors are interests, values and ideologies that civil society, including political parties, articulates. Analytically, they operate on the input side of the policy process. For example, where public opinion is less tolerant of inequality and more supportive of government action to redress it, welfare state retrenchment will be more difficult.[7] To capture ideologies and values the resistance index includes measures of the strength of social democratic and Christian democratic parties. This is because numerous studies have shown that where these parties are strong, welfare states are generous, albeit in different ways (Esping-Andersen, 1990; van Kersbergen, 1995; Huber and Stephens, 2001). I also include the strength of right parties, which are associated with smaller welfare states.

Table 10.3 Public spending

Country	1980–97	1980–90	1991–97	Country	1980–97	1980–90	1991–97
Average social spending as % GDP				Government spending as % GDP			
Australia	15	13.3	17.8	Australia	27.6	26.8	28.9
Austria	26.3	24.8	26.9	Austria	39.6	38.8	41.1
Belgium	27.6	27.4	28	Belgium	39.3	40.1	38.1
Canada	17.2	16	19	Canada	33.2	31.9	35.4
Denmark	30	29	31.5	Denmark	44.4	43	46.5
Finland	26.4	22	32.5	Finland	37.5	32.6	46.4
France	27.3	26.2	29.1	France	40.9	40.5	41.9
Germany	26.6	25.6	28.1	Germany	37	35.6	37.7
Ireland	19.7	19.8	19.5	Ireland	31.8	33.2	29.2
Italy	23.3	21.2	26.7	Italy	35.3	34.8	36.2
Japan	12.2	11.5	13.4	Japan	21.2	20.7	21.9
Netherlands	29.1	29.5	28.5	Netherlands	41.8	42.8	40
New Zealand	20.1	19.8	20.6	New Zealand	NA	NA	NA
Norway	26.3	23.5	28.3	Norway	35.5	34.4	37.2
Sweden	32.9	31.1	35.7	Sweden	47.8	46.3	50.4
Switzerland	20.6	18.3	24.4	Switzerland	28	26.6	31.1
UK	21.3	20.2	23	UK	34.5	33.8	36.4
USA	15.3	14.5	16.6	USA	29.2	29.3	29.2
Mean	**23**	**21.7**	**25**	**Mean**	**35.5**	**34.9**	**36.6**
Variance	**38.1**	**35**	**36.7**	**Variance**	**49.1**	**45.6**	**53.9**

Source: OECD Social expenditures database 1980–97.

Source: OECD Historical Statistics, various years.

Institutions are important because they influence access to the political process. A number of studies have linked concentration of political authority to variations in welfare spending (Pierson, 1994). One well-supported finding is that federal systems are less generous spenders (Huber *et al.*, 1993) This is often explained in terms of Tsebelis' (1995) hypotheses that the greater the concentration of power, the fewer the veto players in the policy process, which makes it easier to change the status quo. Federal systems spread power, which should make radical increases and decreases in welfare spending more difficult.

Another institutional arrangement that has been linked to retrenchment is system of interest intermediation (Swank, 2001). Corporatist patterns of interest intermediation give labour organizations (and others) established channels of information and influence, which they can use to pressure governments to maintain, if not expand, social spending. Pluralist systems of interest intermediation do not embody a social norm of consultation, nor do they guarantee access to particular groups. As regards welfare state development, it is argued that pro-spending (that is, anti-retrenchment) groups have less access to the policy process in pluralist systems, so policy is less influenced by their views (Swank, 2001). Therefore, there should be less retrenchment in corporatist states.

Electoral systems and concentration of political authority are other institutions that have been linked to the politics of retrenchment because of their consequences for access to political arenas (Swank, 2001). Majoritarian systems, in which the candidate who gets the largest number of votes in a district wins, encourages the formation of two-party systems and single-party governments (Lijphart, 1999). Proportional systems encourage the development of multi-party systems (Duverger, 1964) and coalition governments. It is rare that a single party wins enough votes to enable it to govern on its own, so parties learn to consult, compromise and co-operate with each other. As a result, a greater number of societal interests are likely to be represented in the policy-making process. Proportional representation thus increases the inclusiveness of the policy process, which ought to make it more difficult to enact retrenchment policies.

Birchfield's and Crepaz's (1998) analysis of veto points is also relevant to the discussion of concentration of political authority and retrenchment. Their conclusions about the impact of various institutional arrangements are similar to those discussed above. They argue that there are different kinds of veto points, and they have different implications for retrenchment politics. Competitive veto points exist when political actors operating in different institutions and independently of each other can veto each other's actions. Institutional structures that create competitive veto points include pluralist interest intermediation, separation of powers, and single-party government. These structures and their veto points make it difficult to adopt generous social policies and inhibit the formation of influential proponents of welfare spending. Collective veto points exist when political actors operate within the same institutions. Corporatism, proportional representation and multi-party government produce this type of veto point. Actors are forced to interact directly with each other, thus increasing the likelihood of negotiation and compromise. Consensus veto points inhibit significant retrenchment by forcing proponents and opponents of growth and retrenchment to interact directly to enact policy.

To measure domestic resistance potential, I constructed a resistance index based on the variables discussed above. States' scores on the index are based on how many resistance-friendly political factors they exhibit. The data is presented in Table 10.4. Each state is assigned a score of high, medium or low on five political factors: strength of pro-welfare parties as measured by Cabinet presence; strength of anti-welfare parties; horizontal power concentration; vertical power concentration; and electoral system proportionality. These scores indicate whether the state's value on a particular variable is above, below or about average. A sixth factor is interest intermediation. States are divided into two groups – corporatist or pluralist. In Table 10.4, for each of the six factors, scores which the theoretical literature links to effective resistance are underlined. The resistance index is produced by summing each state's resistance factors. The index varies between 0 and 6. For party strength, if a state has one or more strong welfare parties (social or christian democrat), this counts as one source of resistance. A weak right-wing party also counts as a source of resistance. The resistance index is presented in the last two columns of Table 10.4. It confirms that resistance potential varies across states.

Exploring relationships: openness, resistance, spending and performance

The analysis presented above does not show convergence with regard to openness, social spending or resistance potential. This means that variation in social spending might be caused by variations in openness and resistance potential. If so, as discussed previously, the globalization literature predicts that open, non-retrenching, generous states (open

Country	Left party strength	CD party strength	Right party strength	Horizontal concentration of power	Vertical concentration of power	Electoral system proportionality	System of interest intermediation	Resistance index, 1980–90	Resistance index, 1991–97
Australia	HH	LL	LL	H	L	H	P	3	3
Austria	HH	MH	LL	M	M	L	C	4	5
Belgium	LH	HH	LL	L	L	M	C	5	6
Canada	LL	LL	HH	H	L	H	P	1	1
Denmark	LM	LL	HH	L	M	L	C	3	3
Finland	HL	LL	LL	L	M	L	C	5	4
France	HM	LL	LH	H	H	H	P	2	0
Germany	LL	HH	LL	M	L	L	C	5	5
Ireland	LL	LL	HH	M	H	M	P	0	0
Italy	LL	HH	LL	L	H	M	P	3	3
Japan	LL	LL	HH	M	M	M	C	1	1
Netherlands	LH	HH	LL	M	M	L	C	4	5
New Zealand	HL	LL	MH	H	H	H/L	P	1	1
Norway	HH	LL	LL	M	M	M	C	3	3
Sweden	HH	LL	LL	M	M	L	C	4	4
Switzerland	MM	HH	LL	M	L	L	C	5	5
UK	LL	LL	HH	H	H	H	P	0	0
US	LL	LL	HH	M	L	H	P	1	1

Notes: Horizontal concentration: H = one-party governments and executive dominance high; L = one-party governments and executive dominance low; M = all other cases mixed.

Vertical concentration: H = federal decentralized systems; L = unitary centralized systems; M = all other cases mixed.

Electoral system proportionality: H = majoritarian system; L = low disproportionate pr system; M = medium disproportionate pr system.

System of interest intermediation: C = corporatist; P = pluralist.

Party strength (% of cabinet seats held, 1980–97): H = above average; L = below average; M = about average. The first letter refers to the period 1980–90; the second covers 1991–7.

Resistance index: Sum of factors in columns 1–7 that are conducive to resistance.

Scores linked to effective resistance by the theoretical literature are underlined.

Sources: See Appendix.

resisters in Figure 10.1) will exhibit poorer economic performance than others. I now use an empirical analysis to look for evidence of these and other relationships. First, I examine whether openness and resistance potential are related to social spending. As regards openness, a considerable amount of the literature argues that it is related positively to social spending, because increased openness creates economic dislocation that is addressed with higher social spending (see, for example, Katzenstein, 1985; Rodrik, 1997). In contrast, globalization literature posits a negative relationship between openness and spending, particularly financial openness. Resistance potential should be associated positively with social spending if domestic political factors continue to influence welfare-state development. If there is no such relationship, then the globalization arguments cannot be rejected. Second, I look for a relationship between retrenchment and different mixes of openness and resistance potential. The expectation is that open retrenchers cut expenditures most, and closed resisters least. Finally, I look for links between economic performance and the four mixes of openness and resistance potential. In conducting the analyses I use bivariate regression analyses (unless indicated otherwise). All variables are at least ordinal level.

The results of regression analyses to test the relationship between openness, spending and resistance are presented in Table 10.5. For the period 1980–97, trade dependence, foreign direct investment and resistance potential are related significantly to social spending. All three relationships are positive, meaning that greater openness and resistance potential are associated with higher levels of spending. The data have also been examined separately for the 1980s and 1990s in light of the argument that these are distinct periods. Foreign direct investment loses significance, while trade dependence retains its positive influence on social spending for the 1980s, but not the 1990s. Only resistance potential has a large, positive effect on social spending for both periods. These results suggest that openness helped to promote high levels of social spending up to the 1990s, but that since then it is domestic political factors that have exerted a large, positive effect on spending. Regression analysis that includes both variables supports this interpretation. In the 1980s, trade dependence is positively related to social spending, while resistance potential is positively related in the 1990s. In short, thus far the evidence supports the argument that domestic political factors influence social spending. There is no evidence that openness is related negatively to social spending, which casts doubt on the globalization argument. On the other hand, in contrast to previous findings, openness no longer seems to be related positively to social spending, which might be interpreted as evidence that the old compatibility between it and generous social policy has declined.

The lower half of Table 10.5 reports the results of regression analyses to test hypotheses linking retrenchment to economic openness and resistance potential.[8] The data provide additional evidence that the 1980s and 1990s are distinct periods. Specifically, retrenchment is not related to indicators of economic openness in the 1980s, but in the 1990s both trade dependence and cross-border portfolio investment exert a significant impact on it. The results are somewhat contradictory, however. Portfolio investment has a negative effect on retrenchment, with higher levels of investment being associated with lower levels of retrenchment, while the trade dependence – retrenchment link is strongly positive, meaning that greater openness is associated with greater retrenchment. The latter link is more robust and holds even when the resistance index is included in the analysis. Resistance potential has no significant impact on retrenchment, despite its powerful impact on level of social spending.

As modelled in Figure 10.1, however, the expectation is that the interaction of resistance potential and openness should influence retrenchment. To test for such a relationship, the countries were split into four groups, based on whether their economic openness was above or below average, as measured by trade dependence, and whether their domestic resistance potential was relatively weak or strong.[9] As shown in Table 10.5, the openness–resistance mix is not significantly related to social spending, but it has a strong negative effect on retrenchment. This means that retrenchment is greatest in open retrenchers (Case 1) and least in closed resisters (Case 4). Put another way, countries with greater levels of openness have greater levels of retrenchment, but within this group the countries with weak resistance potential are more retrenchment-prone than those with strong resistance potential. The least retrenchment occurs in less open states with highly resistant domestic institutions. Once again, the 1980s and 1990s are different, and the openness–resistance mix matters for retrenchment only in the 1990s.

A final analysis to be conducted here is to examine the relationship between the openness–resistance mix and economic performance. Are resisters punished economically? This is an important question, because it has implications for the future viability of resistance. If globalization arguments are correct, then economic performance ought to

Table 10.5 Determinants of public expenditure

	Social spending as percentage of GDP				Government spending as percentage of GDP		
	1980–97	1980–90	1991–7		1980–97	1980–90	1991–7
Trade dependence	0.419	0.563	0.310	Trade dependence	0.358	0.486	0.247
Direct investment	0.337	0.152	0.362	Direct investment	0.276	0.181	0.294
Portfolio investment	0.130	-0.131	0.174	Portfolio investment	-0.057	0.292	0.933
Resistance index	0.518	0.528	0.551	Resistance index	0.385	0.186	0.429
Openness–resistance mix	-0.174	-0.352	0.003	Trade dependence +	0.256	0.420	0.110
Trade dependence +	0.273	0.433	0.134	Resistance index	0.297	0.194	0.390
Resistance index	0.424	0.380	0.504				

Retrenchment

	1980–97	1980–90	1991–7
Trade dependence	0.368	0.084	0.564
Direct investment	0.298	0.136	0.359
Portfolio investment	-0.158	0.216	-0.457
Resistance index	-0.095	-0.037	-0.128
Openness–resistance mix	-0.375	-0.153	-0.504
Trade dependence +	0.452	0.108	0.693
Resistance index	-0.248	-0.072	-0.369
Portfolio investment +	-0.060	-0.073	0.028
Resistance index	-0.144	0.228	-0.467

Notes: All figures are standardized beta coefficients. One underline indicates significance at the .05 level. A double underline indicates significance at the .01 level be stable or good where resistance is weak and retrenchment possible, because governments respond positively to demands for a smaller welfare state, which in turn encourages investment, work and efficiency. Alternatively, where domestic institutions hinder retrenchment, economic performance should suffer as investors take capital out of the country or stop investing, and domestic producers lose competitiveness relative to their counterparts in retrenchment-successful states. If this is true, then resistance is probably a temporary strategy and not viable in the long term. Finally, if the empirical analysis does not show convergence or support these performance predictions, then it calls into question the correctness of arguments about the long-term instability of generous welfare states and openness.

Since retrenchment varies depending on the openness–resistance mix, if the globalization arguments is correct, then performance should also vary with it. The results of the analysis are presented in Table 10.6 and Figure 10.2. Looking first at Table 10.6, there is no significant relationship between openness–resistance mix and any of the performance variables. However, retrenchment is related positively to GDP growth in the 1990s and negatively to inflation in the 1980s. It is unclear how to interpret this. While it is plausible that lower social spending can lead to higher economic growth (for example, if it leads to lower production costs which promote investment), GDP growth can lead to lower social spending because of a decline in unemployment. Figure 10.2 sorts the countries into the four different openness–resistance mixes and summarizes their economic performance in the 1980s and 1990s. As expected given the results presented in Table 10.6, Figure 10.2 shows that in the 1990s it is open retrenchers, particularly the Republic of Ireland, that exhibit high growth. The other three groups are quite similar, although closed retrenchers perform the worst. Note, however, that this is not true for both periods. In the 1980s, average GDP growth was better in Case 4 than in the other categories. Again, we have uncovered evidence that the 1990s are different.

The stability of the open welfare state?

How can the findings presented above be interpreted, and what do they suggest about the political stability of the welfare state? First, the analysis shows that states continue to vary with regard to both openness and spending. Only on a few indicators have states become more similar. In addition, despite increased openness, few states have in fact reduced average social spending as a per cent of GDP. Only in the

Table 10.6 Determinants of economic performance

	GDP growth			Unemployment			Inflation		
	1980–97	1980–90	1991–7	1980–97	1980–90	1991–7	1980–97	1980–90	1991–7
Retrench	0.249	−0.128	0.518	0.156	0.199	0.114	−0.286	−0.507	−0.115
Openness-resistance mix	−0.026	0.329	−0.351	0.025	−0.087	0.175	0.185	0.149	0.295

DOMESTIC SOURCES OF RESISTANCE

		STRONG		WEAK	
		Case 2: Open resisters		**Case 1: Open retrenchers**	
		Austria		Canada (1990s)	
		Belgium		Ireland	
		Denmark			
		Netherlands			
		Norway			
	HIGH	Sweden			
		Switzerland			
			1980–90	*1991–7*		*1980–90*	*1991–7*
		GDP	2.2	1.9	GDP	3.6	4.4
		Unempt	5.0	6.3	Unempt	15.8	11.8
		Inflatn	5.4	2.5	Inflatn	8.8	2.1
ECONOMIC		Retrench	−0.26	<u>−0.13</u>	Retrench	−0.18	<u>0.16</u>
OPENNESS		**Case 4: Closed resisters**		**Case 3: Closed retrenchers**	
		Australia		Canada (1980s)	
		Finland		France	
		Germany		Japan	
		Italy		New Zealand	
				UK	
	LOW			US	
			1980–90	*1991–7*		*1980–90*	*1991–7*
		GDP	3.8	1.7	GDP	2.6	2.1
		Unempt	6.9	10.7	Unempt	7.2	7.5
		Inflatn	7.2	3.1	Inflatn	6.7	2.3
		Retrench	−0.36	<u>−0.53</u>	Retrench	−0.24	<u>−0.23</u>

Figure 10.2 Openness–resistance and economic performance
Note: Underlined variables are correlated significantly with context. Retrenchment is opera-
tionalized as cuts in spending, so positive numbers reflect cuts, while negative numbers are
increases. In other words, positive retrenchment is spending decreases, and negative
retrenchment is increased spending.

Netherlands and the Republic of Ireland were spending levels as a
percentage of GDP lower in the 1990s than they were in the 1980s. In
other words, variation across states regarding changes in social
spending is a variation in the size of increases rather than a variation
in decreases. This is not to say that states have not cut particular
programmes – of course they have. Moreover, it says nothing about
effort compared to need. The point is rather that there is no evidence
that increasing openness has forced states to reduce overall social
spending (or spending more broadly) as a percentage of GDP. Virtually
all states have increased both spending and openness. This means that
retrenchment is more a matter of lower, or no, increases in spending
than overall cuts.

The analysis revealed little relationship between level of social spending and various measures of openness, which casts doubt on arguments suggesting that openness leads to lower spending. On the other hand, trade dependence – repeatedly shown in previous studies to be related positively to greater social spending – had no such effect on spending in the 1990s. Resistance potential as measured by the resistance index had a large positive effect on level of social spending in both the 1980s and 1990s. Taken together, these results suggest that domestic factors became more important determinants of spending levels in the 1990s. However, this is not necessarily a positive development for supporters of generous welfare spending because, historically, trade dependence has been linked positively to generosity.

The analysis leads to a different conclusion regarding retrenchment. In contrast to their lack of significance in the 1980s, both trade dependence and portfolio investment had a significant impact on retrenchment in the 1990s. The overall picture is mixed, however, because while trade dependence is related positively to retrenchment, portfolio investment is related to it negatively. The first finding tends to support the globalization argument, while the second refutes it in so far as greater cross-border investment is associated with less rather than more retrenchment. The analysis presented here supports a modified globalization argument, one that recognizes the importance of different mixes of openness and domestic resistance potential. Retrenchment is greatest in open retrenchers, where openness is high and resistance potential low, and it is lowest in closed resisters, where resistance potential is high and openness low. Furthermore, retrenchment is greater in open resisters than closed retrenchers. This casts doubt on the ideology-driven retrenchment argument, which states that it is ideology rather than openness that drives retrenchment. This might be because even in states with low resistance potential, established programmes create 'client groups' who resist spending cuts strongly. It might also be because, in these states, levels of spending tend already to be low, so there is much less room to make any cuts.

Finally, the analysis does not provide evidence that states are punished economically for refusing to cut social spending. Openness–resistance mixes are not related to GDP growth, unemployment or inflation. It is more difficult to interpret the findings on retrenchment. While retrenchment does not affect unemployment or inflation performance, it is linked positively to GDP growth. As noted above, however, it is difficult to know the direction of the relationship. Do growth rates have an impact on social spending, or is it the reverse (as globalization arguments suggest)? Economic trouble led to increasing social expenditure in Finland and Sweden in the 1990s, while good economic performance seems to have had the opposite effect in the Republic of Ireland. In the Netherlands and Denmark, however, it may be that changes in social spending impacted on growth. Further analysis, including more qualitative analyses of particular cases is needed. Of particular importance is to trace the timing and nature of changes in spending and economic performance trends.

A central question raised in the first section of this chapter was whether the open, generous welfare state is stable. If resistance is possible, but the price is negative economic performance then it is reasonable to conclude that resistance is a temporary response. This is true for various reasons, not least because voters punish governments for poor economic performance (Garrett, 1998). In the face of poor performance and voter discontent, retrenchment would eventually be implemented. The evidence presented here is consistent with a modified globalization argument with regard to cross-national variation in retrenchment. More open states are more prone to retrenchment, but domestic resistance potential plays an important role in limiting it. At the same time, it is also possible to reject arguments that non-retrenchers are punished in the form of poorer economic performance. At best there is some indication that they might experience somewhat lower growth rates, but even this is not entirely clear. There is no evidence that they suffer higher levels of inflation or unemployment. Moreover, if economic equality is used as a measure of performance, then the non-retrenchers perform considerably better (data not shown here).

The analysis presented here provides considerable evidence that the relationships between openness, retrenchment and openness–resistance mixes were not the same in the 1990s as they were in the 1980s. It is therefore important to conduct additional analyses that include data from the end of the 1990s and beyond in order to shed further light on these relationships. Case-study research can also shed further light on the links between the demands of mobile capital, domestic resistance and capital's response to resistance. None the less, based on the evidence provided here, the answer to the overarching question – whether open, generous welfare states are stable – must be yes, it appears so. Since there is no evidence that they suffer a worse economic performance, there is no reason to suppose that voters will abandon parties that resist retrenchment. In fact, the opposite is to be expected. Retrenchment is politically costly, as Pierson (1994) lucidly points out, and Dutch political parties can verify (Hemerijck *et al.*, 2000). Given this, plus ageing populations, longer education and lack of economic decline as punishment for failing to retrench, it is hardly surprising that retrenchment defined as lower levels of spending is rare.

Appendix

Table A10.1 provides information on political institutional variables. The first two columns present data on the concentration of political power. The horizontal dimension is the distribution of power at the national level. The frequency with which a state is governed by a single party majority government is used to measure horizontal concentration. A majority government is one that controls a legislative majority. The data refer to the percentage of Cabinets between 1945 and 1996 that were a single-party majority (Lijphart, 1999). Higher numbers indicate a greater concentration. Another indicator of the horizontal concentration of political authority is executive dominance over the legislature. To measure this I use Lijphart's (1999) scale of executive dominance. It is based on Cabinet longevity, with higher numbers indicating more dominant executives. Legislatures that are formally independent from the executive are least dominated by the executive and assigned a rank of one. Two measures of vertical concentration of political authority, defined as concentration of power at the national level as opposed to other governmental levels, are also presented in Table A10.1. The first is whether the state has a federal or a unitary political structure. The other is decentralization (distributing political responsibility among different levels of government via regular legislation).

Electoral systems are important for welfare state development because electoral rules have an impact on the viability of small parties. Majoritarian (pluralist) electoral systems encourage the formation of two-party systems and single-party, majority governments because they award electoral victory to the party or person with the most votes, regardless of how few those might be. Proportional representation encourages the formation of small parties, because parties are awarded seats on the basis of the percentage of votes received (usually above some specified threshold). Thus a party need not 'win' (get the most votes) anywhere in order to gain seats in the legislature, or even in government. A more nuanced way of measuring an election system's consequences for smaller parties is to examine the degree of proportionality. This refers to the difference between a party's share of the votes in an election and the number of seats it gets, and it is

Table A10.1   Domestic variables – political institutions

Country	Horizontal concentration of power		Vertical concentration of power	Election system characteristics		Interest intermediation	Cabinet seats (% held) 1980–97		
	One-party governments	Executive dominance		Type	Proportionality		Left	CD	Right
Australia	81.9	5.6	federal, decentralized	majoritarian	9.26	2.66	80	0	20
Austria	41.4	5.4	federal, centralized	proportional	2.47	0.6	67	26	5
Belgium	37.5	1.98	federal, decentralized	proportional	3.24	1.25	29	49	22
Canada	91.0	4.9	federal, decentralized	proportional	11.72	3.56	0	0	57
Denmark	30.2	2.28	unitary, decentralized	proportional	1.83	1.0	27	2	79
Finland	12.8	1.24	unitary, decentralized	proportional	2.93	1.31	34	1	19
France	62.5	5.52	unitary, centralized	majoritarian	21.08	2.84	50	0	40
Germany	36.2	2.82	federal, decentralized	proportional	2.52	1.38	13	66	0
Ireland	58.9	3.07	unitary, centralized	proportional	3.45	2.94	16	0	81
Italy	10.0	1.14	unitary, centralized	mixed	3.25	3.12	22	47	3.0
Japan	48.1	2.47	unitary, decentralized	mixed	5.03	1.25	5	0	93
Netherlands	25.3	2.72	semi-federal	proportional	1.3	1.19	20	49	25
New Zealand	99.5	4.17	unitary, centralized	pluralist	11.11	3.0	39	0	61
Norway	63.1	3.17	unitary, decentralized	proportional	4.93	0.44	65	6	24
Sweden	47.5	3.42	unitary, decentralized	proportional	2.09	0.5	64	3	12
Switzerland	4.1	1.0	federal, decentralized	proportional	2.53	1.0	28	28	28
UK	96.7	5.52	unitary, centralized	plurality	10.33	3.38	0	0	100
USA	81.2	1	federal, decentralized	plurality	14.91	3.3	0	0	75
MEAN	51.55	3.19			6.33	1.93	31	15	41

Notes/Sources: Horizontal concentration of power = % of one-party, majority governments 1945–96; executive dominance based on longevity 1 = least dominant. Source: Lijphart, 1999.

Vertical concentration of power = federal or unitary structure, centralized or decentralized system. Source: Lijphart, 1999.

Electoral system = majoritarian, proportional, pluralist, or mixed; proportionality indicator measures discrepancy between parties' vote results and seat results. Source: Lijphart, 1999.

Interest intermediation = higher numbers more pluralist Source: Siaroff, 1999.

significantly higher in majoritarian systems than under proportional representation.

Whether or not interest groups have a chance to participate in policy formation is influenced by systems of interest intermediation. It is common to distinguish between pluralist and corporatist systems. States are scored on a pluralist–corporatist scale from one to four (Siaroff, 1999), with higher values indicating greater pluralism.

Finally, Table A10.1 reports data on political party strength, measured by a party's percentage of Cabinet seats. Powerful social or christian democratic parties promote welfare spending, while strong right-wing parties have the opposite effect.

Notes

1   Retrenchment refers to policy changes that eliminate programmes, limit eligibility and/or benefit levels, or otherwise reduce social protection and services.
2   A full consideration of the links between these variables requires more analysis than I present here. Therefore, the results are suggestive rather than conclusive.
3   See Garrett (1998), especially 'Introduction', for a review.
4   Quinn's index is available through 1993. Data from Kastner and Rector (2000) show that few states changed capital market regulations during 1994–7, which supports the assumption that the 1993 Quinn scores reflect financial openness accurately through the 1990s.
5   The spending categories are old-age cash benefits, disability cash benefits, occupational injury and disease benefits, sickness benefits, services for the sick and elderly, survivors' benefits, family cash benefits, family services and active labour market policies, unemployment benefits and public spending on health and housing. Data are from the OECD's Social Expenditures Database.
6   For a further discussion of the domestic political variables used here, see the Appendix on page 000.
7   Attitudes and values are not necessarily independent of existing policies (Svallfors, 1999; Rothstein, 1994), but once they exist they are an important domestic political factor in understanding policy development.
8   Retrenchment is measured as average annual percentage change in social spending.
9   Trade dependence is used because it is significant more often than other measures of openness. States with resistance index scores above 3 are classified as having strong resistance potential.

References

Barr, N. (1998) *The Economics of the Welfare State*, 3rd edn, Stanford: Stanford University Press.

Birchfield, V. and Crepaz, M. M. L. (1998) 'The Impact of Constitutional Structures and Collective & Competitive Veto Points on Income Inequality in Industrialized Democracies', *European Journal of Political Research*, vol. 34, no. 2, pp. 175–200.

Duverger, M. (1964) *Political Parties: Their Organization and Activity in the Modern State*, 3rd edn, London: Methuen.

Esping-Andersen, G. (1990) *Three Worlds of Welfare Capitalism*, Cambridge: Polity Press.

Garrett, G. (1998) *Partisan Politics in the Global Economy*, Cambridge University Press.

Garrett, G. and Mitchell, D. (2001) 'Globalization, Government Spending and Taxation in the OECD', *European Journal of Political Research*, vol. 39, pp. 147–77.

Hemerijck, A, Unger, B. and Visser, J. (2000) 'How Small Countries Negotiate Change: Twenty-Five Years of Policy Adjustment in Austria, the Netherlands, and Belgium', in F. W. Scharpf and V. A. Schmidt (eds), *Welfare and Work in the Open Economy. Vol. II*, Oxford University Press.

Huber, E. and Stephens, J. D. (2001) *Development and Crisis of the Welfare State: Parties and Policies in Global Markets*, Chicago: University of Chicago Press.

Huber, E., Ragin, C. and Stephens, J. D. (1993) 'Social Democracy, Christian Democracy, Constitutional Structure and the Welfare State', *American Journal of Sociology*, vol. 99, no. 3, pp. 711–49.

IMF (2001) *International Financial Statistics Yearbook*, Washington, DC: IMF.

Kahler, M. (1998) 'Modeling Races to the Bottom', Paper delivered at the American Political Science Association Annual Meeting, Boston, Mass., 3–6 September.

Kastner, S. and Rector, C. (2000) 'Veto Players and Capital Control Liberalization in Parliamentary Democracies', Paper presented at the Annual Meeting of the Mid-West Political Science Association, Chicago, April.

Katzenstein, P. (1985) *Small States in World Markets: Industrial Policies in Europe*, Ithaca, NY: Cornell University Press.

Lijphart, A. (1999) *Patterns of Democracy: Government Forms and Performance in 36 Countries*, New Haven, Conn.: Yale University Press.

McKenzie, R. B. and D. R. Lee (1991) *Quicksilver Capitalism: How Rapid Movement of Wealth Has Changed the World*, New York: The Free Press.

Mishra, R. (1999) *Globalization and the Welfare State*, Cheltenham: Edward Elgar.

OECD (1985) *Historical Statistics 1960–1983*, Paris: OECD.

OECD (1992) *Historical Statistics 1960–1990*, Paris: OECD.

OECD (1996) *Historical Statistics 1960–1994*, Paris: OECD.

OECD (1999) *Historical Statistics 1960–1997*, Paris: OECD.

OECD (2000) *Social Expenditure Database 1980–1997*, Paris: OECD.

Pierson, P. (1994) *Dismantling the Welfare State? Reagan, Thatcher and the Politics of Retrenchment*, Cambridge University Press.

Pfaller, A., Gaugh, I. and Therborn, G. (eds) (1991) *Can the Welfare State Compete? A Comparative Study of Five Advanced Capitalist Countries*, London: Macmillan.

Quinn, D. (1997) 'The Correlates of Change in International Financial Regulation', *American Political Science Review*, vol. 91, no. 3, pp. 531–51.

Rodrik, D. (1997) *Has Globalization Gone Too Far?*, Washington, DC: Institute for International Economics.

Rothstein, B. (1994) *Vad Bör Staten Göra?*, Stockholm: SNS.

Scharpf, F. (2000) 'The Viability of Advanced Welfare States in the International Economy: Vulnerabilities and Options', *Journal of European Public Policy*, vol. 7, no. 2, June, pp. 190–228.

Siaroff, A. (1999) 'Corporatism in 24 Industrial Democracies: Meaning and Measurement', *European Journal of Political Research*, vol. 36, pp. 175–205.

Simmons, B. (1999) 'The Internationalization of Capital', in H. Kitschelt, P. Lange, G. Marks and J. D. Stephens (eds), *Continuity and Change in Contemporary Capitalism*, Cambridge University Press.

Steinmo, S. (1994) 'The End of Redistribution? International Pressures and Domestic Tax Policy Choices', *Challenge*, November–December, pp. 9–17.

Svallfors, S. (1999) 'The Middle Class and Welfare State Retrenchment: Attitudes to Swedish Welfare Policies', in S. Svallfors and P. Taylor-Gooby (eds), *The End of the Welfare State: Responses to State Retrenchment*, London: Routledge.

Swank, D. (2001) 'Political Institutions and Welfare State Restructuring: The Impact of Institutions on Social Policy Change in Developed Democracies', in P. Pierson (ed.), *The New Politics of the Welfare State*, Oxford University Press.

Tsebelis, G. (1995) 'Decision Making in Political Systems: Veto Players in Presidentialism, Parliamentarism, Multicameralism and Multipartyism', *British Journal of Political Science*, vol. 25, pp. 289–325.

Van Kersbergen, K. (1995) *Social Capitalism: A Study of Christian Democracy and the Welfare State*, London: Routledge.

Name Index

Åberg, Y.   158
Ackum Agell, S.   173, 186
Adsera, A.   130
Aitken, B.J.   82, 83
Alesina, A.   154, 164
Allende, S.   41
Andersen, T.M.   130, 131
Andvig, J.C.   70
Assarsson, B.   175

Barr, N.   214
Becker, G.   55
Behrenz, L.   172, 202
Ben Bella, M.A.   30
Bentzel, R.   98
Bergen, P.L.   58
Berlin, G.   47, 51, 53
Bevelander, P.   197
Bhagwati, J.   5–7, 24–43
Bin Laden, O.   58
Birchfield, V.   223
Björklund, A.   179, 185
Black, S.   40
Blanchard, O.   175
Blank, R.M.   48–9, 51
Boberg, K.   160
Bodansky, Y.   58, 68
Boix, C.   130
Bonoli, G.   167
Bordo, M.   74
Borjas, G.J.   196
Bourdieu, P.   24, 34–5
Braconier, H.   81, 87, 89–90
Brainard, S.L.   75, 81
Brainerd, E.   40
Budd, J.W.   82
Bukharin, N.   36
Bush, G.W.   72

Calmfors, L.   174, 184, 186
Cameron, D.   130
Cancian, M.   49, 51
Cardoso, H.F.   27–8

Carling, K.   119
Carr, C.   56
Carr, D.   76
Chomsky, N.   30
Clark, A.E.   158
Crepaz, M.M.L.   223
Cusack, T.R.   130

Delander, L.   172, 202
Delsen, L.   129
Derrida, J.   31–2
Dixit, A.   67
Doms, M.E.   82
Drago, R.   159
Drezner, D.   37
Duverger, M.   223

Eagleton, T.   31
Edin, P.-A.   203
Edquist, H.   123
Ekberg, J.   9, 185, 195–211
Ekholm, K.   6, 8, 12–13, 74–92
Engbersen, G.   158
Esping-Andersen, G.   151, 221
Esposito, J.L.   66, 67, 68

Fälldin, T.   14, 105
Fanon, F.   32
Farah, C.E.   63, 64
Feenstra, R.C.   79
Feldt, K.O.   105
Feliciano, Z.   82
Fisher, I.   70
Forslund, A.   175
Freeman, R.B.   112
Friedman, D.   24
Friedman, M.   35
Friedman, T.   24
Fukuyama, F.   29

Galbraith, J.K.   35
Garrett, G.   128, 130, 133, 134, 144,
        145, 214, 215, 233

Globerman, S.   82
Green-Pedersen, C.   5, 128–46
Grogger, J.   53
Grossman, G.   67
Grubb, D.   173
Gruber, J.   159
Gueron, J.   51
Guevara, C.   30, 32
Gustafsson, B.   209
Gustavsson, B.-Å.   205

Hammarstedt, M.   197
Hanson, G.H.   79
Harkman, A.   119
Harrison, A.   41, 82, 83
Haveman, R.   54
Heckman, J.J.   173
Helpman, E.   75, 76
Hemerijck, A.   129, 233
Henrekson, M.   116–18, 119, 123,
    164, 185
Hirschleifer, J.   56, 57
Hobsbawm, E.   67, 70
Hobson, J.M.   131
Holmlund, B.   184
Horstmann, I.   75
Howenstine, N.G.   82
Huber, E.   130, 132, 167, 217, 221, 223
Hume, D.   33
Huntington, S.P.   68

Iversen, T.   130, 137

Jaeger, A.   175
Jakobsson, U.   164
Jansson, P.   175
Jensen, J.B.   82
Johannisson, B.   205
Johansson, P.   159, 185
Jonasson, E.   9, 16, 19, 118, 172–92
Jones, E.   137, 142

Kahler, M.   215
Kahneman, D.   166
Katzenstein, P.   213, 226
Keller, W.   83
Khan, C.   56
Kijphart, A.   223, 234–5
Kite, C.   21–2, 128, 133, 145, 213–36

Kitschelt, H.   135
Klein, N.   38
Konings, J.   81, 89–90
Krugman, P.   27, 76
Kumm, B.   58–9, 64
Kurzer, P.   145

La Fontaine, O.   135
Lankes, H.P.   84
Layard, R.   158, 172, 175
Leamer, E.E.   121
Lee, D.R.   215
Leibried, S.   128, 130
Lenin, V.I.   8, 36
Lewis, B.   68
Lidbeck, Å   115
Lind, D.   123
Lindbeck, A.   5, 16, 17, 18, 20, 21,
    98, 103, 119, 149–69, 173, 175,
    178, 185, 187, 202
Lindblad, H.   175
Lipsey, R.E.   82
Loprest, P.   51
Lucas, R.E. Jr.   8
Lundahl, M.   6, 10, 55–72
Lundborg, P.   121
Lundh, C.   202, 210
Lundin, M.   173, 186
Lundius, J.   67
Luxemburg, R.   33

MacKenzie, L.W.   97
Macmillan, H.   19
Markusen, J.R.   75, 76
Martin, J.P.   173
Maskus, K.   76
McKenzie, R.B.   215
Mishra, R.   214, 215, 216
Mitchell, D.   214
Modig, A.   160
Moene, K.O.   70
Moffit, R.   157–8
Mosley, L.   128, 131, 132
Murphy, A.   81, 89–90
Murray, R.   102
Myrdal, G.   153–4

Nader, R.   26, 30, 38
Naipaul, V.S.   32

Nannestad, P.   137, 140
Nasrallah, S.H.   64
Navarro, P.   57
Nkrumah, K.   28
Nyberg, S.   157

Ohlsson, M.   185
Ohlsson, R.   184, 197, 204–5
Olson, M.   66
Omar, M.M.   58
O'Rourke, K.H.   7, 20
Österberg, T.   210

Palme, M.   159, 185
Palme, O.   14
Palme, P.   102, 105, 108
Pareto, V.   56
Parkinson, M.   175
Pauly, M.   51
Pempel, T.J.   97
Pereira de Queiroz, M.I.   67
Persson, M.   116–18, 159, 165, 185
Persson, T.   151, 154
Pettersson, L.   9, 16, 19, 107, 118, 172–92
Pfaller, A.   214
Pierson, P.   133, 151, 223, 233
Prebisch, P.   27
Putnam, R.   34

Quinn, D.   132, 218

Radcliffe-Brown, A.R.   33
Rankenhaeuser, M.   153
Rathbone, A.   59, 66
Rawls, J.   32–3
Reuter, C.   62, 66, 70
Ricardo, D.   1, 8
Rieger, E.   128, 130
Riker, D.   81
Robertson, Sir D.   32
Rodrik, D.   130, 154, 213, 226
Rooth, D.O.   185, 202, 206, 210
Rowley, C.K.   59, 66

Said, E.   34, 35
Scharpf, F.   214
Schön, L.   98
Schröder, H.   135

Schwartz, H.   128, 129
Scott, K.   197
Sharon, A.   68
Shaw, G.B.   31
Siaroff, A.   235–6
Simmons, B.   215
Sinn, H.-W.   163
Slaughter, M.J.   80, 82
Smith, A.   17, 32, 35
Snower, D.-J.   175, 202
Snower, D.S.   151
Södersten, B.   1–22, 96–126, 178
Solow, R.M.   5, 8, 45–54
Soros, G.   30
Spencer, A.   57
Stalin, J.   56
Steinmo, S.   215
Stephens, J.   130, 132, 167, 217, 221
Stigler, G.J.   57
Stiglitz, J.   27
Summers, L.   175
Sunkel, O.   28
Swank, D.   128, 130, 131, 133, 134, 167, 223
Szanyi, M.   84

Tabellini, G.   151, 154
Thoursie, S.   160
Thygesen, N.   137
Toirkens, J.   137
Trujillo, R.   56
Tsebelis, G.   223
Tullock, G.   61–2
Turgenev, I.S.   32
Tversky, A.   166

van Kersbergen, K.   134, 135, 137, 140, 143, 144, 221
van Wijnbergen, C.   142
Venables, A.   75, 84
Vickrey, W.   33
Vilhelmsson, R.   210
Visser, J.   129

Wadensjö, E.   197, 198, 206, 209
Wallerstein, I.   36
Weibull, J.W.   155
Weiss, L.   130, 132, 133
Wildavsky, A.   150

Williamson, J.G.   7, 20
Wise, D.A.   159
Wolfe, A.   37
Woodcock, G.   58
Wooden, M.   159

Yeaple, S.R.   83
Young, A.   8

Zeile, W.J.   82

Subject Index

Afghanistan   58, 64
Africa   7, 21
age distribution   185
agents   61–72
aggregation fallacies   25–9
Aid to Families with Dependent
    Children   *see* Temporary
    Assistance to Needy Families
al-Qaeda   57–8
Albania   84
Anti-Sweatshop Coalition   30, 39
anti-business   42
anti-capitalism   6, 8, 24, 29–35, 36,
    42
anti-corporation   6, 24, 36–8
anti-globalization   6–8, 24–43
    aggregation fallacies   25–9
    anti-capitalism   29–35
    anti-corporations   36–8
    confrontation   39–43
    political alliances   39
Argentina   29
Astra-Zeneca   123
Australia   1, 3, 200, 201
    stability of globalized welfare state
        219, 220, 221, 222, 225, 235
Austria   218, 219, 220, 222, 225, 235

Baader–Meinhof gang   58
Baltic States   84
bargaining   175
Belgium
    immigration   196, 201
    stability of globalized welfare state
        217, 218, 219, 220, 221, 222,
        225, 235
benefits   157
    cheating   160
    see also sick leave/sick pay;
        unemployment
benign impact   28
benign intent   28
Bosnian immigrants   203–7

brainwashing   62
Brazil   29–30
Bretton Woods system   19, 98
Bulgaria   84
Bush Administration   39
business cycle   184–5

Canada   8, 82, 175, 200, 201
    stability of globalized welfare state
        218, 219, 220, 222, 225, 235
capital   3–4
    flows   2, 3, 7, 26–7
    mobility   215
    value   156
capitalism   6–7, 8, 24–5, 26, 31, 36,
    40, 42–3
case loads reduction   46–8
catch-up effect   178
Center on Policy Attitudes   28
Central and Eastern Europe   12–13,
    75, 83–91
cheating   17
child care   152, 153
Chile   7
China   4
Christen Democratisch Appèl (CDA)
    137, 142, 143, 144
Christian Democrats   16, 151, 221,
    224
    Netherlands and Denmark   135,
        137, 139, 142, 144
Clinton–Blair neoliberalism   34
cointegration test   190–1
Cold War   4
Communism   4
competition   77–8, 79, 90, 214–15
conservatives   111
consumer theory   71
convergence   217–24
Corn Laws, repeal of   2
corporations   40, 41, 42
cost–benefit   61, 62
Czech Republic   84, 85, 86

Davos meeting   29
demographics   184–5
Denmark   2, 4, 5, 14, 15–16, 167
   immigration   196, 200, 201, 203, 209
   stability of globalized welfare state
      219, 220, 221, 222, 225, 235
   and Sweden   111, 115
   taxation and government spending
      108, 109, 110
   unemployment and non-
      employment   177, 178
   see also Netherlands and Denmark
depreciation   123
deregulation   179
devaluation   14, 103–6, 112, 120
disabled people   186–7
'discouraged worker effect'   119
discrimination   200
disincentive effects   165, 167
displacement issue   53
domestic resistance   216–17, 221–2,
   224–9, 231, 232, 233
   index   224, 227, 232
   potential   225
dual economy   120–3
dynamics of welfare state   17–18,
   149–69
   reforms and retreat   164–8
   social norms and political
      preferences   156–64
   virtuous and vicious dynamics
      153–6
   welfare-state arrangements,
      expansion of   149–53

early retirement   159–60
Earned Income Tax Credit   48, 54
East Asian financial crisis   26–7
economic and monetary union   141
economic openness   214, 216–18,
   224–34
economic performance   227, 229,
   230, 231
economically benign   40
educational attainment   85, 184,
   186, 198–9
electoral systems   223
empirical evidence on home country
   effects   79–83

employment   46, 81–2, 90, 92, 125
   patterns   100–2, 120
   see also Sweden: employment and
      non-employment
entrepreneurship   163–4
Environics International   27
Ericsson   123
Europe   3, 5, 9, 28, 81
   and American welfare reform   45,
      46, 50, 53
   dynamics of welfare states   151, 152
   immigration   195, 196, 199
   unemployment and non-
      employment   172, 175, 176,
      177, 184, 186
   see also Central and Eastern Europe;
      European; Northern Europe;
      Southern Europe; Western
      Europe
European Community   175
European Free Trade Area   176
European Monetary System   137
European Monetary Union   179
European Union   84, 85, 86, 100,
   105, 123, 159
   Council Meeting   6
   unemployment and non-
      employment   176, 177, 178
Euskadi ta Askatasuna (ETA)   58
exchange-rate policies   2, 123, 137,
   142
exports   120–2, 123, 124, 125,
   217–18, 219

factor cost advantages   84
factor prices   3
Far East   28
financial
   difficulties   164–5
   flows   218, 220
   openness   218
   vulnerability   165
financing of welfare state   108–11
Finland   20, 167, 196
   stability of globalized welfare state
      219, 220, 221, 222, 225, 233, 235
   unemployment and
      non-employment   177, 178,
      186

First World War   4
fiscal policies   2
foreign direct investment   12, 74, 88, 89, 220
   horizontal   75–6, 77–8, 80, 82, 84, 88
   multinational enterprises   13, 84
   stability of globalized welfare state   218, 226
   vertical   75–6, 77, 79, 80, 83, 84
France   2, 4, 129, 177
   immigration   20, 196, 201
   stability of globalized welfare, state   219, 220, 222, 225, 235
free-rider problem   66, 71

G8 countries   6
Gap   38
General Agreement on Tariffs and Trade   *see* World Trade Organization
general equilibrium   97
Germany   2, 4, 16, 99, 103, 125, 145
   immigration   196, 201
   inflation   105, 112, 113
   interest rates   137, 138, 139, 141, 142, 143
   macroeconomic policy   129, 133, 135,
   stability of globalized welfare state   219, 220, 222, 225, 235
   unemployment and non-employment   175, 177
Global Exchange   30–1, 38
gold standard   3
government
   sector   100–2
   spending   218–29
gradualism   150
Great Depression   4, 98
Greece   13, 85, 86
gross domestic product   4, 15, 111, 115–16, 120, 123, 165, 231
   foreign direct investment   220
   government spending   221
   retrenchment   229
   social spending   222
   Sweden   11, 98, 102, 104, 108, 172
   trade exposure   217–18, 219

gross national product   150, 154, 209

Harkin Child Deterrence Bill   42
headquarters activity   76
Heckscher–Ohlin sectors   120, 121, 122
'history dependence'   151, 152
Hizbollah guerillas   57
Hong Kong   4, 7
human-capital option   52
Hungary   84, 85, 86

ideological factors   221
illegitimacy   46
immigrants/immigration   20–1, 184–5
   Bosnians   203–7
   first-generation   195
   second-generation   195, 196, 210–11
   see also Sweden: immigrants
imperialism   7, 8, 36
imports   217–18, 219
income   115–20
   distribution   162–3
   effects   196
India   7, 31, 43
indoctrination   64
Indonesia   29
inflation,   112, 125, 137–9
insider–outsider theory   151, 175, 201–2
Institute for the Labour Market Policy Evaluation   173
institutional
   arrangements   223
   changes   202
   factors   185
integration policy   201, 202–7
interest intermediation   223
international capital markets   131–2
international financial markets   144
International Labour Organization   42
International Monetary Fund   38
International Programme for the Eradication of Child Labour   42
international trade theory   97

investment   *see* foreign direct
    investment; portfolio
    investment
'in-work benefits'   152
Iran   57
Ireland   4, 177, 218
    stability of globalized welfare state
        219, 220, 222, 225, 235
Ireland, Republic of   22, 178
    stability of globalized welfare state
        221, 229, 231, 233
Irgun gang   10, 58
Irish Republican Army   10, 58
Islam/Muslims   11, 57–8, 59, 67–8
Israel   10, 30, 58, 71, 72
Italy   4, 159, 218, 219, 220, 222,
    225, 235
    unemployment and non-
        employment   177
ITT   41

Japan   4, 7, 40, 97
    stability of globalized welfare state
        218, 219, 220, 221, 222, 225,
        235

Keynesianism   15–16, 19, 98, 99,
    134, 135
know-how   91
knowledge capital model   76

'la belle époque'   7
labour   3, 82, 91, 92
    costs   85
    demand   79
    -force participation   178–83
    market   178–83, 197–200; changes
        184–5; policy   173–8, 202;
        procedures   205–6;
        programmes   186
    see also multinational enterprises
        and labour markets; skilled
        labour; unskilled labour
lags   17–18
'last parenthesis'   119
Latin America   1, 3
Lebanon   57
leisure   115–20
Liberal Democratic Party   97

Liberals   16, 142
long-run effects   79–80
Luxembourg   177, 178

Maastricht   16
macro policies   120
macroeconomic policy   129, 133,
    134, 135–43, 144
Malaysia   4
malign impact paradigm   28
malign intent paradigm   28
Manpower Demonstration Research
    Corporation   47, 51, 52, 53
martyrdom   66
Marxism   32
micro versus macro   106–8
Middle East   21, 205, 206
migration   2, 7
    see also immigrants/immigration
monetary system   3
Mongol empire   56
moral hazard   17, 157, 158, 159,
    160, 162
multinational enterprises   12–13,
    37–8, 40, 41
    and labour markets   74–92
    empirical evidence on home
        country effects   79–83
    expansion into Central and Eastern
        Europe   83–91
    theory of multinational enterprise
        75–9

Nazism   4
Netherlands   2, 4, 5, 14, 15–16, 22
    anti-globalization   43
    dynamics of welfare states   158,
        159, 167
    immigration   196, 200, 201, 203
    stability of globalized welfare state
        218, 219, 220, 221, 222, 225,
        231, 235
    and Sweden   111, 115
    taxation and government spending
        108, 109, 110
    unemployment and
        non-employment   177, 178
    see also Netherlands and Denmark

Netherlands and Denmark 128–46
  globalization and welfare state
    130–3
  macroeconomic policies
    (1973–2000) 135–43
  networks 205–6
New Zealand 167, 218, 219, 220,
  222, 225, 235
Nike 38
non-acceleratiing inflation rate of
  unemployment 175
non-employment *see* Sweden:
  employment and non-employment
non-governmental organizations
  34, 42
Nordic countries 96, 151, 152, 195–6
North America 1, 3, 28
  see also Canada; United States
North-South divide 27–9
Northern Europe 87, 88, 89, 90
Norway 4, 196
  dynamics of welfare states 152–3,
    159
  stability of globalized welfare state
    219, 220, 222, 225, 235
  unemployment and non-
    employment 177, 178

oil crisis 2, 13, 15, 19, 103, 217
  Netherlands and Denmark 137,
    139
  unemployment and non-
    employment 175, 179
old-age care 152, 153
Organisation for Economic Co-
  operation and Development
  (OECD) 13, 21, 22, 45, 102,
  115, 120, 123
  immigration 196, 200
  multinational enterprises 80
  stability of globalized welfare state
    217
  taxation and government spending
    108, 109, 110
  unemployment and non-
    employment 172, 173, 177,
    179
Organization for Oil Producing and
  Exporting Countries 13, 27

outsourcing 79–80
overshooting 154–5

Palestine 58, 68, 72
Paradise 63–4, 66–7, 70
performance 224–9
Perron test for unit roots and
  structural change 187–91
Personal Responsibility and Work
  Opportunity Reconciliation Act
  45, 46, 47, 48, 51
Pharmacia Corporation 123
Poland 84, 85, 86
policy
  factors 102–3
  failures 178
politics/political
  alliances 39
  authority 223
  domestic 214–17
  institutions 235
  party 134
  preferences 156–64
poor tax (*zakāh*) 64
portfolio investment 218, 227, 232
Portugal 1, 4, 13, 85, 86, 177
poverty 8–9, 45–6, 51
principal 58–61, 62, 64, 71
principal–agent problem 58–9, 63,
  71
production 87, 131
  activity 76
  costs 85, 88
productivity 78, 83, 108, 120
  spillovers 82
profits 79
  repatriation 78
Progress Party 140
public expenditure 222, 228

Quinn scale 219
Qur'ān 63–6

race 46
Rand Corporation/Report 53
recruitment of agents 60
recruitment cost curve 61
Red Brigades 58
regression analysis 226–7

religion   11
  see also Islam/Muslims; Qur'ān
relocation   77–8, 88, 90, 202, 203–4
retrenchment   213–17, 221, 223,
  226–7, 229, 231–3
risk for retaliation or regression   59
Romania   84
Ruckus Society   24
Russian Federation   84

savings   163–4
Scandinavia   4, 130, 132
self-sacrifice   63
September   11, 2001 6, 10, 55–6,
  57–8, 59
sex   46
Shii   66
Shining Path   58
short-run effects   81–2
sick leave/sick pay   115–20, 126,
  158–9
Singapore   4
single parents   160
skilled labour   77–8, 80, 85, 87
Slovakia   84
'snake'   137
social democrats   14, 15–16, 102,
  106, 108, 111, 119, 151
  Netherlands and Denmark
    129–30, 134–7, 139–45
  stability of globalized welfare state
    221, 224
social norms   17–18, 156–64, 185,
  187
social spending   218–29, 231, 232,
  233
socially malign   40
socioeconomic developments   165
South Korea   4, 7
South-East Asia   7
Southern Europe   87, 88, 89, 90
Soviet Union   4, 31, 56, 97
Sozialdemokratische Partei Deutsch-
  land (SPD)   145
Spain   4, 10, 13, 58, 85, 86, 177
spending   224–9
spillovers   78, 83
  productivity   82
  technology   79

stability of globalized welfare state
  213–36
  convergence   217–24
  openness, resistance, spending and
    performance   224–9
  opennness   229–34
  retrenchment and domestic politics
    214–17
Stern gang   10, 58
Stockholm School of Economics   55
striking power curve   59, 60
structural change   187–91, 201
subcontracting   80
Sudan   58
suicide bombers   58, 62, 65–6,
  68–70, 71
Sunni   66
Sweden   2, 4, 5, 9, 16, 22, 96–126
  challenges of a new era   99–100
  devaluation   103–6, 139
  dual economy   120–3
  dynamics of welfare states   152–3,
    159, 160, 163, 164, 166–7
  employment and non-employment
    172–92; labour market, changes
    in   184–5; labour market and
    labour-force participation
    178–83; labour market policy
    and non-employment   173–8;
    Perron test for unit roots and
    structural change   187–91
  employment patterns and the
    government sector   100–2
  financing of welfare state   108–11
  general equilibrium   97
  growth, strains and crisis   111–15
  immigrants   20–1, 195–211;
    explanations   200–2;
    integration policy   202–7; in
    labour market   197–200; in
    welfare system   207–9
  Immigration Board   202
  income and leisure   115–20
  Labour Market Policy Board   202
  macroeconomic policy   133, 141
  micro versus macro   106–8
  multinational enterprises   80, 81,
    85, 86, 87, 88, 89–90
  non-employment   177

policy factors   102–3
stability of globalized welfare state
    219, 220, 221, 222, 225, 233,
    235
success and a new era   97–9
unemployment   18–20, 177
welfare state   13–15
Switzerland   196, 219, 220, 222, 225,
    235

Taliban   58
taxation   131, 155–6, 157, 165
technology   91
    -driven sectors   120–1
    spillovers   79
    transfers   78, 79, 82
telegraph   3
Temporary Assistance to Needy
    Families   49–51
terror groups   55
terrorism   10–12, 55–72
    agents   61–72
    principal   58–61
    September   11, 2001 57–8
theory of comparative advantage   1, 8
theory of efficiency wages   174–5
trade   130–1
    arm's-length   80
    dependence   226–7, 232
    exposure   217–18, 219
    free   2, 7, 26–7
    sanctions   41–2
    unions   130, 133, 137, 140
transportation   3
Turkey   29, 85
turnover costs   202
two-period utility function   63

unemployment   18–20
    benefits   158
    insurance   119
Union Meuniere   41
unit roots   187–91
United Kingdom   1, 2–3, 4, 141
    dynamics of welfare states   152,
        158, 167
    immigration   20
    stability of globalized welfare, state
        218, 219, 220, 222, 225, 235

unemployment and non-
    employment   175, 177, 178
United States   2, 3, 4, 5, 7, 8, 45–54
    anti-globalization   30, 42
    case loads reduction   46–8
    Congress   41
    dynamics of welfare states   152, 153
    immigration   20, 200, 201
    multinational enterprises   79, 80,
        81, 82, 83
    poverty   45–6
    productivity   100
    stability of globalized welfare, state
        217, 219, 220, 221, 222, 225,
        235
    Temporary Assistance to Needy
        Families   49–51
    unemployment   19; and
        inflationary pressure   98; and
        non-employment   173, 175,
        178
    welfare reform   8–10
    welfare-to-work schemes   51–3
unskilled labour   77–8, 80, 85

veto points   223–4
voting behaviour   161–2

wages   12, 13, 83, 91, 92, 112
    costs   81–2, 85, 90
    formation   175
    ratio   87
    real   3–4
    -setting mechanisms   105
Wassenaar agreement   16
welfare effort   218–29
welfare reform   8–10
welfare reform act (1996)   *see* Personal
    Responsibility and Work
    Opportunity Reconcilation Act
welfare-to-work schemes   51–3
Western Europe   1, 2, 4, 8, 96
    multinational enterprises   12–13,
        75, 83–4, 85, 88, 89, 91
    unemployment   19; and
        inflationary pressure   98; and
        non-employment   174
'Whole Sweden' strategy   203
work-first option   52

working conditions   12
World Bank   33, 38, 41
World Economic Forum   25, 27, 28, 29

World Trade Center   39
World Trade Organization   6, 30, 34, 38, 39

Globalization and the Welfare State

Books are to be returned on or before
the last d   below

Also by Bo Södersten

A STUDY OF ECONOMIC GROWTH AND INTERNATIONAL TRADE
INTERNATIONAL ECONOMICS (*Third Edition, with Geoffrey Reed*)

Translations
INTERNATIONELL EKONOMI (*Swedish*)
ECONOMIA INTERNAZIONALE (*Italian*)
ECONOMIA INTERNATIONAL (*Portuguese*)
A KÜLGAZDASÁG (*Hungarian*)